GENTLEMEN
SCIENTISTS

AND

REVOLUTIONARIES

PREVIOUS BOOKS BY TOM SHACHTMAN

NON-FICTION

American Iconoclast: The Life and Times of Eric Hoffer (2011)
Airlift to America (2009)
Rumspringa: To Be or Not To Be Amish (2006)
Terrors and Marvels (2003)
'I Seek My Brethren' (2001)
Absolute Zero and the Conquest of Cold (1999)
Around The Block (1997)
The Most Beautiful Villages of New England (1997)
The Inarticulate Society (1995)
Skyscraper Dreams (1991)
Decade of Shocks, 1963–1974 (1983)
The Phony War, 1939–1940 (1982)
Edith and Woodrow (1981)
The Day America Crashed (1979)

FICTION

Driftwhistler (1983)
Wavebender (1982)
Beachmaster (1981)

COLLABORATIVE WORKS

Building Tall, with John L. Tishman *(2011)*
The Forty Years War, with Len Colodny *(2009)*
Dead Center, with Shiya Ribowsky *(2006)*
Torpedoed!, with Edmund D. Pope *(2001)*
Justice Is Served, with Robert K. Ressler *(1994)*
I Have Lived in the Monster, with Robert K. Ressler *(1993)*
Whoever Fights Monsters, with Robert K. Ressler *(1991)*
The Gilded Leaf, with Patrick Reynolds *(1988)*
Image by Design, with Clive Chajet *(1987)*
Straight to the Top, with Paul G. Stern *(1986)*
The FBI-KGB War, with Robert Lamphere *(1984)*

FOR CHILDREN

The President Builds a House (1989)
Video Power, with Harriet Shelare *(1988)*
America's Birthday (1987)
Parade (1986)
The Birdman of St. Petersburg (1983)
Growing Up Masai (1981)

GENTLEMEN SCIENTISTS

AND

REVOLUTIONARIES

The FOUNDING FATHERS *in*

the AGE *of*

ENLIGHTENMENT

TOM SHACHTMAN

palgrave
macmillan

GENTLEMEN SCIENTISTS AND REVOLUTIONARIES
Copyright © Tom Shachtman, 2014.

First published in 2014 by PALGRAVE MACMILLAN® TRADE in the United States—a division of St. Martin's Press LLC, 175 Fifth Avenue, New York, NY 10010.

Where this book is distributed in the UK, Europe and the rest of the world, this is by Palgrave Macmillan, a division of Macmillan Publishers Limited, registered in England, company number 785998, of Houndmills, Basingstoke, Hampshire RG21 6XS.

Palgrave® and Macmillan® are registered trademarks in the United States, the United Kingdom, Europe and other countries.

ISBN: 978-1-137-27825-8

Library of Congress Cataloging-in-Publication Data

Shachtman, Tom, 1942–
    Gentlemen scientists and revolutionaries : the founding fathers in the age of enlightenment / Tom Shachtman.
        pages   cm
    Includes bibliographical references and index.
    ISBN 978-1-137-27825-8 (alk. paper)
    1. Science and state—United States—History—18th century. 2. Science and state —United States—History—19th century. 3. Technology and state—United States—History—18th century. 4. Technology and state—United States—History—19th century. 5. United States—History—18th century. 6. United States—History—19th century. 7. United States—Intellectual life—18th century. 8. United States—Intellectual life—19th century. 9. Founding Fathers of the United States. I. Title. II. Title: Founding fathers in the age of enlightenment.
    Q127.U6S46   2014
    509.2'273—dc23

                                                                    2014002006

A catalogue record of the book is available from the British Library.

Design by Letra Libre, Inc.

First edition: October 2014

10 9 8 7 6 5 4 3 2 1

Printed in the United States of America.

Research for this book was conducted with the assistance of a grant from the Alfred P. Sloan Foundation's program for the Public Understanding of Science and Technology.

For my grandchildren;

and in memoriam,

Robert K. Ressler (1937–2013)

as the province of the elite, the urban, and the solitary.[2] However, in the American colonies, where the population was sparse, the colleges few, and the libraries small, it was nearly impossible for a gentleman—or for anyone else—to become enlightened in the absence of extensive contact with like-minded others with whom to share the joys and pains of investigation and discovery. Nonetheless, a particularly American Enlightenment spread, aided by an atmosphere of greater religious toleration than that of Europe, by colonial governmental and social structures loose enough to encourage individual curiosity, and by a frontier culture that ranked as cardinal virtues independence, comparative reasoning, and sharing one's thoughts. "The poorest labourer upon the shores of the Delaware thinks himself entitled to deliver his sentiments in matters of religion or politics with as much freedom as the gentleman or scholar," an assistant at Christ Church in Philadelphia wrote in midcentury. "Indeed, there is less distinction among the citizens of Philadelphia than among those of any civilized city in the world."[3]

Two centuries after Kant's essay on enlightenment, Michel Foucault asked, in his critique of that essay, "whether we may not envisage modernity rather as an attitude. . . . And by 'attitude,' I mean a mode of relating to contemporary reality; a voluntary choice made by certain people; in the end, a way of thinking and feeling; a way, too, of acting and behaving that at one and the same time marks a relation of belonging and presents itself as a task."[4] To me, Foucault's definition best characterizes the form of enlightenment in the American colonies as the gentlemen scientist Founding Fathers knew it. To them, enlightenment had a particularly scientific cast. All of them had a scientific outlook: all understood natural processes as obedient to the sort of laws that Newton had elucidated—as rational, as predictable.

Today, however, the centrality to the Founding Fathers of their enlightened, scientific outlook has been obscured. While most twenty-first-century Americans are aware that young George Washington was a surveyor, they do not know the extent to which scientific and technological interests guided him throughout his life, for instance in his championing of complex engineering projects to conquer the Potomac River by locks, canals, and steam vessels; or in his experimental farming techniques, so advanced that a contemporary agrarian expert considered him to be America's most "scientific" farmer; or that during the Revolutionary War, and against the wishes of the Continental Congress, Washington ordered doctors to use a still-experimental vaccination technique to prevent his troops from being decimated by smallpox, an action identified by some historians as his most important in preserving the American enterprise.

John Adams gained such a strong and continuing sense of excitement about the natural universe from his studies in astronomy, fostered at Harvard under the tutelage of his science professor, John Winthrop, that thirty years later he would confess to a friend that while in his adult life he had not had enough time for science, "Whenever any Thing of the kind however has accidentally fallen in my Way, it has revived the fond Attachment of my Youth, and given me more pleasure than I can account for."[5] He founded one of America's two scientific societies, the American Academy of Arts and Sciences, and wrote into the Massachusetts state constitution public support of science and the arts.

Thomas Jefferson became president of the leading scientific organization, the American Philosophical Society (APS), before he became president of the United States and continually studied stars and planets, insect pests, and native tribal languages. To ready the Lewis and Clark expedition, he asked leading APS experts on anatomy, botany, and anthropology to tutor Meriwether Lewis in how to conduct fieldwork properly. So deep and sustained were Jefferson's scientific interests that he spent a considerable part of his fortune acquiring scientific instruments, fossils, and parcels of land that he thought geologically unique. Toward the end of his days, he wrote that his "passion" had ever been the "physical and mathematical sciences," from which he had been unfortunately "drawn" by "the history of the times."[6]

James Madison took up meteorology and stargazing primarily to please Jefferson; Tom Paine was a relentless scientific popularizer and the designer of a remarkable piece of early technology, an iron span bridge; Alexander Hamilton's understanding of anatomy impressed a leading physician of the age. Hamilton's 1791 *Report on Manufactures,* in combination with the first federal patent law, encouraged Eli Whitney, Robert Fulton, Oliver Evans, and others whose technologies strongly affected the early economic growth of the United States of America.

The terms "science," "technology," and "scientist," as we understand them today, were not in use in the Founders' era. There was no distinction between science and technology, the latter being considered as the more practical, usually mechanical product resulting from scientific inquiry. The title "scientist" did not exist prior to 1833, when British scientist and historian William Whewell coined it. Before then, newspapers, magazines, books, and speeches either referred to a specific field of study by name, such as astronomy, or in the aggregate plural as "the sciences," a label that encompassed a wide variety of fields including rhetoric and political science. Dr. Samuel Johnson in 1755 identified the "curious of nature" as "inquisitive, attentive, diligent, accurate, careful not to mistake, exact, nice, subtle, artful, rigorous." Such men (and a few women) expressed their "genius" by engaging in "speculation"—making educated guesses about natural phenomena. "Natural philosophy" and "natural history," the terms regularly used to denote science in the writings of the Founding Fathers and in the contemporary *Philosophical Transactions* of the London-based Royal Society, seem to us interchangeable. But natural philosophy then referred to what we might term the hard sciences, the mathematically based disciplines of physics, astronomy, chemistry, optics, and hydraulics. Natural history encompassed the soft sciences of botany, anthropology, anatomy, and, to a lesser extent, biology—what Foucault has called "the science of the characters that articulate the continuity and the tangle of nature."[7]

It is also important to note that the Founding Fathers' science was in no way opposite to their religion. The notion that science and religion were antithetical is a nineteenth-century construct. In 1874, American historian and scientist John William Draper, in his *History of the Conflict between Religion and Science*, thought he had consigned that notion to the dustbin by precisely identifying the main reason that the Founders had been more oriented to scientific understandings of the world than to the explanations and rationales proffered by organized religion: while religion always supports the power of groups, institutions, and establishments, science always supports the power of ideas—and the conception of the United States of America was very much an idea.[8]

To split the Founders' religious beliefs from their scientific ones creates a schism that did not exist in the Founding Fathers' time. The Founders saw and felt no space between their faith in science and their faith in a Deity. Although most of the Founders were not traditional Christians as were their neighbors who regularly attended a single church and believed in all its teachings, the Founders did share a set of religious tenets. These included faith in a single God and in a heaven, as well as an acceptance of the mythic truth of, and to varying degrees the literality of, the Book of Genesis's chronicle of the earth's and humanity's beginnings. The Founders' religiosity has generally been labeled Deism; but historian of religion Gregg L. Frazer, after an exhaustive review of their writings, concludes that the beliefs of the key Founders did not fit within any established categories, including Deism; rather, they shared a "hybrid belief system mixing elements of natural religion, Christianity, and rationalism, with rationalism as the predominant element."[9]

Their faith was in tune with the times. During the eighteenth century "as never before," historian Carl Becker suggests, "'Nature' . . . stepped in between God and man; so that there was no longer any way to know God's will except by discovering the 'laws' of Nature." "The Puritan Ethic as it existed among the Revolutionary generation," historian Edmund S. Morgan agrees, had "lost for most men the endorsement of an omnipresent angry God. The element of divinity had not entirely departed, but it was a good deal diluted. The values and precepts derived from it, however, remained intact."[10]

John Adams, who was raised as a Puritan Congregationalist and was more traditionally religious than most of the Founders, until the eve of the Revolutionary War regularly attended the church of his forefathers but preferred non-religious explanations for phenomena. In college he became an enthusiastic stargazer. He confided to his diary that observations of the heavens and study of Newton spurred him to awe regarding "the amazing harmony of our solar system," and to a firmer belief that "the Stupendous Plan of operation was projected by him who rules the universe, and a part assigned to every particle of matter, to act in this great and complicated Drama."[11] Adams believed in Newton's laws of motion as well as in revelation and occasional divine intervention—but in later life he no longer agreed with the notion, fundamental to Christianity, that Jesus was more than an extraordinary moral leader. For that reason, in 1773 he joined a Unitarian church.

Two men with whom Adams was frequently at odds philosophically, Franklin and Jefferson, held many of the same tenets regarding religion and science.

By the age of fifteen, Franklin wrote in his *Autobiography*, he had become a doubter of organized religion but kept his doubting in check until he chanced upon printed lectures that tried to debunk Deism: "They wrought an effect on me quite contrary to what was intended by them, for the arguments of the Deists, which were quoted to be refuted, appeared to me much stronger than the refutations; in short I soon became a thorough Deist."[12] In his twenties, he set out his religious beliefs in a ten-page liturgy, complete with a hymn. "I think it seems required of me, and my Duty, as a Man, to pay Divine Regards to SOMETHING," he wrote, for "when I stretch my Imagination thro' and beyond . . . the visible fix'd Stars themselves, into that Space that is every Way infinite, and conceive it fill'd with Suns like ours, each with a Chorus of Worlds for ever moving around him, then this little Ball on which we move, seems, even in my narrow Imagination, to be almost Nothing, and my self less than nothing, and of no sort of Consequence." He prayed to be "preserved from Atheism and Infidelity, Impiety and Profaneness."[13]

Toward the end of Jefferson's life, he completed the "Jefferson Bible," extracts from the New Testament that conveyed Jesus's moral teachings but not those parts recounting miracles or apostolic testimony as to his divinity. This project proved, he later wrote, that he was a Christian in that he was in agreement with Jesus's principles if not with his divinity. One of Jefferson's most famous lines is, "I have sworn upon the altar of God eternal hostility against every form of tyranny over the mind of man." As displayed on the wall of the Jefferson Memorial in Washington, DC, it is read by countless visitors, most of whom presume that it expresses a political imperative; but Jefferson penned it in specific rejection of repeated pleadings from Dr. Benjamin Rush to return to standard, church-based religious worship. Like Franklin, Adams, and Madison, Jefferson believed that established-church doctrines and practices were tyrannical in their attempts to limit the ways in which an individual could or should worship the Deity.[14]

Washington, an intensely, purposefully private man, carried everywhere a pocket-sized copy of a seventeenth-century Anglican prayer book and was occasionally seen reading it. But he was careful never to say or to write much about his religious beliefs. He repeatedly requested that citizens, soldiers, and legislators be respectful of those who professed religions other than their own, and he attended churches of many different denominations more as a concomitant of his public offices than as an expression of faith. In his speeches, letters, and other writings, Washington avoided mention of Jesus and of miracles and did not cite specific passages of the Bible. When out of the public eye, his church attendance declined, and if communion was offered during services, he either refused it or skipped church on those Sundays when communion was on the agenda.[15]

Madison was the most faithful to the religion of his father and remained a sometime adherent even after his marriage to the former Quaker, Dolley Payne Todd; but Madison was also the author and champion of the most definitive constitutional provisions separating church and state. James Monroe, who served as one of Washington's wartime lieutenants, and for whom Washington's conduct as president was the most important model for his own in that office, followed a similar pattern of visiting many churches but in private not being very religious. Alexander Hamilton and Aaron Burr were the least overtly religious of the Founding Fathers. Hamilton had gone through an early period, influenced by the clergyman Hugh Knox, in which he embraced a Protestant faith that he later pointedly discarded. Burr, son of a clergyman, was raised in a religious household but as an adult had almost nothing to do with organized religion.

RELIANCE ON RATIONAL AND RIGOROUS LOGIC, and on the need for experimentation, reproducible proof, and peer review—all aspects of a search for truth—were central to the Founders' understandings of their surroundings and to their dreams and plans for the new country. This book is an attempt to explore and chart that territory.

Since the significance of the Founders to history derives mainly from their roles as public patriots, I have used as guides the works of philosophers Jürgen Habermas, Foucault, and others regarding performance and the public sphere. The science-influenced works of the Founding Fathers reflect what Habermas identifies as the "communicative bases" of a society's leaders as well as—another important quality for Habermas—the genuineness of their self-expression. These matters are also essential to Foucault's distinction between the true participants in a discussion and polemicists who are "obstacles to the search for truth."

"The American Revolution," historian Gordon S. Wood writes, was "as radical and as revolutionary as any in history, if we measure the radicalism by the amount of social change that actually took place—by transformations in the relationships that bound people to each other." Those transformations include rejection of monarchism, of a state religion, and of a class system based on both, as well as getting rid of primogeniture and other patriarchal laws while explicitly accepting and promoting representative democratic governance and egalitarian social goals.[16]

To conceive of and to complete such a broadly transformative revolution requires leaders primed for change and willing to experiment. Had the Founders shared an obedient-to-authority, orthodox religious outlook, they might never have undertaken such a radical revolution, rebelling against Great Britain, its king, its state-sponsored church, and its hierarchical, anti-egalitarian colonial society. Their science-mindedness made them more willing to consider a multiplicity of new ideas.

Critical support for the American Revolution came from the vast majority of the populace that were neither university trained nor members of the socioeconomic elite; and it is important to note that many colonists who agreed with the Founders on the need to separate politically from Great Britain did not have a scientific outlook.[17] Still, by the mid-1770s a substantial fraction of the populace did agree with the leadership's science-influenced viewpoint. Together these leaders and followers constituted a group very like the "experimental polity" identified by historians of science Steven Shapin and Simon Schaffer, "said to be composed of free men, freely acting, faithfully delivering what they witnessed and sincerely believed to be the case. It was a community whose freedom was responsibly used and which publicly displayed its capacity for self discipline."[18] To a remarkable degree, those attributes of mind and behaviors among the denizens of the scientific laboratories and universities in seventeenth-century England studied by Shapin and Schaffer fit with those of the creators of that eighteenth-century revolutionary, experimental entity, the United States of America. Such a commonality of outlook was not accidental or unexpected, for Francis Bacon, as much a hero to the Founders as he was to the scientists of seventeenth-century England, had been convinced of the considerable overlap between scientific and democratic impulses, as summed up in his statement, "However governments may vary, there is but one state of the sciences, and that will be forever democratical and popular."[19]

In 1759, French mathematician Jean d'Alembert wrote that the world was in the midst of a period when "the kind of enthusiasm which accompanies discoveries, a certain exaltation of ideas which the spectacle of the universe produces in us . . . have brought about a lively fermentation of minds, spreading through nature in all directions like a river which has burst its dams."[20] D'Alembert's description aptly expresses the effect that the intellectual excitement of science had on America's Founding Fathers, whose science-based thoughts and actions were critical to the nation's birth and early health—far more so than were religious doctrine or economic considerations.

ONE

CHILDHOODS *of the* FOUNDING FATHERS

THE TERM "FOUNDING FATHERS" USUALLY REFERS to four senior patriots, three of whom became president: in the order of their births, Benjamin Franklin (1706–1790), George Washington (1732–1799), John Adams (1735–1826), and Thomas Jefferson (1743–1826). Membership in the Founders is often extended to James Madison (1751–1836), Alexander Hamilton (1755–1804), Aaron Burr (1756–1836), and James Monroe (1758–1831). I shall press the case for elevating to Associate Founder, for their scientific thinking, John Bartram (1699–1777), David Rittenhouse (1732–1796), Tom Paine (1737–1809), Benjamin Rush (1746–1813), and Charles Thomson (1729–1824), but will hold them aside for the moment to first consider the backgrounds and childhoods of the better-acknowledged octet.

In sharp contrast to the childhoods of later generations of middle- and upper-class Americans, the early years of Franklin, Washington, Adams, Jefferson, Madison, Hamilton, Burr, and Monroe, as with most of their contemporaries, were stolid and purposeful, far from carefree or idyllic even in those families with money. All eight were of British descent; all were Protestants; save for Hamilton, all were born in the North American colonies; and, save for Burr, they had fathers with little formal education.[1]

Washington, Jefferson, Burr, and Monroe became fatherless before they reached adulthood. Hamilton hardly knew his father; and while the fathers of Franklin and Adams survived into their sons' middle years, the sons definitively rejected the life paths set out for them by their sires. Only Madison's father lived to see his son, James Jr., fulfill his paternal expectations.

The condition of fatherlessness was then common. Average life expectancy for white men and women in the American colonies remained steady at forty-six years throughout the eighteenth century. Nearly half of the white children born in the southern colonies became fatherless, motherless, or both by age twenty-one; in the northern colonies the percentage of children who lost one or both parents was smaller but still significant.[2] Though the loss of a parent was common, American family histories of the colonial era universally acknowledge that it was traumatic for a child; and while most widowed parents did remarry within a few years of a spouse's death, bereaved children remained emotionally scarred for life.[3]

For sons in the American colonial culture, the early loss of a father was particularly difficult since the primogeniture laws and church practice mandated that male children were to be taught by fathers rather than by mothers and were to be led by their fathers through their major life choices of vocation, spouse, political and church affiliation, and residence. According to one study of familial structures,

> Sons were often regarded as extensions of their fathers; young or newly born sons were commonly described by their fathers as "my hope" or "my consolation". . . . Men were thought to have superior reason, which made them less likely than women to be misled by the "passions" and "affections" to which both sexes were subject. . . . Fathers had to restrain their children's sinful urges and encourage the development of sound reason.[4]

From birth to age five or six, children were clothed in dresslike gowns; by age seven, approximately when schooling began, boys were switched to clothing resembling that of an adult male, while girls remained in dresses—a change emphasizing that men were dominant and adult but that women were subordinate and childlike. Fathers, not mothers, had the responsibility of instructing sons at home or arranging for their early schooling. Later on in the sons' lives, fathers directed them into apprenticeships or to other ways of earning their livelihoods, superintended their marriages, and bestowed or bequeathed property to them. That many sons dutifully and regularly sought their fathers' counsel is reflected in the thousands of surviving letters from sons to fathers, in contrast to the few hundred extant letters from sons to mothers.[5]

Literate fathers of lesser economic means taught their prepubescent sons to read and write at home; better-off fathers sent the sons to schools, usually those run by local clergy, who were often graduates of British universities and the most literate men in a community. In such early-grade schools, the revolutionary cohort learned what was, then as now, the basis of science: mathematics. Franklin, Washington, Adams, Jefferson, and Hamilton came to love mathematics and to rely on it. Although Franklin twice flunked basic math and never mastered geometry, in his adulthood he became adept enough to create "magic squares" of numbers; Adams remembered enough mathematics so that he could teach his son John Quincy rudimentary calculus; Washington's surveying was dependent upon mathematical precision; Hamilton used his facility with numbers to escape a stultifying childhood in the Caribbean for New York. Jefferson's embrace of mathematics translated into his measuring and comparing by ratio many aspects of his daily life; while teaching mathematics to his grandson, he revealed why he liked it: "We have no theories there, no uncertainties remain on the mind; all is demonstration and satisfaction."[6]

Fatherlessness has been explicitly acknowledged in modern times as emotionally roiling and as a largely negative influence on children. But some modern studies show that the effects of fatherlessness on "high achievers" may not be as bad as they are upon those who never reach prominence. Studies of mathematical and scientific geniuses of the nineteenth and twentieth centuries reveal that a disproportionately high fraction, in some fields a quarter, in others a third, had lost one or both parents during childhood in an era when losing parents was significantly rarer than in prior centuries. Individuals who managed to surmount the difficulties attendant on an early parental death went on to accomplishment more often than did their contemporaries. This modern study echoes the lesson that Jefferson, who lost his father at age fourteen, understood from the experience: "The whole care and direction of myself was thrown on myself entirely, without a relation or friend qualified to advise or guide me." Willing and able to rely on his own decision-making processes, Jefferson grew up quickly.[7] Fatherlessness, I believe, was one of the most important bases for the Founding Fathers' predilection for adopting mind-sets primed for independence, rebelliousness, and new ideas.

One of the most distinctive characteristics of high achievers is their willingness to break with convention. This trait is better acknowledged in scientific than in political work, for significant scientific breakthroughs are seldom incremental in nature and usually involve a rejection of or a serious alteration to prior theories and accepted wisdom. While Isaac Newton—hero to all of the Founding Fathers—famously wrote, "If I have seen further, it is by standing on the shoulders of giants," his accomplishments owed far more to his eagerness to disprove and transcend some of those giants' less rigorously scientific understandings of the universe. To make their Revolution, the Founding Fathers similarly had to overturn the patriarchal form of government under which the colonies labored, as well as many of its accompanying conventions and social structures.

Able to choose between fealty to the older, religious-dictated worldview and acceptance of the possibilities inherent in the newer, science-based one, the Founders gravitated toward the new—in part because just at that moment it was eminently possible for them to embrace the new without danger to their souls. Adopting scientific thinking did not require them to be irreligious or in any way to deny God as the First Cause of the universe. In their view, the breathtaking scope of God's design and its fabulous, intricate details had been revealed and illuminated by the scientific discoveries of the previous two centuries. In consequence, the then-current scientific worldview encouraged the rejection only of what was distasteful, unsupportable, or unduly shackling in religious explanations, and it retained and even burnished a reverence for God. That worldview had moved toward the aims for science that the quite religious Francis Bacon had set out in 1620 in *The New Atlantis:* "the knowledge of Causes, and secret motions of things, and the enlarging of Human Empire, to the effecting of all things possible." A hundred years after Bacon wrote, his vision was perhaps more characteristic of the conception and expectations of science in the American colonies than of science in the British Isles.[8]

"THE BEAME AND CHAINE balke no Truthes nor blaunch Un-truths . . . Take away Number, Weight, Measure you exile Justice and reduce and haile-up from Hell the olde and odious Chaos of Confusion." Sarah S. Hughes cites this ancient quotation about surveying in her study of Virginia colonial surveyors to underscore the idea that surveying was then considered a thrillingly exact practical science and exploration into the barely known, aspects that contributed to its respect by the community, and certainly by the young surveyor George Washington.[9]

George Washington was a child of a second marriage; his father, Augustine, had remarried after being widowed. When George was three, the family moved to Fredericksburg, where he may have first been taught by his father's tenant, a Mr. Hobby, who later claimed credit for his instruction, prior to attending a school run by the Reverend James Marye. Two hundred pages of Washington's schoolboy notes survive; they are largely taken up with copyings from mathematics textbooks and exercises in geometry, trigonometry, rudimentary economics, record keeping, and surveying.[10] It is likely that Washington also received informal education from his half-brother and idol, Lawrence, fourteen years older, who had attended the Appleby School in England and may have stayed on as an instructor before returning to Virginia. George's own school attendance ended abruptly in 1743 when his father died. The tall eleven-year-old then came more directly under the influence of Lawrence, then twenty-five, and of Lawrence's father-in-law, Lord William Fairfax, who served as Washington's model for acting as a gentleman.

George's next schooling of record was four years later, when he attended the College of William & Mary for a short session that, given the school's fiat, must have been devoted to training and licensing as a surveyor rather than to the classical education that the college provided to regular students. William & Mary held an exclusive grant to license surveyors in Virginia and had reason to assert that privilege, which was an important source of revenue for the college from licensees bound by contract to turn over to it a sixth of their fees. But Lord Fairfax was a powerful man who held sway over five million acres granted to him by the king, and within that domain he independently exercised the right to employ, if not to license, surveyors. In 1748, Washington worked as an apprentice for George William Fairfax, the son of Lord Fairfax's cousin, on a survey into the Shenandoah Valley, and on a second one for the city of Alexandria, of which Lawrence was a trustee. A few days after the plan for Alexandria was completed, George Washington was commissioned as a full surveyor.

Surveying was a way of introducing order and reason into the wild western Virginia frontier—and into the life of a young and largely adrift practitioner of the craft. In Virginia, surveying had evolved into a gentleman's calling that brought cash and prestige to such men as Peter Jefferson, father of Thomas, and John Henry, father of Patrick, both senior surveyors when Washington was a neophyte. "Whatever the defects of their education," Hughes concludes, "the gentlemen surveyors were numbered among the colony's practical-minded intellectual elite, the minority who collected books and subscribed to newspapers."[11]

From 1749 to 1752, Washington put in a few months each year as a surveyor during amenable weather, taking along an experienced chainman whom he paid directly rather than, as per custom, having the several chainmen paid for by the client whose property was being surveyed. Washington and a crew of three or four were often at work far from European civilization at a time when Native Americans understood the meaning of surveyors' hacked marks on trees and sometimes followed those marks to a camp and killed or kidnapped the surveyors.

Washington did most of his surveying work on the frontier, at the western edge of Frederick County. His regular kit included expensive state-of-the-art equipment, such as a two-foot "Gunter's scale." Although Washington appears to have enjoyed using his surveying skills and commanding a small band of men, his letters suggest that his main purpose in surveying was income. "A Dubbleloon is my constant gain every Day that the Weather will permit my going out, and some time Six Pistoles," he wrote to a friend. Aside from paying his chainman, he kept all of the £100 or so he earned each year, sending none of it to the College of William & Mary.[12]

A few entries in his diaries and notes convey his modest appreciation of the natural surround, but more of them deal with the need to conquer it for the settlers' use. He conceived a lifelong interest in reshaping the rapids and falls of the Potomac River for a commercial route to the lands of the West. Returning from a trip along the Potomac, he observed to a friend, "There is no obstacle other than the shallowness of the water to prevent Craft from passing," and imagined that one waterfall "may be much amended by digging a channel on the Maryland side abt 2 Miles from this and ½ Mile below the Mouth of the Shannondoah."[13] He used part of his profit from surveying to make a first land purchase, 1,459 acres along Bullskin Creek in Frederick County.

In all that Washington later did he incorporated surveying's essentials—faith in numbers, precision, accuracy, and rigor, and the need to double-check every assessment. He ceased his surveying in November 1752 when he had an opportunity to take over Lawrence's military commission; but also, the supply of unsurveyed lands on the western Virginia frontier was dwindling. Additional pressure to yield his surveying assignments may have come from William & Mary; under a new royal governor, the college was reasserting its sole right to license surveyors, taking it back from Lord Fairfax.

The previous year, Washington had cut short his surveying season to accompany Lawrence, ill with tuberculosis, on a journey to Barbados, in whose balmy atmosphere his brother's health was expected to recover. George kept a diary on this thirty-seven-day voyage, recording his advancing knowledge of the "riggan," his new eating experiences of dolphins and "barracootas," and what occurred when the sea-going equivalent of a survey was inaccurate:

> We quitted our beds with surprise and found ye land plainly appearing at bout 3 leagues distance when by our reckonings we shou'd have been near 150 Leagues to the Windward we to Leeward abt ye distance above mention'd and had we been but 3 or 4 leagues more we shou'd have been out of sight of the Island run down the Latitude and probably not have discover'd Error in time to have gain'd land for 3 Weeks or More.

On Barbados, Washington observed flora, fauna, and society, and read a local natural history book and commented in his diary on crops, means of production, and yield per acre compared to what he obtained in Virginia. Lawrence's health did not markedly improve and on November 17 George was "strongly attacked with the small Pox," becoming so ill that he did not write again in the diary until December 12. Lightly scarred in the face, he understood that a scientific fact had been imprinted on his body, evidence that he had acquired immunity from smallpox for life. [14]

Lawrence died soon after their return to Virginia, and George took over Lawrence's responsibilities with the militia and devoted himself to agriculture at Mount Vernon, the estate he inherited from Lawrence and enlarged after his 1759 marriage to Martha Custis, the wealthiest widow in Virginia. On Mount Vernon's acres he struggled to replace the land-exhausting crop of tobacco. He recorded in a diary that he and his smith,

Peter, made "several efforts to make a plow after a new model—partly of my own contriving," but did not then succeed. He cultivated new crops, flax and hemp, obtained equipment for turning those crops into cloth, and within three years the plantation was making all of the cloth needed for his numerous slaves' everyday garb. He also conducted what he styled "experiments" of various mixes of manures, seeds, and planting schemes. A typical entry, March 24, 1760: "In the Evening, in a Bed that had been prepared with a mixture of Dung on Saturday last, I sowed Choice Lucerne, and Rye Grass Seeds in the Garden, to try their Goodness, doing it in the following Order: at the end next the Corner were two Rows of Clover Seed; in the 3rd, 4, 5, and 6th Rye Grass—the last Row thinnest Sowd; 7th and 8th Barley (to see if it woud come up)." Within a few days he was grafting cherries, plums, apples, and planting Madeira grapes; in May he experimented with different soils in which to plant oats and "watch their growth and different changes till Harvest."[15]

IN EARLY CHILDHOOD, John Adams later wrote, "the most indolent man I ever knew," a teacher, "gave me a disgust to Schools, to books and to study." When Adams was switched to another school, the master "neglected to put me into Arithmetick longer than I thought was right, and I resented it." So he found a textbook, mastered it, and surpassed the class in the subject, taking care to conceal this accomplishment from his father so as not to be chided for a reciprocal neglect of Latin, a prerequisite for the ministerial studies his father wanted him to pursue. Only after Adams found a third school amenable did he agree to accept instruction and become reconciled to attending Harvard, at his father's request. The senior Adams was perhaps unaware that just then, as historian Michael N. Shute writes, Harvard "was exercising new autonomy from clerical restriction, and experimenting in science, aesthetics, and other areas." These experiments did not sit well with some students; as one put it in *The American Magazine and Historical Chronicle*,

> *Now algebra, geometry,*
> *Arithmetic, astronomy,*
> *Opticks, chronology, and staticks,*
> *All tiresome parts of mathematics,*
> *With twenty harder names than these*

Disturb my brains, and break my peace. . . .
Our senses are depriv'd by prisms,
Our arguments by syllogisms.
If I should confidently write,
This ink is black, this paper white,
They'd contradict it, and perplex one
With motion, light, and its reflection.[16]

Adams's most seminal experience at Harvard, while he was engaged in obtaining a classical education, was a single course given by astronomer John Winthrop. It strongly affected him. "Mathematicks and natural Phylosophy attracted most of my attention" in college, Adams wrote in his autobiography, adding that he owed to these studies "some degree of Patience of Investigation, which I might not otherwise have obtained," and for which he was later celebrated. Winthrop's course featured attempts to relate scientific principles to the sort of problems encountered by farmers, lawyers, and accountants, as well as to more lofty matters of truth, skepticism, proof, and healthy argument. Adams brought the canons of scientific inquiry to a wide variety of subjects, testing them in the ways he believed scientists tested their hypotheses—as he related in a letter written a few years after graduation to a classmate regarding the Roman orator Cicero: "The Art of the sublime, like the Art of natural philosophy, is founded [formed?] in a science, and Experiment and Observation are the natural means of improving both. We must make Trial of the Effects of . . . different Ideas, and of different Sentiments, on the human Senses, Passions, Imagination, and Understanding."[17]

Adams would still later recall for his son John Quincy his delight in mounting to the highest point of Harvard's buildings of an evening to use Winthrop's telescope and his thrill as it brought into focus the moons of Jupiter.

Winthrop was a great-grandson of John Winthrop Jr., governor of Connecticut and a noted alchemist, part of the Hartlib Circle that in the seventeenth century had connected by correspondence most of the world's scientists.[18] The great-grandson followed the family's scientific tradition, in 1738 becoming Harvard's second Hollis Professor of Mathematics and Natural Philosophy. By the 1750s Winthrop was regularly contributing reports of celestial observations to the Royal Society. He taught his pupils so well that even after a three-decade hiatus from math and science, Adams could spend a year in Paris teaching his son geometry, trigonometry, algebra, and conic sections, and attempted "a sublime Flight and endeavoured to give him some Idea of the Differential Method of Calculation of the Marquis de L'Hospital and the Method of Fluxions and infinite Series of Sir Isaac Newton."[19]

Winthrop's natural philosophy course included such then-current topics as electricity. While teaching Adams, Winthrop had to abbreviate his course in order to travel to Philadelphia to meet Benjamin Franklin, whose electrical prowess had stunned the scientific arbiters of London and Paris.[20] Another student of Winthrop's recalled him as such a good tutor that "every subject he handled . . . each new lecture seemed a new revelation," an attribute that "at once commanded both respect and love"; and a sometime student, Benjamin Thompson, who became Count Rumford, a giant of physics, also acknowledged Winthrop as a fine teacher.[21]

Adams graduated from Harvard but rejected a ministerial future and was instead studying law in mid-November 1755 when a fairly substantial earthquake occurred. Known as the Cape Ann earthquake, it is today estimated at a magnitude of 6.0–6.3 on the Richter scale and was likely a distant echo of the much larger earthquake that had leveled the city of Lisbon two weeks earlier. The four-minute Cape Ann quake so jolted Adams, who was in Braintree, that he chose that day to begin a new diary. He "awoke out of my sleep in the midst of it. The house seemed to rock and reel and crack as if it would fall into ruins about us. 7 Chimnies were shatter'd by it within one mile of my Fathers house." Adams was interested to know what Winthrop thought about the quake. The professor made his analysis known in a lecture at Harvard's chapel in late November. By then, ministers had already labeled the quake an instance of divine retribution for human sin and claimed that it had been set off by those newfangled devices, Franklin's lightning rods, which had dared to lure God's fire from the heavens and direct it deep into the earth, provoking the eruption. Winthrop explained the quake to his audience in purely scientific terms. Beneath the earth's surface, Winthrop said, was "a compages of a vast variety of solid substances, ranged in a manner that to us seems to have not much of regularity in it. Here we find earths, stones, salts, sulphurs, minerals, metals, &c, and a great number of inferior species under each of these general heads, blended and intermingled with each other. Many of these are combustible, or of a texture proper to be turned by fire into flame and vapor." Winthrop described the quake as shaped like a wave, suggested that it had rattled through the various subsurface strata, and attributed its cause to what we would today call a tectonic shift, a geologic concept not yet elucidated in Winthrop's time. Adams's notes on the margin of the printed version of Winthrop's lecture show the student agreeing with the professor: "The Invention of Iron Points to prevent the Danger of Thunder has met with all that Opposition from the Superstitions, Affectations of Piety, and Jealousy of New Inventions, that Inoculation to prevent the Danger of the Small Pox, and all the other Usefull Discoveries, have met with in All Ages of the World."[22]

If Adams had ever seriously considered a career in science, he talked himself out of it in 1758, arguing to his diary that if a person was "not instructed to contemplate the Heavens, he will instruct himself to contemplate Cockle shells and Pebblestones," and wondering whether, if one chose "the study of Nature, for the business of your life, should you not inquire in the first Place, what is the End of that study? Is it to improve the Manufactures, the Husbandry, or the Commerce of Mankind, or is it to adorn a Library with Butterflies of various sizes, Colours and shapes?"[23]

PETER JEFFERSON WAS NOT highly literate but recognized the need for his son to become so. He sent Thomas, at nine, to a boarding school run by the Reverend William Douglas, who taught him a bit of Latin, Greek, and Scottish-accented French. After Peter's death in 1757, the four-teen-year-old Jefferson was switched to another boarding school, operated by a clergyman with a similar Scottish background, the Reverend James Maury. At that time the products of the Scottish Enlightenment, men who had learned from Edinburgh philosophers Adam Smith, David Hume, and their followers, were filling many of the teaching slots at American schools. "In demanding that experiment not inherited truth define the business of living, the Edinburgh philosophers stamped the West with its modern scientific and provisional character," historian James Buchan writes. "They created a world that tended toward the egalitarian and, within reason, the democratic."[24] Both the Reverend Maury and Jefferson's later teacher, William Small, were products of the Scottish Enlightenment.

During his two years with Maury Jefferson continued his French, Latin, and Greek, became close friends with his future brother-in-law, Dabney Carr, and may also have met another later close friend, James Madison, a cousin of the future president of the same name. Maury introduced Jefferson to scientific matters, including Newtonian astronomy. Jefferson was probably permitted to use Maury's library and to explore the landscape with his teacher. Maury's likely targets of exploration are suggested by a box that he sent a correspondent around this time, containing what the recipient described as "a piece of antediluvian mud petrified with the perfect print of a cockle shell upon it, taken from the top of one of the Great [Blue Ridge] Mountains, and a piece of sea-coal as good as any in Whitehaven, taken out of a broken bank."[25]

At age sixteen, wanting to attend William & Mary, Jefferson attempted to convince the executors of his father's estate that he should do so by recourse to mathematical reasoning. "So long as I stay in the Mountains the Loss of one fourth of my Time is inevitable," since it was taken up with entertaining company, and he argued that he could more profitably and economically socialize in Williamsburg, "& by that means Lessen the Expences of the Estate in Housekeeping."[26] Among the friends to more easily entertain at the college were Carr and neighbor John Walker.

In Williamsburg, Jefferson was most fortunate to encounter William Small, "a man profound in the most useful branches of science, with a happy talent of communication, correct and gentlemanly manners, and an enlarged and liberal mind," as Jefferson would describe him, adding that being a student of Small's "fixed the destinies of my life." To instruct and inspire an extraordinary pupil requires a no less extraordinary teacher. By all accounts, Small, just nine years older than Jefferson, was that. Small was much more of a product of the Scottish Enlightenment than was Maury. Small's college, Marischal, in Aberdeen, had experimented with new ways of instruction and with subject matter that included more science and less religion, consciously following the Baconian plea to rid schools of the pedagogical system in which "philosophy" came "down to us in the persons of master and scholar instead of inventor and improver." Marischal had begun to employ experts in various fields to teach individual courses. Small's biographer, Martin Claggett, writes that this systemic change was accompanied by a push "to make the study of the sciences more natural and progressive, and to prepare . . . students to be useful in life" by means of scientific demonstrations and instruction in using scientific measuring devices. After graduating from Marischal, Small moved to London, where he is believed to have taken courses in medicine before crossing the Atlantic. He owed his appointment at William & Mary to a furor that had brought about the firing of previous instructors for their effrontery in demanding payment for services in tobacco, the general medium of exchange, rather than in the colony's scrip. The new governor had insisted that the replacement be a layperson and not an Anglican. Small fit that bill. When Jefferson arrived, Small had been at William & Mary for several years and had recently, after the death of its president, begun directing its courses.[27]

Jefferson took all of his courses with Small, but more than that, and "most happily for me," as Jefferson wrote in his *Autobiography*, Small "made me his daily companion when not engaged in the school, and from his conversation I got my first views of the expansion of science & of the system of things in which they are placed." Jefferson later lauded Small "as a father. To his enlightened and affectionate guidance of my studies while at college, I am indebted for everything."[28]

To the annoyance of Small's fellow faculty members, the Scot disdained the food served at the college and habitually took evening meals at the homes of some of the capital's wealthier, more literate, and more accomplished men. Jefferson soon joined Small at the tables of Lieutenant Governor Frances Fauquier and lawyer George Wythe. The governor, then fifty-seven and the elder statesman of the four, was a man of science; his father had immigrated to England to work directly with Newton; the governor knew a fair amount about physics, mathematics, and economics and was a Fellow of the Royal Society. Wythe, who would become Jefferson's law tutor and mentor, was also scientifically inclined, participating in astronomical observations with Small and Jefferson's fellow student, John Page, whose family mansion, Rosewell, was nearby.

Wythe and Page had also been fatherless in their youths. That was one bond between them and Jefferson, and the three were also united by their respect for Small. Other Jefferson and Small table companions included the colony's printer, William Hunter, who shared the title of colonial postmaster with Benjamin Franklin of Philadelphia, and Peyton Randolph. The table on most evenings consisted solely of Jefferson, Small, Wythe, and Fauquier, a "*partie quarrée*," Jefferson later wrote, to whom he "owed much instruction," being privy at these dinners to "more good sense, more rational and philosophical conversations, than in all my life besides. They were truly Attic societies."[29]

In the formal classes that Small introduced under the new system, William & Mary professors lectured in the mornings and in the afternoons answered student questions and performed demonstrations of scientific principles. Classes were held six days of the week, with alternating days for moral and natural philosophy.

After two years of classes, Jefferson remained in Williamsburg to study law under Wythe. The following year Small, having been denied the presidency of William & Mary, returned to England, amid controversy but with an important commission from the college, to buy enough science-demonstrating and -measuring equipment to teach a much larger compass of science courses. The attention paid by Small to the purchase suggests that he hoped to return to the college. He never did. In a parting shot at him, the college's check for severance was accompanied by a nasty letter: "If the Malevolence of disappointed Ambition will allow a fair and candid Exercise of [reflection], it must convince you that you received more Civilities & Indulgences here than you had the least Pretence of Right to expect.... [You were] Master of Art enough to insinuate yourself into the Fav'r of some of the principal Gentlemen of the country, most of whom, tho' they had not Penetration enough to see thro' your Disguise at first, are now thoroughly convinced of the Delusion."[30]

Small disproved the accusations of incompetence and incompatibility once he had relocated to Birmingham as a medical doctor, validating his introductory from Benjamin Franklin, which attested that Small was "both an ingenious Philosopher & most worthy honest man." In Birmingham, Small became a prime influence on the mainstays of the Lunar Society, Matthew Boulton and his manufacturing partner James Watt, ceramicist Josiah Wedgwood, and chemist Joseph Priestley. Small's influence on Watt was considerable, encouraging him to publish his improvements to the steam engine, which enabled it to become the most important technological innovation of the century. Small died in 1775 at the age of forty-one. As Jefferson moved through life (he later told his grandson), when faced with difficult decisions he would routinely ask what William Small would advise him to do in such a spot, and whether his actions would still earn the teacher's approbation.[31]

So let us cherish the image of Adams and Jefferson—whose personalities and political philosophies would clash in profound ways—in their college days, mounting to the roofs in the darkest hours of the night to peer through their teachers' telescopes at distant celestial bodies and experience the wonder of nature and the enlightenment that came from understanding the heavens as scientists did. For what these future Founders obtained through their telescopes was more than beautiful sights, it was verification of the workings of universal laws as elucidated by human genius. And what they learned from professors such as Small and Winthrop was more than information, it was a cast of mind that viewed everything through scientific frames.

DESPITE THE BEST EFFORTS of Small, Winthrop, Yale's Thomas Clap, and a few other science-minded professors, scholasticism based on the writings of Aquinas and Aristotle "continued to be the philosophic teaching of [most] American universities and colleges down until well on in the nineteenth century," according to historian of education James J. Walsh. In those institutions, students were required to defend or attack in "public disputations" about a hundred theses, usually of the moral and ethical sort. However, by the 1760s, the occasional scientific thesis made the lists at the leading colleges: "Heat is produced by the transverse agitation very rapidly of very small particles." "The *ignis fatuus* (or will-o'-the-wisp) is not due to the ignition of meteors." "Earthquakes are caused by subterranean heat." "There is such a thing as transmutation of metals." Although Clap emphasized science during his tenure at Yale, the college did not have any "Theses Physicae" until 1770, when several questions in physics, chemistry, astronomy, mechanics, and biology were included.[32]

There were no such science theses at the College of New Jersey in the time of James Madison. The eldest of twelve children of the wealthiest tobacco planter in Orange County, Virginia, James learned basic mathematics and science between the ages of eleven and sixteen at a boarding school run by yet another Scot, Donald Robertson. After two additional years of preparatory courses at home, under the Reverend Thomas Martin, Madison matriculated at the College of New Jersey, in Prince Town, in 1769. Later to be renamed Princeton, this was the last top-tier American bastion of teaching the classics without edging over at all into natural philosophy or natural history. Although mathematics and geometry were taught, the college had neither books about, nor adequate machinery to demonstrate, physical and mechanical principles, and so the basic study of mathematics did not lead, as it did at Yale, Harvard, William & Mary, and King's College in New York, to more detailed consideration of the knowledge obtainable through scientific observation. Madison condensed four years of college into two, thus graduating prior to the college's first attempts to purchase the books and equipment needed to teach science, which began in 1772.[33] After completing his undergraduate courses, Madison remained on campus an additional year, concentrating on mastering Hebrew to supplement his Latin and Greek. His major revelation while at college was that religious doctrine could be open to question and that observance could be practiced in a way other than the rigid Protestantism of his father and rural Virginia. Several classmates went into the Presbyterian ministry, and he asked one to send a copy of the Pennsylvania charter's article about religious toleration, explaining that "Religious bondage shackles and debilitates the mind and unfits it for every noble enterprise, every expanded prospect."[34] He obtained the Pennsylvania material so that he could write a similar statute for Virginia.

ALEXANDER HAMILTON'S CHILDHOOD, on Nevis and other Caribbean islands, was terrifying, and his birth father was mostly absent from it. By the time Alex was fourteen and his brother James was sixteen, virtually every one of the relatives who had charge of him had died, including his mother, uncle, grandmother, and cousin. By that age, however, Hamilton could read, write, and do some elementary math, and came under the guidance of clergyman Hugh Knox, who was also a doctor, apothecary, and journalist. Hamilton's computational abilities served him well in a junior position with a trading company, enabling him to take over tasks usually done by older, better-educated men. When he was seventeen, a hurricane struck the island, and he wrote a detailed descriptive letter about it: "The roaring of the sea and wind, the fiery meteors flying about . . . the prodigious glare of almost perpetual lightning, the crash of falling houses, and the ear-piercing shrieks of the distressed, were sufficient to strike astonishment into angels." Knox helped get the letter published. It was so clearly the work of a young man of promise that a collection was taken up to provide money for Hamilton to go to New York and attend college.[35]

Lacking appropriate academic preparation, he was sent first for additional training to the well-known Elizabethtown Academy; that city was then New Jersey's capital and in it Hamilton divided his time between absorbing the classics and making himself known to high-placed families who could assist his rise. The Elizabethtown Academy taught elementary sciences and served as a preparatory school for the College of New Jersey. Hamilton would later claim that he had been unable to convince that college's new president, Reverend John Witherspoon, to allow him to advance from freshman to sophomore and sophomore to junior when he felt ready to do so rather than taking courses one semester at a time, and so moved to Manhattan and King's College. The story may be apocryphal since Madison had managed to complete the usual four years in two. At King's, Hamilton studied mathematics with Robert Harpur, a Scottish mathematician, and anatomy with Dr. Samuel Clossy, an Irish surgeon. In later years Dr. David Hosack, Hamilton's physician, would describe his friend's understanding of human physical anatomy as rather complete and unsurpassed among laymen.[36]

Aaron Burr had academic parents. His father was a former president of the College of New Jersey, and his mother was the daughter of the famed preacher Jonathan Edwards. But by the age of two, Burr and his sister, Sally, were orphaned and sent to live with Dr. William Shippen Sr. in Philadelphia. They were shortly moved to Elizabethtown by their uncle, Timothy Edwards, and the precocious Burr attended the academy there until admitted to the College of New Jersey at age thirteen in 1769. Unlike Madison, Burr must have absorbed enough in the way of technology to later be able to turn his hand to making guns and to design a steamboat.[37]

Monroe, fifteen years younger than Jefferson, followed Jefferson's path to a mid-Virginia boarding school and then to William & Mary. When Monroe was sixteen, his father died, as had Jefferson's when he was fourteen. At the Campbell boarding school, Monroe's progress in mathematics was judged faster and more thorough than that of other students, including his classmate, future Chief Justice John Marshall. Proceeding to William & Mary in 1774, Monroe learned science, although without the benefit of William Small. An equally celebrated young teacher was then in charge of the science courses, Reverend James Madison, Jefferson's friend. Because Small had obtained for the college the finest set of scientific instruments in the colonies, these were available for use. Monroe's college career was cut short when the agitation in the colonies grew to the point of shutting down the school's operation, after which he joined the 3rd Virginia Regiment of the Continental Army as a junior officer.

BY MODERN STANDARDS, the science learned by the Founding Fathers was rather basic. A great deal of it was still based on underlying principles that had survived since ancient Greece. Empedocles (c. 490–430 BC) had identified the four elements of the universe as Earth, Water, Air, and Fire; singly or in combination, these accounted for the composition of all things in, on, or above the earth; science was a matter of understanding those "elements," combinations, and actions. Aristotle added a fifth element, the Aether—a divine element not accessible to humankind—which he believed made up the sun, moon, stars, and other celestial bodies. The Empedocles-Aristotle conception survived the collapse of the ancient world and was reasserted in the thirteenth century by Thomas Aquinas. In the seventeenth century, Francis Bacon and René Descartes undermined it, citing the astronomical discoveries of Copernicus and Galileo. The more emphatic thrusting aside of the Aristotelian conceptions resulted from further seventeenth- and early eighteenth-century discoveries that relied on rigorous experimentation and measurement. American astronomer David Rittenhouse would precisely identify why the Aristotelian understandings of the universe were eclipsed by those of Isaac Newton: "because [Newton] pretends not to be of Nature's privy council, or to have free access to her most inscrutable mysteries," as Aristotle did, Newton was therefore more readily able to "discover the immediate causes of visible effects [and] to trace those causes to others more general and simple."[38] The same could be said of William Harvey in discovering the circulation of the blood, and of Robert Boyle in understanding the relationships of volume, pressure, and temperature. Boyle encapsulated the difference between old and new methods in his famous assertion that had he believed Aristotle's saw that nature abhorred a vacuum, he never would have sought to create one.

Until around 1750, the vast majority of Europeans and American colonists knew little about the advances of Newton, Boyle, Harvey, or Robert Hooke, and still held a biblically based view of the natural world, one almost completely independent of science. Hanging onto the Aristotelian notions of Earth, Air, Water, and Fire well past the time when the four-elements conception had been discarded by leading scientists, the colonists did so not only because of lack of information about what science had learned in the recent past, but also because what I term the deconstructive discoveries of science had not yet been made. Air was thought of as a single entity since oxygen and nitrogen had yet to be identified as its more basic components. Arguments in geology regarding the composition of Earth were less about physics or chemistry than about theology, pitting those who believed in a volcanic origin of continents against those who believed that Noah's flood had shaped its current configuration. Water, too, was still thought of as an indivisible element. As for Fire, nothing had suggested that it was not basic and elemental, although scientists were arguing over the precise nature of "phlogiston," an immaterial substance that they believed was released during combustion. By the 1820s, Earth, Air, Water, and Fire would all be deconstructed, and even schoolchildren would know that each contained multitudes of more basic elements. That very large change developed contemporaneously with, and had an effect on, the events and attitudes chronicled in this book.

At the start of the period, the opening decades of the eighteenth century, the old Aristotelian few-element conception was already crumbling, but many natural philosophers were reluctant to let it go. There is evidence of the transition to the later, more properly descriptive conception in a textbook by John Questebrune, initially written for a Scottish lord in 1720 and used in Philadelphia in the 1740s. The sophistication of the text marks the author as a reasonable and knowledgeable teacher of the sciences. But his descriptions often rely on Aristotelian terminology. He identifies "bitumen" as "a kind of Oily Earth form'd of an airy & fat exhalation condensed by the Coldness of the Earth into an oleaginous liquor; and sometimes when mixed with many serene particles made Solid." He concedes in his text that no one up-to-date in the sciences could continue to believe that Earth consisted of a single element, "since there are a 1000 mixtures," and he was also willing to subdivide Water into mineral water, sea water, and water containing "dissolutions"—dissolved substances— but in many other passages of this exquisitely lettered book, he adhered to the older formulation.[39]

Assisting in the retention of the few-elements conception of the physical world was continued reliance on the book of Genesis as a literal record of the creation of the universe. While many knowledgeable people had long since accepted the Copernican concept that the sun, rather than the earth, was the center of our solar system and understood that the earth and other planets revolved around the sun, other aspects of received biblical wisdom about creation survived in their thoughts. For instance, many accepted a precise date on which God had established and fixed the earth in the firmament: during daylight hours on October 23, 4004 BC. Irish Archbishop James Ussher, working from biblical and historical sources, had calculated that date in 1654, and his work had since become accepted as dogma. Newton too had attempted to calculate the earth's age; positing that the earth had begun as a ball of molten iron, Newton determined that it had taken 42,964 years to cool below incandescence and an additional 96,670 years to drop to the then-current temperature.

Newton's laws of motion, Copernicus's conception of the earth as revolving around the sun, and Hooke's discoveries of previously invisible creatures were all seen as further proofs of God's plan of nature and his intricate, near-infinitely detailed designs. Mankind's continuing task was the discovery of those designs. Accordingly, what remained as problems for science vis-à-vis religion arose not from the basic belief in the existence of God's plan but from interpretations of scripture that had fused with religious practice. Ussher's supposedly biblically based, precise identification of the earth's age was one such amalgam. Three other such sticking points provided difficulties for the Founders: the denial of the possibilities of extinction, of evolution, and of the existence of separate races of mankind. Eighteenth-century Christians held to the beliefs that each plant and animal on earth had existed in its current configuration, unchanged, since Genesis—that none had evolved or become extinct—and that all human beings on earth were the descendants of Adam and Eve. The Founders' generation of scientifically literate men struggled with these outdated and hampering pseudoscientific concepts as they simultaneously fought a political struggle against similarly arthritic and restricting forms of governance.

TWO

"VARIOLA" *in* BOSTON,

1721–1722

BENJAMIN FRANKLIN'S CHILDHOOD AND ROUTE TO scientific thinking differed markedly from those of the other Founding Fathers. Born a quarter century prior to Washington and Adams and two generations earlier than Jefferson and Madison, he was also not born a gentleman or of relatively wealthy parents and did not receive very much in the way of classical education.

He entered the world in 1706, to the joy of the Boston candler Josiah Franklin and his second wife, Abiah, who had lost three earlier products of their union to disease, and became a member of a household full of siblings, the nearest in age seven years his senior. Benjamin attended Boston Latin until the age of ten; despite teachers' recognition of his brightness and his excelling in some classes, he had done well in neither mathematics nor deportment and had not learned Latin, to the dismay of his father, who dreamed of his becoming a minister. For a few months he attended a less prestigious academy but then ceased formal schooling. After a brief period of working with his father and considering indentures with tradesmen in a variety of fields, at age twelve he was formally bound as a "printer's devil" to a half-brother, James. Recently returned from London, James Franklin had learned there the most advanced printing methods and had come home to use them in starting his own business. Young

Benjamin signed a particularly onerous apprenticeship arrangement designed to keep him in harness until he turned twenty-one.[1]

Memoirs are often burdened by the sort of hindsight that seats in remembered early incidents the justification of later stances. Among the problematic elements of Franklin's *Autobiography* is material implying that his father had not been thrifty enough to afford Harvard's tuition for his son. That myth held until recent Franklin biographers offered a more logical reason: Josiah Franklin had early on detected Ben's antipathy to organized religion and did not want to waste money sending him to an institution for producing ministers. As biographer Walter Isaacson points out, "Anecdotes about [Franklin's] youthful intellect and impish nature abound, but there are none that show him as pious or faithful."[2]

Writing under the pseudonym "Silence Dogood," a fusty, moralistic widow, Franklin would depict Harvard as attracting students "little better than Dunces and Blockheads," who had somehow managed to get past gates guarded by "two sturdy Porters named *Riches* and *Poverty.*" What students learned was to "carry themselves handsomely, and enter a Room genteely, (which might as well be acquir'd at a Dancing-school)," and when they graduated, "after Abundance of Trouble and Charge," they were "as great Blockheads as ever, only more proud and self-conceited," and motivated by "Pecunia."[3]

Released from formal school, Franklin read voraciously on his own, devouring the complex arguments and vocabulary of William Petty's *Political Arithmetic,* John Locke's *Essay Concerning Human Understanding,* and a bound volume of Joseph Addison and Richard Steele's *The Spectator.* These three were notably suffused with science, Petty employing mathematical models and proofs in the studies of economics and political maneuvering, and Locke insisting on sensory evidence as the basis of human ideas. *The Spectator* championed the genius of Bacon, Boyle, and Newton while satirizing the pomposity of the Royal Society. In combination, biographer Joyce Chaplin writes, these volumes taught Franklin "that the sciences were essential to knowledge and a route to fame."[4]

Franklin also learned as a youth that minds untrained in science could also experiment. He later recalled for Swedish botanist Peter Kalm an experiment done by his father, Josiah: noticing that herring would spawn in one particular stream that led to Massachusetts Bay but not in another, Josiah had guessed that the activity had to do with the geographic location where the fish had been hatched. To test the theory, one year at spawning time he transported fish to the second stream, where they spawned and died; the following year, as Josiah had predicted, their offspring returned to the second stream.[5]

ON APRIL 22, 1721, slightly more than a hundred years after the first Pilgrims landed on Plymouth Rock, the merchant ship HMS *Seahorse* arrived in the port of Boston from Isla de Tortuga. Regular disease-defense procedures, instituted after prior smallpox epidemics, mandated that ships were to moor in mid-harbor and not disgorge passengers, crew, or cargo until inspected. But a clearly ill black seaman was soon discovered on land. A red flag was planted in front of the building where he lodged, with the legend, "God have mercy on this house." Within a few days, others of the crew showed signs of infection.[6] These were not subtle. According to contemporary Boston physician Zabdiel Boylston, smallpox symptoms included "Purple Spots, the bloody and parchment Pox, Hemorahages of Blood at the Mouth, Nose, Fundament, and Privities; Ravings and Deliriums; Convulsions, and other Fits; violent inflammations and Swellings in the Eyes and Throat; so that they cannot see or scarcely breathe, or swallow any thing, to keep them from starving."[7]

By June, an epidemic was sweeping through the city, much as earlier ones had done in 1677, 1690, and 1702. In those years, 10 percent of the colony's population died in the epidemics. In 1721, 900 of Boston's 10,700 residents fled to the countryside. At least as many were affected by the disease and quarantined. The extensive quarantines disrupted commerce and pushed the town council to decree that disease-ridden victims were to be henceforth isolated in prisons and hidden from the public; shortly, the council would limit the length of time that funeral bells could toll for the same reason—to prevent full-scale panic.

It was in this crisis atmosphere that James Franklin decided to print and publish a new newspaper, the *New England Courant*. He did so in part because he had recently lost the contract to publish the *Boston Gazette*, and in part because of the controversy already begun over how to lessen the impact of the epidemic—a controversy that he believed would sell newspapers.

On one side of it was the most famous Bostonian of the time, the writer, preacher, and natural historian Cotton Mather, son of the famed Puritan divine Increase Mather. Back in 1689–1692, Cotton Mather had been an enthusiastic principal in the Salem witch trials, instrumental in urging the court to have the alleged witches killed. By the second decade of the new century, and aspiring to membership in the Royal Society, Mather had evolved a more scientific approach to life, seeking to emulate Robert Boyle, with whom he had corresponded, and stressing the need to heal the sick, preserve life, and daily to "do good." In 1713 the Royal Society accepted his communications on the hybridization of plants, and he became a corresponding member, permitted to add F.R.S. to his name, which he did.[8] In 1716 in response to having read several *Transactions* articles on smallpox, Mather reported to the Royal Society a conversation about smallpox with his slave from the Sudan, Onesimus, who told him that "he had undergone an Operation, which had given him something of ye Small-Pox, & would forever præserve him from it." This conclusion matched the reports of two Greek physicians and other RS correspondents on the subject of "variolation" for smallpox—the cause of the disease then being labeled *variola*. The technique involved inserting pus from an infected person under the skin of an uninfected person and then isolating the inoculated individual during the period when the disease was highly communicable.

On June 6, 1721, Mather commenced an action in regard to smallpox for which he had been preparing for decades, building on his correspondence with Boyle about the disease and on his prior championing of the palliative programs of the English physician Dr. Thomas Sydenham over the frequently fatal treatments utilized by most other physicians. That day Mather dispatched a private letter to the dozen physicians in Boston, extolling the "Wonderful Practice" of variolation, enclosing the information from Onesimus and the articles in the *Transactions*, and urging them to variolate their patients to prevent further spread of the epidemic.[9]

Often the voice of reason shouts but gets no response. Mather had just one positive reply to his letter, from his friend, Zabdiel Boylston, a botanist and surgeon who had performed the first successful mastectomy in the American colonies. At Mather's urging, Boylston proceeded to "artificially infect" his son, two slaves, and members of Mather's family. After doing so, Boylston invited the other Boston physicians to observe the inoculated patients, but they declined the opportunity, believing that the procedure hastened the onset of the disease rather than stopping its spread. Boylston's invitation did, however, deliberately make his efforts public—the town authorities had made what he called too "slight and trifling a Representation" of the disease, given its virulence, rapid spread, and substantial risk of death, and that was why he dared something new.

James Franklin was determined that the *New England Courant* would be satirical and completely independent of the authority of the town council and the governor—the first such independent journal in the Massachusetts colony. To make headway in the controversy about variolation, he already possessed an asset, Dr. William Douglass, the only college-trained physician in Boston—the other eleven, including Boylston, had learned their craft as apprentices. A 1705 graduate of Edinburgh, Douglass had further studied medicine in Paris, Leyden, and Utrecht before moving to Boston in 1718, possibly on the advice of his fellow Edinburgh medical graduate, Cadwallader Colden, who had similarly emigrated to Philadelphia. His sense of superiority to the non-college-trained doctors in Boston was pronounced: "A young man without any liberal education, by living a year or two in any quality with a practitioner of any sort, apothecary, cancer doctor, cutter for the stone, bonesetters, tooth-drawer, etc., with the essential fundamental of ignorance and impudence, is esteemed to qualify himself for all the branches of the medical art," he later wrote.[10]

Douglass catalogued the methods used by Boston's non-trained physicians to ameliorate smallpox, among them washing the pustules with sheep dung, to contrast these to his own approach: "The Cure of the Small Pox, properly speaking, is to manage the infecting *Miasma* in the first period or *Apparatus* of the disease." In his view, during the 1721 epidemic, Boston was unduly turned into a laboratory for study of the disease by the experimentation done by Bolyston and Mather.[11] But what Douglass sought in decrying inoculation—and in dismissing Mather—was not so much to warn the public about an untested technique but to protect his turf, so that Mather and others who were untrained in physick would not usurp the exclusive right of trained doctors to diagnose and treat patients.

Douglass's article in the premier issue of the *New England Courant*, dated August 7, 1721, was anonymous and was keyed to the news that Boylston's inoculated son had contracted a bad case of the pox: "The bold Undertaker of the Practice of the Greek old Women, not withstanding the Terror and Confusion from his Son's Inoculation-Fever, proceeds to inoculate persons from seventy years of age and downwards." Douglass did not mention Boylston by name; nor did he name Mather when he went on to criticize the clergy for interfering. He reported that the Boston selectmen had unanimously condemned inoculation as a "dubious" matter that should be stopped immediately. A second article in the *Courant*'s premier issue more directly attacked Mather, deriding Puritan clergymen who "pray hard against sickness, yet preach up the Pox!"

There was a case to be made for Douglass's medical viewpoint that variolation only worked properly if receivers were uninfected, had been prepared for the inoculation by ten days of diet and supervised treatment, and if after inoculation they were isolated until the period of high infectiousness had passed. But Douglass and the *Courant* did not make this case, perhaps judging that the readers of the *Courant* could not be swayed by scientific argument. Mather contributed to this race-to-the-bottom by complaining to a rival newspaper of the "scandalous paper called the *Courant*, full-freighted with nonsense, unmanliness, raillery." Boylston tried to be factual, asserting in an advertisement his claim that those he variolated were doing well and, therefore, that no one should be afraid of being inoculated. Douglass railed against "the blind Conduct of *Empiricks* and *Montebanks*" who lacked the theoretical knowledge and understanding of disease causation that were ingrained in university-trained physicians.[12] He topped all such articles in an essay echoing satirist Jonathan Swift, "A project for reducing the Eastern Indians by Inoculation," a plan to pay a bounty of £5 to anyone who inoculated a Native American that later died of the smallpox, and double that amount to the inoculator for each one that survived and spread the disease.

At three o'clock one morning, a lit "granado" was tossed into Mather's house with a message attached: "I'll inoculate you with this, with a Pox on you," but the grenade did not explode.[13] Hanging parties with nooses scoured the town for Boylston, and some newspapers called for the execution of any physician who practiced inoculation; for fourteen days Boylston hid in a concealed place within his home and visited his patients only at midnight and in disguise.[14]

The rhetoric and the death toll mounted in tandem. The *Courant* denounced the practice of variolation "as an infusion of malignity into the blood . . . a species of poisoning; an interference in the prerogatives of Jehovah, whose right it was to wound and heal; an attempt to thwart God, who sent the smallpox as a punishment for sins, and whose vengeance would thus be provoked all the more."[15]

An anonymous pamphlet, *A Friendly Debate; or, a Dialogue Between Academicus and Sawny & Mundungus, Two Eminent Physicians,* undermined Douglass's reputation. He attributed the scurrilous dialogue to Mather, but its author was soon revealed as a young science student of Mather's at Harvard, nineteen-year-old Isaac Greenwood—one of those who had been successfully inoculated by Boylston.[16]

Through the many publications about the variolation controversy, the Boston public was almost unwittingly educated about a scientific matter that materially involved them. Chief among those so edified was apprentice printer Benjamin Franklin, age sixteen, who read many of the materials as he composed them for printing. It was not until April 1722, however, as the epidemic was waning, that he joined the fray in a glancing way in his "Silence Dogood" letters. The ostensible author of the letters, the crusty widow, parodied Mather in claiming to have "an excellent Faculty [and a] natural inclination to observe and reprove the Faults of others."[17] Franklin, in studying Mather closely enough to make fun of him, also learned from him: the Mather pamphlet, *Bonifacius: Essays to Do Good,* which furnished the name and character for Silence Dogood, also contained Mather's rules for personal behavior, many of which Franklin soon adopted.

In 1723, James Franklin went beyond what the town council could accept as responsible criticism, not in regard to their conduct concerning smallpox but to their attempts to prevent piracy. Arrested and jailed, he decreed that the *Courant* would be published under Benjamin's name and, to make that arrangement legal, released Ben from his indenture.

From the variolation brouhaha, Benjamin Franklin learned the value of newspaper-based controversy for raising scientific literacy and the need for scientific testing and evidence in combating disease. He was thoroughly convinced by the results of the experiments, figures showing that during the epidemic 5,889 of Boston's 10,700 people contracted smallpox, and of these 844 died—a death toll that included only a handful of the 280 inoculated by Boylston, a fatality rate for the uninoculated of 14.1 percent, and of the inoculated, of 2.2 percent.[18]

Community-wide controversies often cause unpleasant consequences for the main actors. Douglass was too much the scientist not to yield to facts, and after statistics revealed how well the variolated survived, he did acknowledge the efficacy of variolation, although at first only to Colden in a private letter. But he had been publicly proved wrong, and after the epidemic the public-advocate part of his career was over. He became quite embittered. Cotton Mather's advocacy of variolation was counter to the opinion of the church, and it led to his being turned down by the overseers of Harvard for the one post he coveted, the presidency of the college. Rejected there, he then announced to a meeting of fellow ministers his complete withdrawal from public affairs. Those responsibilities lifted, he further embraced science and its future. He wrote to Greenwood, the most "ingenious" member of his science study club at Harvard, who had gone to London for further study, "I shall consider you as my son, and appear with more zeal to gett your proposals answered, than if you were by Nature so." At Mather's instigation, Greenwood met with wealthy merchant Thomas Hollis, who shortly endowed the first scientific chair at Harvard, for Greenwood to occupy.[19]

What Mather and Boylston accomplished in Boston during 1721–1722 was a triumph for American medicine and for scientific boldness and experimentation; their large-scale trial of variolation set the stage for one of the most important advances in the history of medicine, the broader use of inoculation as disease prevention. The British also held a trial of variolation in stages; first, six condemned prisoners were infected with pus; when they recovered, the royal family agreed to try the technique; thereafter it was adopted wholesale. On Boylston's visit to London, the Royal Society celebrated him, elected him as a Fellow, and published his article on smallpox prevention by variolation. The tone in the article was reflexive but angry at those who had prevented the technique's further use—Douglass, the Boston selectmen, and the *Courant,* though not mentioned by name—since wider use of variolation might have saved hundreds of lives.[20]

As important for the story being traced in this book, the entire affair of the smallpox epidemic and the attempt to prevent its ravages by means of a scientific treatment had taken place in the public eye through the mediation of the press. From then on, in the American colonies, there was increased understanding that news of scientific matters need not be confined to publications intended for the elite—this was a fit subject for popular consumption. For instance, to rouse public support for improved sanitation and treatment of sewage to prevent yellow fever, Douglass's correspondent Cadwallader Colden took to the newspapers in New York and thereby pressured the city's councils to reform.

Public discussion of the 1721–1722 smallpox epidemic contributed to the eclipse of the pattern of the first hundred years in the colonies, during which the religious hierarchy had dominated the public's thoughts in regard to medicine and other scientific activities as it did in every other field of endeavor. From then on, the shift away from religious-based instruction in many arenas quickened.

When James Franklin returned home from his time in jail, the brothers quarreled, and shortly afterward the seventeen-year-old Benjamin Franklin quit the printing house and Boston and found his way to New York and then to Philadelphia.

THREE

GODFATHERS *of* AMERICAN SCIENCE

THERE ARE DISTINCT, RECOGNIZABLE, ASCENDING stages of mastery in dealing with scientific information. The trio of observation, collection, and description constitute what historian of science John V. Pickstone labels the "notebook stage," the most basic, lowest stage. Notebook observers record their surroundings "not chiefly for meaning, nor necessarily for use, but for the wonder of it or from a compulsion to identify and collect," he writes. Analysis and experimentation are more advanced phases and usually do not occur simultaneously with the notebook stage, as the taker of inventories has not yet applied his or her intelligence to positing or discovering why and how one observed thing differs from another.[1]

This chapter traces the personal journeys of the colonial "notebook culture" stalwarts who directly influenced Franklin and helped to construct the scientific milieu in which later-born Founding Fathers studied and operated.

AFTER THE WANING of the 1721–1722 smallpox epidemic in Boston, and despite the shift in Harvard's curriculum toward more science, Philadelphia soon supplanted Boston as the center of scientific activity. Philadelphia became the main port of entry for what social historian E. Digby

Baltzell identifies as the "anti-authoritarian ideals of equality and democracy," the transatlantic trade in scientific facts and ideas, as well as being the locus of a "Quaker ethic [that was] egalitarian and experimental as against the hierarchical and deductive nature of [Boston's] Calvinism."[2]

During the rule of William Penn and his lieutenants, a historian of the Quakers writes, "the search for an understanding of the creation and insight into its beauty, sincerity and genuineness led many Quakers to scientific pursuits, particularly botany and ornithology. . . . Science seemed closer to reality than did art."[3] Philadelphia's leading scientist in the 1720s, and America's first scientific godfather, was James Logan, Penn's former secretary, a bibliophile and polymath whose curiosity ranged from mathematics and astronomy to Greek and Persian classic literature. Among his protégés were John Bartram and Benjamin Franklin. Logan's primary connection in London, who would also become Bartram's and Franklin's mentor and the second godfather, was the Quaker merchant Peter Collinson.

Born in Ireland in 1674 of Scottish-Quaker parentage, Logan early in life became a schoolteacher and a book collector. In 1699, after selling his books to finance a passage to the New World, he was introduced to William Penn and agreed to become Penn's secretary in Philadelphia. Logan also became a fur merchant, a trade he detested as "a nauseous drudgery, to which nothing but the profit could reconcile a man of any spirit."[4] He channeled those profits into gentlemanly pursuits, amassing a personal library that included scientific books in English, Latin, and French, among them the first copy in the colonies of Newton's *Principia,* and tomes in Hebrew, Arabic, and German, languages that he could also read. He enjoyed the proximity and intellectual companionship of Cadwallader Colden, another young physician-scientist, until New York's governor, a similar gentleman-scientist, lured Colden to that colony. A loner, Logan was never an aspirant to the fellowship of the Royal Society, whose resources and comparable minds might have boosted his inquiries. He did correspond with other astronomers, including the royal astronomer in Greenwich and counterparts in Amsterdam and Leyden. "I have a Strong Inclination to make some experiments about the Parallax of our Great Orb viz the Earths about the Sun," he wrote in 1716, but to do those experiments required more widely distanced observations points (and more accurate time-pieces) than he could muster. The absence of intellectual companionship hurt Logan's progress less than the inadequacy of available scientific equipment. He could not prove his theory that violin strings and pendulums obeyed the same laws of motion, as no pendulums large enough to test that theory existed in the colonies. Others later proved his guess correct, and he received no credit for the discovery.[5]

Not initially interested in botany, Logan changed his attitude in 1726 upon being transfixed by English cleric William Wollaston's posthumous book *The Religion of Nature Delineated*. Known to have had its second edition set and read by printer's apprentice Franklin (who wrote a refutation of it) in London, and to have been perused by Bartram, owned by Jefferson and Washington, and likely read by Adams (who recommended it to his son), *The Religion of Nature Delineated* enlarged on arguments made earlier by John Ray in a very popular book, *The Wisdom of God Manifested in the Works of Creation*. As had Ray, Wollaston contended that there was no difference between the book of nature and the book of God, the Bible. Wollaston's contribution was to identify man's principal task as the delineation of nature's laws, or "truths." "*They who are capable to discerning truth, tho not all truths, and of acting conformably to it. . . . It is the duty of such a being sincerely to* endeavour *to practice reason.*"[6] Wollaston extrapolated from this a theory that new generations of life were demonstrations of God's continuing activity in world affairs.

Logan agreed with Wollaston that God infused the divine (male) spirit into an "animalacule" that then found a ready (female) receptacle, and designed an experiment to test the theory. It was elegantly simple— as, throughout the history of science, many critical experiments have been. Logan had observed on stalks of maize "a kind of adventitious dust, scarce belonging to the plant, as if lodged there by dew from the air," a "farina" that seemed akin to the male animalcules described by Wollaston and also noted the kinship between unripe kernels of the maize and unfertilized eggs. So he embedded four groups of maize plants in separated hillocks. Leaving one group unadulterated as a control, he modified the others. From a first he removed all the tassels; from a second he cut off only parts of those silks. He wrapped the third group's stalks, tassels and all, in muslin to prevent entry of "farina." When harvested, the wrapped plants and those whose tassels had been entirely removed showed no ripe kernels of corn; the plants from which only parts of the silks had been removed displayed ripe kernels in proportion to the amount of silk that had remained, and the control group had a full complement of ripe kernels. "From these experiments," Logan concluded, "it is very plain that the farina emitted from the summits of the styles [tassels] is the true male seed, and absolutely necessary to render the uterus and grain fertile."[7]

He repeated the experiment the next spring—but then waited eight years before sending his observations to Collinson, who had them read at the Royal Society. In his letter, Logan made no mention of the religious bases for his thesis. He first dismissed previous European work on propagation for not having "applied all the care that was requisite in the Management" of their experiments, which had perhaps led the Europeans to the erroneous conclusion that maize reproduced without farina. He then described his own experiments, whose results were consistent with his propagation theory. The Fellows voted to publish an abstract in the next *Philosophical Transactions.* The abstracted article was clear and definitive, but its publication in 1736 enraged Logan because it was overly condensed and contained several errors that were obvious only to him. He was also upset when the ship captain who carried Logan's letter to London and was present when it was read at the Royal Society told him that during the reading, "there was two thirds of them imployed at discussing a Germain cabbage and looking for the Small fibers in the root of an turnop."[8]

Yet the abstract stunned Carl Linnaeus, the Swedish naturalist, also a Collinson correspondent. Linnaeus praised Logan to Collinson as "*inter Naturae Mystas heroa,*" a hero for piercing a prime mystery of nature. What Logan had done was nothing less than provide a much-needed experimental justification for Linnaeus's epochal classification and nomenclature of the plants. Foucault reminds us that Linnaeus's codifying by sexual characteristics was not simply a substitution of a new system for an outdated one; the new classification eclipsed the old-style grouping together of various plants simply because they appeared to resemble one another and substituted a new system based on more fundamental functional similarities and differences—it replaced irrationally based groupings with rationally based ones, exemplifying the correct and helpful application of Enlightenment reasoning to the natural world.[9]

While the British scientific establishment paid little heed to Logan— or, initially, to Linnaeus—the Dutch, further advanced in botany, encouraged Logan to expand his treatise and, when he did so, printed it for wide circulation. It was eventually retranslated into English. Two additional

Logan letters appeared in the *Philosophical Transactions,* conveying his thoughts on the nature of lightning and why the moon appeared larger at the horizon than when high in the sky. Very few scientists in any age have three articles on varying subjects published in a short span of years in the most prominent scientific journal.

Logan might have had a larger impact on colonial science had he sought pupils or acolytes. His earliest American protégé was an accidental one, the Philadelphia glazier and self-taught astronomer Thomas Godfrey who, after completing the repair of a window at Logan's home, asked to borrow the *Principia.* Godfrey was one of the "leather apron" men convened by the young entrepreneur Benjamin Franklin in 1728 in a "Junto" that met regularly to discuss ideas. Godfrey rented lodgings from Franklin, and the two were somewhat friendly, although as time passed Franklin found the glazier lacking in gratitude and manners. When Logan had first learned of the Junto's existence, he had written that the members were "base and lying lackeys" of Governor Sir William Keith, the official who had mentored Franklin but who had been an enemy of Penn and of Penn's widow and, therefore, of Logan. However, Logan undertook to champion Godfrey in London. The British government had offered a generous monetary prize to the developer of any instrument that would make it easier for ships to navigate accurately. Godfrey had made an ingenious device that might qualify for part of the prize, an improvement to the standard mariner's quadrant. Using two mirrors set at a particular angle, it could produce an image of the sun that when juxtaposed to the horizon gave a very good estimation of a ship's latitude, even if the vessel was pitching. Logan tried it out and then sent a letter about it to Edmund Halley, who had succeeded John Flamsteed as royal astronomer, flattering Halley that Godfrey's implement built on "thy great genious" to enable a "certain method for observation practicable on that unstable element the sea."[10]

Hearing nothing from Halley, Logan then read in the next *Philosophical Transactions* an account of a decidedly similar quadrant created by the Royal Society's vice president, John Hadley. Halley and Hadley had been backing an English clockmaker, John Harrison, whose further innovations would eventually be awarded the bulk of the longitude prize.[11] Part of that prize should have been Godfrey's, Logan believed, and wrote thus to three other Fellows. They agreed that at least Godfrey's contributions and the affidavits submitted on his behalf deserved a hearing from the Royal Society or else, as one put it, "We must believe that all the people in Pennsylvania combined to impose on the Society, which no reasonable man will do."[12] The Society was shamed into publishing the letters and awarding Godfrey £200; but because the Fellows had been told that Godfrey was a heavy drinker, they gave him the gift in the form of a specially made clock.[13]

Logan's more significant protégé was John Bartram of Kingsessing. Before 1734, when Bartram began his efforts in earnest, only 300 of the estimated 10,000 plants of the American colonies had been collected and sent to England for classification and propagation in nurseries. Between then and 1776, around 600 new American plants were found and sent— half by Bartram.[14]

Logan's association with a third protégé, Franklin, had begun by the time of the Library Company's formation in 1731, and Logan eventually became Franklin's "intellectual peer as well as his client," biographer Chaplin writes, something that "would never have happened had Franklin not become both a property holder and a man of letters whom Logan could take seriously."[15] In short, Franklin was accepted by Logan as a gentleman with whom the pursuit of scientific truth could be properly discussed. Soon they were sharing their intellectual efforts. Logan allowed Franklin to read and critique parts of his unpublished treatise on ethics and epistemology. Begun as a "Proposal to Myself," it had evolved into *The Duties of Man Deduced from Nature*, a riff on Wollaston's title and thesis, and based on an attempt to separate "Logical Truth when our words really agree with the Things spoken of whether we believe them to be so or not—and Moral [truth] when we speak as we think whether our Thoughts be true or otherwise."[16] Franklin, evidently sure of Logan's friendship, pulled no punches in his critique, faulting Logan's "dilate manner of writing" and defending a Logan target, Thomas Hobbes, whose *Duties of Man* Franklin touted as "somewhat nearer the truth" than Logan's Quakerism. Franklin also submitted his own writings to Logan for approval and went out of his way to print Logan's translation of Cicero's *Discourse on Old Age*, a gesture that resonated deeply after the older man suffered a stroke on top of a crippling injury. During Logan's last years, Franklin visited him regularly, and Logan intrigued him into first solving and then creating magic squares, dubbing Franklin's productions "astonishing."[17]

Franklin's road to colloquy with Logan, and eventually to collaboration with Collinson, was long. He had taken the first step, the formation of the Junto, less than a year after returning from London in 1726, and based on ideas from Mather's *Bonifacius: Essays to Do Good*. At each meeting, members were required to stand, hold a hand over the heart, and properly answer four questions, among them, "Do you love mankind in general of what nation, religion or profession soever they be?" and "Do you love Truth for Truth's sake and will you endeavour impartially to find it and freely communicate it to others?"[18] Proper responses to these questions certified the responders as aspiring gentlemen, from whom such attitudes were expected—in contrast to lower-class practices of openly expressing bias against other races, creeds, or nationalities, and of refusing to accept truths that contradicted prior beliefs. The Junto was a big step forward for more than the individuals involved; from the time of the Junto on, chroniclers of the era assert, "Science at Philadelphia never hesitated to enlist the skills of the craftsman, and the gardener, the engineer and the architect, the teacher, the artist, the printer or the merchant. The democratic implications of such an approach are nearly as obvious as the practical nature of the results."[19]

The democratic implications only extended to males. Franklin's sister, Jane Mecom, their letters reveal, was as intellectually capable of comprehending the science of the times as any of the Junto fellows. Franklin wrote more to her than he did to any other correspondent. But Jane lacked schooling, mathematics, and a base of knowledge in the sciences, and so while Franklin discussed with her complex moral and civic matters, he did not tell her very much about his experiments or scientific aspirations.[20]

In 1731, when the Franklin-led Junto group established the Library Company, Logan advised the new group on what books to buy and steered them to Collinson as the purchaser. Among the first books bought were a copy of the *Principia* and a half dozen other scientific tomes. Gifts to the Library Company from members included works by Locke and Bacon and, from the Proprietor, an "air-pump" that could produce a vacuum. Through these materials, Franklin's ingenuity in science was encouraged, and eventually his reputation as a scientist would be made through Collinson.

PETER COLLINSON OF LONDON never conducted a critical experiment but was a far more influential patron of American science than was Logan. Every colonist of scientific aspirations corresponded with this textile "mercer" and countinghouse owner who, following in the tradition of Samuel Hartlib a century earlier, undertook to interconnect the world's scientists by correspondence. By the 1730s, the Royal Society and its European counterparts had superseded the need for Hartlibian correspondence by regularly issuing the *Philosophical Transactions* and similar periodicals. However, Collinson, a very active member of the Royal Society, seized on the palpable need to promote scientific activity by the periphery to contribute to the center and to the body of scientific knowledge. Historian Raymond P. Stearns suggests that Collinson's success as an interlocutor stemmed from his not being a scientist and therefore being more willing to cultivate and celebrate the truly ingenious. After a Royal Society brouhaha over the precise membership status of Cotton Mather, Americans were no longer permitted to become full voting members and found it less easy to submit signed articles, so many midcentury American contributions were published as letters to members, a large proportion of these letters to Collinson.[21] Several other English and Continental science-minded men also corresponded with various American colonists, but Collinson's efforts were the most prolific, diligent, and wide-ranging. He personally sponsored seventy-six men for membership, including most of the Society's distinguished foreign members.

His most important American correspondent was John Bartram. William Bartram later recalled that his father's collecting and nurturing of plants had started as an outgrowth of his Quaker sensibility: "While ploughing his fields, and mowing his meadows, his inquisitive eye and mind were frequently exercised in the contemplation of vegetables; the beauty and harmony displayed in their mechanism; and the admirable order of system which the great Author of the universe has established throughout their various tribes."[22] In Great Britain, plant collection and investigation was mostly limited to men of sufficiently noble birth or income. Even in America, Bartram's ruminations might have remained of only local interest had he not been touted to Collinson as a potential source of new plants. During their first exchanges, the Londoner over-instructed the colonist on how to construct boxes to hold seedlings, nuts, and dried animal specimens, while the provincial was overly deferential and undemanding.

Logan had to remind Collinson that Bartram was not a gentleman of leisure but a farmer with a family "that depend wholly on his daily labour, spent on a poor narrow spot of ground, that will scarce keep them above the want of the necessaries of life. You, therefore, are robbing them while you take up one hour of his time without making proper compensation for it." When Collinson sent reference books in English but refused to send a copy of Linnaeus's *Systema Naturae,* ostensibly because it was in Latin, Logan offered to translate Linnaeus for Bartram because "thou wilt . . . be fully able to deal with [the theoretical implications] thyself." By separate letter Logan chided Collinson for withholding the Linnaeus. Collinson soon sent the Linnaeus book directly to Bartram, and thereafter their affairs were more businesslike. However, Collinson reminded Bartram that he must "proceed gently in these curious things, which belong to a man of leisure, and not to a man of business."[23]

Collinson sought from Bartram solely "notebook-stage" observations but promised that the exchanges would make him a better analyst: "What I have further to propose . . . is thy own Improvement in the knowledge of plants, for thou shall Send Mee another Quire of Duplicates of the Same Speciments. I will get them Named by Our Most knowing Botanists & then Return them again which will improve thee More than Books."[24] By 1736, Bartram felt able to request an annual stipend rather than submitting bills. Collinson agreed because one of the more important of his sixty patrons, Lord Robert Petre, had read a Bartram letter, "admired thy plain Natural Way of writeing & thy observations & Descriptions," and was willing to put up ten guineas a year, which Collinson matched. For their money they wanted a lot: for instance, in a single shipment, 500 swamp laurel cones, 200 chestnuts, and a peck of dogwood berries.[25] Shortly, Collinson had Bartram letters read at the Royal Society and published in the *Philosophical Transactions.*

While with Quaker correspondents Collinson discussed politics and Quaker minutia, he did not do so with Bartram, who had quit the Quakers upon realizing that he did not believe in Jesus's divinity. But Collinson unhesitatingly asked Bartram to do such difficult tasks as determine whether the rattlesnake killed birds by fang and venom or by charming them, a subject of importance to the Royal Society. Collinson came to appreciate that Bartram deliberately searched for "ye most desolate craggy dismal places I can find where no mortal ever trode," as Bartram had written.[26] Collinson felt comfortable touting Bartram to a southern colonial botanist as "more knowing in Science than any you have Mett With," and cautioning the southerner to disregard Bartram's shabby habiliment and heed his conversation.[27]

Mainly through Collinson's efforts in support of Logan, Bartram, Colden, and others, and by introducing them to other Americans of similar interests, he—and by extension the Royal Society—encouraged the growth of American science even as he and the Society downplayed the importance of the individual colonists' contributions. As important, by alternately deprecating and praising these Americans, the Royal Society engendered in them a palpable sense of the need for colonial as well as for personal independence.

FRANKLIN AND COLLINSON DID NOT correspond directly, even though Franklin was the soul of the Library Company. But Franklin did seek out Bartram for scientific training and collaboration. They shared a common interest in the Native Americans. The Tuscarora had killed Bartram's father, and he frequently voiced his hatred toward that tribe, but he became an expert on Native Americans and discussed them also with Logan and Colden, similar students of the indigenous. In all of these colonists' plant foraging and anthropological searches they displayed a distinctly American scientific trait: seeking to understand plants and animals as they existed in the wild, in situ, rather than studying them under cultivation in gardens, hothouses, and menageries, as the British did. Bartram published more about Native Americans than about botany, some of it in Franklin's *Poor Richard Improved,* and more of it in his lone book, *A Journey from Pennsylvania to Onondaga* (1743). The Onondaga tribe altered his preconceptions by being "subtle, prudent and judicious" while continuing to be "indefatigable, crafty, and revengeful in their wars, the men lazy and indolent at home, the women continual slaves."[28]

Bartram frequently ventured beyond the notebook stage in colloquys with men whose primary scholarly connection was not the Royal Society, such as the Dutch scholar Jan Frederik Gronovius, with whom he discussed his contention that some islands were likely to be the tips of undersea mounts, citing as evidence that he had found fossils in American mountains that had clearly once been seashells. An indication of what Bartram might have accomplished in analysis had he been more seriously prodded comes through a typical note accompanying a requested chimney swallow's nest:

> I thought of ye glutinous matter which they glued ye sticks together with was ye gum of our chery tree but yesterday when drying it with a coal fire held to it I found . . . by ye stinking smell it emitted like burnt animal substance I believe it is a kind of saliva. . . . I think thay are ye foolishest of birds in ye place they chuse to build their nests in which is in chimnies & when thair young is grown heavy almost big enough to fly thair weight with ye first rain that comes relaxes ye glue & down cometh ye nest &r ye young one two ye latter of which commonly makes a fine regale for our cats which soon notice of thair downfall by ye squaling noise thay make.[29]

In 1739, Bartram wrote to Collinson with an idea for an American version of the Royal Society but was slapped back: "Had you a Sett of Lerned, Well Qualified Members to Sett out with, it might Draw your Neighbors to Correspond with you. Your Library Company I take to be an essay toward such a Society. But to Draw Learned Strangers . . . to teach Sciences, requires Salaries . . . [and] Publick as well as proprietary assistance, which can't be at present complied with, Considering the Infancy of your colony."[30] Yet four years later, in 1743, when Franklin proposed the same idea—through Bartram as co-sponsor—Collinson was more welcoming.

Franklin, who had become relatively wealthy, was intent on achieving fame beyond that attainable through writing. He had begun work on a "Pennsylvania Fireplace," a convection system able to warm an entire room better than a regular fireplace because it took advantage of the principles of heat rise and air circulation. His accompanying pamphlet cited a half dozen learned references, and the text referred in familiar terms to works of Boyle, Newton, and Stephen Hales, whose *Vegetable Staticks* was the scientific book of the moment. But in 1743 Franklin did not have the stature as a scientist to propose an American scientific society on his own; for that he needed Bartram as partner. Still, the preamble of the charter of the American Philosophical Society was quintessentially Franklinian:

> The first Drudgery of Settling New Colonies, which confines the Attention
> of People to mere Necessaries, is now pretty well over, and there are many
> in every Province in Circumstances that set them at Ease, and afford Lei-
> sure to cultivate the finer Arts and improve the common Stock of Knowl-
> edge. To such of these who are Men of Speculation, many Hints must from
> time to time arose, many Observations occur, which if well-examined, pur-
> sued and improved, might produce Discoveries to the Advantage of some
> or all of the British Plantations, or to the Benefit of Mankind in General.[31]

The aim of the APS echoed Bacon's credo for *The New Atlantis,* using almost exactly similar words: to pursue "all philosophical Experiments that
let light into the Nature of Things, tend to increase the Power of Man over
Matter, and multiply the Conveniences or Pleasures of Life."[32]

Overall, this prospectus for the American Philosophical Society was
an elegant, gentlemanly plea for Americans to be allowed to graduate
from notebook culture to the higher stages of analysis and experiment.
Bartram, in agreement with Franklin on the need for the Society, disagreed with Franklin's reliance on men of leisure as its main members.
In a letter to Colden he tried to explain the difficulties of obtaining new
members of the APS only from among the leisured:

> Ye first Class are those whose thought & study is intirely upon getting &
> laying up large estates, & any other attainment that don't turn immediately
> upon that hinge they think is not worth their notice. The second Class are
> those that are for spending on Luxury all they can come at. . . . Ye third
> class are those that necessity obliges to hard labour & Cares for a mod-
> erat & happy Maintenance of their family, & these are many times ye most
> curious, tho deprived mostly of time & materials to pursue their natural
> inclinations.[33]

Together, Franklin and Bartram knew two dozen like-minded colonists—mostly Collinson correspondents, and mostly gentlemen—of
adequate intellectual wherewithal to merit membership. Logan, solicited
for membership, demurred, his frailty melding with his general reluctance to join organizations. Bartram had cautioned that they would have
to "jog along" without Logan.[34] Franklin helped the enterprise through
his position as an assistant postmaster; but despite their efforts, within

a few years the American Philosophical Society became moribund. This failure, ascribed to the dearth of scientifically knowledgeable individuals, was equally attributable to the founders' reluctance to acknowledge that the health of the Royal Society depended on merchant members like Collinson who underwrote its activities in exchange for the privilege of associating with scientific leaders.

More of a colonial overreaching, in the eyes of the British scientific establishment, was Cadwallader Colden's thesis on gravity. Colden was a physician, physicist, chemist, politician, Native chronicler, and botanist—Linnaeus called him "Summus Perfectus"—but his assertion, in a book-length treatise called *An Explication of the First Causes of Action in Matter and the Cause of Gravitation* (1745), that he had found the cause of gravity took him into rarified territory occupied only by Newton and Gottfried Wilhelm Leibniz. Franklin, Logan, and Bartram, shown the manuscript, told Colden it was beyond their competence.[35]

Newton had described gravity in terms of mutual attraction of celestial bodies but simply stated that it operated through the "aether." Colden speculatively identified the composition of the aether as small, tightly packed elastic bodies that transmitted any and all actions imposed on them but did not originate activity—he imagined it composed of light. Such an imagining was not out of line in an era in which explanations involving invisible fluids were in vogue. But in describing inertia, Colden transgressed. Newton had labeled inertia a "passive principle by which bodies persist in their motion or rest, receive motion in proportion to the force impressing it, and resist as much as they are resisted." To Colden's logical mind, inertia had to be an active force—since there could not be a negative power.[36]

Colden's book made some good points, but—as European experts, overlooking those good points, quickly pointed out—it failed to take into consideration that Leibniz and Leonhard Euler had corrected certain of Newton's errors, and it was therefore laughable. Collinson distributed copies and solicited responses; there were not many he could send to Colden, he later confided to Franklin, because readers had such a negative opinion of it that out of politeness they said nothing. Colden's book deserved better. Had it been written by a Royal Society Fellow it would have been read with respect, and even if eventually rejected, it would have brought honor to the author for the attempt. Physician and botanist Alexander Garden of

Charles Towne commiserated with Colden, comparing his troubles with those of Linnaeus: "You have not been the first whose works had been denied the countenance of English Society: They appear to me to be either too lazy or too indolent to examine or too conceited to receive any new thought from any one but an F.R.S." Later, Franklin, similarly wounded by criticism of his electrical work, would observe to Colden, "I see it is not without reluctance that the Europeans will allow that they can possibly receive any instruction from us Americans."[37] The poor reception of Colden's treatise, of Godfrey's lunar sextant, of Bartram's classifying, of Logan's botanizing, and of the nascent American Philosophical Society reinforced the Royal Society's bias that while colonists could add to botanical stocks, they could not promulgate theories or undertake the sort of critical experiments done by Boyle, Hooke, and Newton—although no one in the British Isles just then was working at that level either.

The Americans' reaction to the disdain was to create their own polity through internal correspondence. Franklin, Colden, Bartram, Garden, and their associates, according to Susan Parrish, a historian of the colonial period, employed language "strikingly similar" to that used by the original members of the Royal Society in the 1660s to separate what they did from Scholasticism; but by the 1740s, Parrish writes, "English and European science more generally was associated with rhetoric, showiness, fancy, unnaturalness, idealization, invention, deception and indolence, whereas the American philosophy was presented in terms of 'Honour,' 'Clearest reasoning and Demonstration,' accuracy of description [and] putting God's works before one's own creation."[38]

IN THE SUMMER OF 1754, several of these usually isolated American men of science, all mentored by Collinson, came together in a private conclave that all had looked forward to for decades. Alexander Garden of Charles Towne and John Bartram of Philadelphia visited Cadwallader Colden at Coldengham, his estate in Orange County, New York. Each had advanced beyond collecting and observation into analysis, but in doing so felt increasingly lonely; during their notebook-stage work they had considered modest direction from London enough interchange for their purpose, but in aspiring to higher-order scientific engagement they understood that they needed more and better discussion to sharpen their ideas. Previously, as Garden wrote to an English correspondent, they had been over-reliant on letters: "Every letter which I receive not only revives the little botanic spark in my breast, but even increases its quantity and flaming force. Some such thing is absolutely necessary to one, living under our broiling sun, else . . . we should [not] rest satisfied before we had half discharged our duty to our fellow creatures, which obliges us, as members of the great society, to contribute our mite."[39]

Garden had come north ostensibly to flee the extreme heat of western Virginia; Bartram had similarly arranged one of his periodic trips in a northerly direction; Colden, more isolated than they because of his seat's remote location, nearly a hundred miles north of New York City, was overjoyed to be the host. Bartram and Garden had met before, and Garden had tattled to Colden an uncharitable but accurate portrait of Bartram at home:

> There was no parting with him for two days, during which time I break-
> fasted, dined and supped, slept, and was regaled on botany and mineralogy,
> in which he has some excellent notions and grand thoughts. His garden is
> a perfect portraiture of himself; here you meet with a row of rare plants
> almost covered over with weeds, here with a beautiful shrub, even luxuri-
> ant amongst briars, and in another corner an elegant and lofty tree lost in
> common thicket.[40]

Garden added that he had taken a bit of pleasure from correcting some of Bartram's erroneous identifications of plants. Colden too had now and then looked askance at Bartram, telling Collinson that while Bartram "is a natural and wonderful observer . . . when I saw him [he] had not acquired sufficient knowledge of the principles of botany as a science."[41] Nonetheless, at Coldengham the three, meeting as equals, talked botany for two days, tramped in the woods, identified some flora, and tried out some minor experiments in Colden's chemical laboratory. Bartram and Colden had been corresponding for years about magnetizing steel, attempting to measure the magnetic field, and testing by fire and chemical decomposition some long-buried "indian bread."[42] At Coldengham, Garden obtained his first glimpse of Linnaeus's *Genera Plantarum* and *Critica Botanica*, which changed his life, for until then he had used outmoded classifications and almost despaired.[43] Colden enjoyed introducing the visitors to his daughter, Jane, to whom he had turned over the cataloguing and identifying of plants, and who was just then classifying some that had escaped the attention of more senior botanists, and even one—a gardenia, named by Linnaeus after Garden—a flowering plant, she insisted, that Linnaeus had not properly understood as a separate species. Only a few women were engaged in the sciences in the colonies, and all were plant collectors and aspiring botanists; Jane Colden was nearly alone in having her work published and lauded by the field's authorities.[44]

When Bartram returned home, he pronounced himself well satisfied with the meeting. Garden produced the most effusive comment in a letter introducing himself to Linnaeus on the strength of what had occurred:

> How grateful was such a meeting to me! and how unusual in this part of the world! What congratulations and salutations passed between us! How happy should I be to pass my life with men so distinguished by genius, acuteness, and liberality, as well as by eminent botanical learning and experience! . . . Whilst I was passing my time most delightfully with these gentlemen, they were both so obliging as to shew me your letters to them. . . . I will not yield to them [in] my ardent desire to imbibe true science from the same source, and to quench my thirst from so pure a spring.[45]

While at Coldengham, Bartram, Colden, and Garden lamented the absence of their own "pure spring" of science, the gentleman scientist whom all considered a friend, Benjamin Franklin, whom Garden had visited in Philadelphia, and who had very recently, and very rapidly, risen so far as a scientist that he was becoming the most famous American in the world.

FOUR

The BOLT *from the* BLUE

"THE SURPRISEING PHENOMENON OF ELECTRICITY Engages the Vertuosi in All Europe," Peter Collinson informed Cadwallader Colden and, separately, the Library Company in 1743. This could justifiably be called "an age of wonders," he added, because of the changes going on in science; interest in the "polypus," the coral whose ability to regenerate astonished London, was ceding focus to "the electric fire . . . surpriseing as a miracle." Colden was too deeply involved in writing his magnum opus on gravity to hearken to the siren call of electricity, but Benjamin Franklin of the Library Company was ready for action.[1]

Franklin's inability to push an American Philosophical Society to full functioning only intensified his desire to do something of importance in a scientific discipline. That yearning had first surfaced during his sojourn in London in 1725–1726, when, as an apprentice printer, he had lingered in coffee shops frequented by Royal Society members and tried and failed to meet Isaac Newton, but was able to press himself on Sir Hans Sloane. Franklin came to understand that in the sciences, to a greater degree than in many enterprises, the superior intellect could be a balance to others' advantages of superior birth, wealth, and schooling. On his voyage home to Philadelphia he wrote his first extended observations of nature. During the ensuing two decades, James Logan, John Bartram, and Cadwallader Colden encouraged him in scientific study while he made his fortune as a printer and author and tested his mettle as a public servant. With his correspondents Franklin discussed the circulation of the blood, the role of the skin in maintaining liquid balance in the human body, whether inertia was a basic property of matter, the genesis of waterspouts and the Gulf Stream, and the mechanics of glassmaking. "I wish I had Mathematics enough to satisfy my self, whether the much shorter Voyages made by Ships bound hence to England, than by those from England hither, are not in some Degree owing to the Diurnal Motion of the Earth; and if so, in what Degree?"[2] He learned enough about physical forces to design the Franklin fireplace, but the lunar tables in his almanacs were derived from others' computations, and he recognized that his lack of advanced math and his ignorance of Latin precluded him from going further in physics or astronomy. He might have done well in chemistry, then struggling to isolate and identify as elements carbon dioxide, nitrogen, and oxygen, and to purify various metals, but no one touted chemistry to Franklin, least of all Collinson, who knew nothing of it. Electricity intrigued Franklin perhaps because, as Joseph Priestley would later write, it "has one considerable advantage over most other branches of science, as it both furnishes matter of speculation for philosophers, and of entertainment for all persons promiscuously."[3]

DESPITE COLLINSON'S CLAIM of electricity being all the rage in Europe, its study was in a state of flux. In the late seventeenth century Newton had been amused by the attraction and repulsion caused by electricity, and he wrote that electricity reminded him of lightning on a small scale; toward the end of his days, in the 1720s, he characterized electricity as "a certain most subtle spirit which pervades and lies hid in all gross bodies."[4] Newton and his followers were fascinated by attraction and repulsion and believed these were the basic components of electrical force. They were not—attraction and repulsion were results of the force, and the inability of the "electricians" who followed Newton to understand that hampered them. The British experimenter and theorist Stephen Gray was a self-educated astronomer; he and the Reverend Granville Wheler were the first to identify the concepts of conduction, insulation, and grounding in reference to electricity. Gray also made the first spectacular parlor demonstration, suspending a boy from a ceiling by means of threads, imbuing his body with static electricity, and having him give shocking kisses to audience members—a feat soon replicated in many drawing rooms.

French electrician Charles Dufay then built on Gray and Wheler's understandings to fashion a theory of the origin and operation of electricity:
"There are two distinct Electricities, very different from one another, one
of which I call *vitreous Electricity,* and the other *resinous Electricity.* The
first is that of Glass, Rock-Crystal, Precious Stones, Hair of Animals . . .
the second is that of Amber, Copal, Gum Lack. . . ." Vitreous substances
attracted resinous ones but repelled other vitreous ones.[5] Dufay's "two
fluids" theory was adopted in France by the Abbé Jean-Antoine Nollet,
in Germany by Ewald von Kleist, in the Netherlands by Pieter van Musschenbroek, and in England by Jean Desaguliers and William Watson. All
would influence Franklin.

Desaguliers, Newton's one-time assistant, began in the 1720s to give
influential lecture-demonstrations on electricity, as well as on other
physical subjects. Isaac Greenwood, the Cotton Mather protégé, took
courses from Desaguliers in London and then returned to teach science
at Harvard, fashioning his own curriculum from that of Desaguliers. By
1742 Desaguliers, as an adherent of the Dufay two-fluids theory, stated
as though it were a fact the wrong-headed conception of attraction and
repulsion as the basic components of electricity: "Electricity is a Property
of some Bodies, whereby they alternately attract and repel small Bodies
when brought near them, and that at sensible Distances, *viz.,* from a quarter of an Inch to the Distance of two or three Foot, and sometimes beyond." Along with other electricians, Desaguliers was unable just then to
do more than describe how he thought that static electricity got from one
"body" to the next. "A Body which is *electrick per se,* does not receive this
Virtue from another *electrick per se* tho' excited, till it is become a *non-
electrick;* which happens when it is made moist; and then it will be made
electrick only by Communication. So that an *electrick per se* may become
non-electrick; and likewise a Body *non-electrick per se* may become *electrick* by Communication." Such convoluted language, common to many
of the era's electrical treatises, reflected—although the electricians did
not know it—their imprecise understanding of electricity's basic nature
and mechanisms. That was why their "experiments" were no more than
demonstrations, and they made no critical tests.[6]

Watson, originally an apothecary, was Desaguliers's rival in lecture
demonstrations of electricity. A Royal Society Copley Medalist, he gave
lectures attended by the Prince of Wales and other nobility. Watson's

concern was the conduction of electricity from one object to another; Nollet, his rival as theorist, thought more about the qualities of attraction and repulsion. Errant findings from experiments never disturbed Nollet's confidence in his theory, but some of Watson's results did perplex the Englishman. He had two men stand, separately, on cakes of wax, which were understood to be non-conducting, and electrified man A, who then touched man B, who felt the shock. However, when the sequence was repeated several times, the power conducted to B diminished with each repetition—and Watson could not explain why.

In 1745–1746, the theories and experiences of all electricians were suddenly upset by the new device that became known as the Leyden jar. Musschenbroek and Kleist independently constructed wired jars that stored static electricity but that also, the men found to their very literal shock, magnified its power. A large jug lined internally and externally with tinfoil, and with a metallic rod connecting to the internal tinfoil through a cork stopper, the Leyden jar was able to store and discharge larger amounts of electricity than had previously been possible. Musschenbroek received such a large jolt from touching his jar that he warned his Académie des Sciences correspondent that the act of putting one's hands on the jar should never be repeated because it was too dangerous for the body and for the mind. "I've found out so much about electricity," Musschenbroek wrote, "that I've reached the point where I understand nothing and can explain nothing." The cause of the electricians' befuddlement, posits J. H. Heilbron, was that the Leyden jar "flagrantly violated received principles of electricity. The electricians were no more able to explain the jar than was the general public who came to witness its power." The latter group included Louis XIV, who at Versailles witnessed Abbé Jean-Antoine Nollet's demonstration that caused 180 soldiers holding hands in a circle to leap simultaneously in the air as the first and last ones touched the jar. Nollet attempted to dismiss the power of the Leyden jar as the exception that proved his rule. William Watson similarly thought that it proved his theory. But all the electricians soon ceased performing any original experiments in electricity. To proceed further, they had to wait for a new idea to emerge.[7]

IN THE EARLY 1740s, Franklin already knew a bit about electricity from Isaac Greenwood. After Harvard had fired Greenwood, ostensibly for drunkenness, he taught his courses for public audiences while in the throes of the downward spiral that would lead to his death in obscurity and poverty. When a promising life ends badly, a focus on the tragedy obscures the achievements. It did so for Greenwood for the two centuries after his death. But historian Theodore Hornberger reopened the issue and evaluated Greenwood's impact on American science as "revolutionary"; having "found the instruction almost wholly book learning, [Greenwood] left it marked by awareness of the prime importance of observation and experiment." He wrote the first American textbook on advanced mathematics, and his courses explained the entire gamut of scientific matters, as he put it in an advertisement, "by means of various instruments and machines, with which there are above three hundred curious, and useful experiments performed."[8]

After Greenwood began offering his course to the public, he and Franklin became friends, or perhaps they renewed an earlier friendship— they might have met in London in 1725, or even earlier in Boston during the smallpox controversy. In 1740, Franklin arranged for Greenwood to lecture in Philadelphia in a room next to the Library Company's quarters, and he later visited him in Boston. The ex-Harvard professor most likely introduced Franklin to the writings of Jean Desaguliers, whose work on electricity featured the notion—doubtless seductive to Franklin—that it was possible to understand Newton's science without having to learn calculus; Desaguliers had repeatedly written of John Locke's managing to understand Newtonian concepts without ever learning the math, a story heard directly from Newton.[9]

Neither Greenwood nor Desaguliers are mentioned in Franklin's *Autobiography;* rather, Franklin attributes his introduction to electricity to a "Dr. Spence," who lectured on it in Boston in 1743. Franklin brought him to Philadelphia to give a similar series and bought his equipment. Franklin's memory was imprecise. Later scholarship has identified a Dr. Archibald Spencer, an anatomist, and found evidence that Franklin purchased Spencer's electrical equipment in the 1750s, well after completing his most important experiments.[10]

In late 1745, Collinson heightened the possibility of someone from the Library Company making a significant contribution to the field of electricity by sending to that institution a vacuum tube for the production of static electricity, directions for its use, and a copy of the April 1745

Gentleman's Magazine that contained a history of electricity experimentation. The article was as important to Franklin as was the apparatus. It was
an English translation of a French pamphlet by a Swiss physiologist that
stressed recent experiments conducted in Germany and at Leyden rather
than those of England and France. Franklin and his associates, in their
first group of experiments, would replicate much of the procedures of,
and make reports in the same language as, the experiments discussed in
the *Gentleman's Magazine*.[11]

Franklin has been lionized as a lone experimenter working in an isolated laboratory, but he had three main collaborators, plus a half dozen
unnamed people who performed as subjects in some of their experiments, and an audience of visitors who came to view the proceedings. His
principal associates were Thomas Hopkinson, a lawyer, one of his original
Junto mates; Philip Syng, a silversmith and Junto member; and Ebenezer
Kinnersley, a Baptist minister, professor of English, and neighbor. Syng
had evidenced an abiding interest in science and medicine beyond his
well-renowned craftsmanship, and he and Franklin were together involved in many public service endeavors, as were Franklin and lawyer
Hopkinson, who was also an agent for London firms and an importer.
Kinnersley was a fiery preacher and scientific tinkerer who had endeared
himself to Franklin even though Kinnersley publicly opposed the teachings of revivalist George Whitfield, whom Franklin had befriended. In
January 1748, Franklin would publish in his *Pennsylvania Gazette* a long
Kinnersley editorial arguing for complete freedom of religion. Franklin's
associates were men of intellect who enjoyed his trust.[12]

Their science was done in a way that left little margin for failure,
working in a makeshift laboratory and with delicate materials imported
from England and the Continent—electricity-generating machines, cakes
of wax, silk cloths, thin wires, improvised Leyden jars, gold-embossed
books, bodkins, and assorted metallic and wooden implements. The
order in which they conducted their initial experiments is not known,
but they were reported in clear, precisely worded descriptions, almost every experiment serving to advance the field of electricity. Franklin often
larded into these records phrases of homespun and naïveté—just as he
would later wear a coonskin cap in Paris salons. The humility had long-
lasting effects, in the case of electricity, on the perception of his experiments and theories, for instance by Priestley, who would influence their

public repute by writing, "It is not easy to say, whether we are most pleased with the simplicity and perspicuity with which these letters are written, the modesty with which the author proposes every hypothesis of his own, or the noble frankness with which he relates his mistakes, when they are corrected by subsequent experiments."[13]

FRANKLIN'S OCCASIONAL ADMISSION of error and his wonder that no one else had bothered to try certain experiments were signs that he regarded the experiments as voyages into unknown territory. Nearly a hundred years earlier, Robert Boyle had charted a similar course into a little-known scientific backwater, that of cold temperatures, a field whose neglect, he wrote, provided an "invitation [to] repair the omissions of mankind's curiosity toward a subject so considerable." As signposts, Boyle had only the wrong guesses of his predecessors; in the absence of accurate thermometers and very little hard information about cold's effects, Boyle proceeded by disproving his predecessors' inadequate theories so he could replace them with his own, which were better able to explain the known facts and the anomalous observations that previous theories had had difficulty in encompassing. Franklin and his associates followed the same pattern. Their electricity experiments were designed to prove or disprove theory. Franklin's own theorizing, however, was at first not done openly, perhaps as a sop to his perceived lack of scientific credentials. The only experiments reported to Collinson, for transmittal to the Royal Society—although Franklin would later assert that the letters had not been thus intended—either directly contradicted or meaningfully augmented European experiments. He took deliberate aim at the theories of Nollet and Watson. In the two-fluids theory, for instance, materials either generated or absorbed the electric charge—they could not do both; Franklin's first experiment challenged that theory by describing the "wonderful Effect of Points both in *drawing* off and *throwing* off the Electrical Fire." Moreover, while Watson and Nollet considered the shape of the materials to be of no consequence, Franklin touted the pointing of the metal as highly significant. He also called attention to his group's professionalism by their use of language. Their reports' form replicated that of the Royal Society, and Franklin's written explanations were clear enough to allow others to easily replicate the work and the results—thus meeting another Royal Society standard:

Place an Iron Shot of three or four Inches Diameter on the Mouth of a clean dry Glass Bottle. By a fine silken Thread from the Ceiling, right over the Mouth of the Bottle, suspend a small Cork Ball. . . . Electrify the Shot, and the Ball will be repelled. . . . If you present to the Shot the Point of a long, slender, sharp Bodkin at 6 or 8 inches Distance, the Repellency is instantly destroy'd, and the Cork flies to it. . . . To prove that the Electrical Fire is drawn off by the Point: if you take the Blade of the Bodkin out of the wooden Handle, and fix it in a stick of Sealing Wax, and then present it . . . no such Effect follows. . . . [But] Lay a long sharp Needle upon the Shot, and you can not electrise the Shot, so as to make it repel the Cork Ball.[14]

To prove that their results were no fluke, the experimenters repeated the sequence with other materials; in each the repelling power of the electrified object was diminished. In a footnote Franklin explained this by an analogy that referenced the four-elements conception of the universe, suggesting that the object's internal electricity "is never really destroyed, as when Water is thrown on common Fire, we do not imagine the Element is thereby destroy'd or annihilated, but only dispersed."[15]

If Franklin presented his first experiments as though undertaken in the absence of a controlling theory, he dissembled. The choice of experiments, their sequence, and the interpretations drawn from the resulting data all argue that Franklin had previously conceived a new theory: of electricity as a single fluid, extant in everything as an excitable potential, a fluid that, like all others, sought equilibrium. Franklin saw evidence of equilibrium in heat and cold circulation, ocean currents, the relationship between man's fiery and rational spirits—and in electricity, observing to Collinson, "There is really no more electrical fire in the phial after what is called its *charging,* than before, nor less after its discharging."[16] Franklin's notions of "drawing off" and "throwing off" were not arbitrarily chosen phrases but identifications of action derived from his intuitive sense that an electrical equilibrium existed. Some objects might at times display more electric potential, at times less, but all such imbalances would eventually be eliminated.

Having a workable theory, adequate equipment, a catalog of prior experiments, and capable assistants enabled Franklin to test theories by critical experiment—precisely what Watson, Nollet, and others had failed to do. The Philadelphians took a new look at a very recent series of Watson experiments whose peculiar results Watson had not successfully explained. When two men, each standing on wax or pitch, were electrified, both were able to shock a third person not standing on insulated material. If, however, during the charging the two men on wax touched each other, then neither would become electrified. And if they touched after the charging, "there will be a stronger Spark between them than was between either of them and the Person on the floor," as Franklin described it. Such results had perplexed Watson, but Franklin's single-fluid-that-seeks-equilibrium theory could explain them. He wrote out the supposition: "That Electrical Fire is a common Element, of which every one of the three Persons [in Watson's experiments] has his equal share before any Operation is begun with the Tube." Only a construct such as a single fluid that seeks equilibrium could allow Franklin to predict all the results of the various experiments and triumphantly sum up, "The Equality [of charge] is never destroyed, the Fire only circulating."

To fully express that new theory he had to coin new terms: "positive" and "negative," and "plus" and "minus." The pairs denoted not two kinds of electricity but two phases of a single fluid, two halves of a whole. Franklin envisioned electricity as a force but not a mechanical force like Newton's motion, momentum, and impact. Franklin's electrical force could not be measured and reduced to laws—that was why he rejected the terms "attraction" and "repulsion," since attraction and repulsion were mechanical actions whose strength could be measured; conversely, positive, negative, plus, and minus were non-mechanical terms.[17]

Hastening to finish off a lengthy letter for a ship about to sail to London, in a packed two-paged paragraph Franklin tersely described more than a dozen experiments, such as electrifying the gilt lines on a leather book's cover, performing variations on the "shocking kiss" with people standing on insulated materials, and constructing a "Counterfeit Spider" that moved when electrified, "appearing perfectly alive." "For my part," he summed up, "I never was before engaged in any study that so totally engrossed my attention."[18]

Franklin's friends were enthusiastic about his work. Logan allowed Franklin to shock him in hopes of relieving his pain. When Syng, a fine craftsman, was able to perfect a way of making glass tubes, akin to the one sent by Collinson, Franklin sent tubes and copies of his other materials to

Colden and to a young Boston merchant, James Bowdoin, enabling them, too, to perform electrical experiments.

Franklin and his group completed their first series of experiments in the spring of 1747 as rumors circulated of an impending attack on the city from Spanish or French privateers. Great Britain was then at war with France and Spain, and Philadelphia, being the colonies' largest and wealthiest city, was a prime target. Shortly after Franklin dispatched his letter to Collinson, privateers attacked, robbed homes within twenty miles of the city, and captured a ship coming to port from Antigua, murdering its captain in the process. In response, Franklin composed a powerful pamphlet, *Plain Truth*, arguing that despite Quaker-led pacifism, Philadelphia must arm itself against future invaders, and he helped form a committee to buy cannon for the city's defense. Those matters were ongoing when the Franklin electricity group resumed experimentation in the fall, producing results that Franklin conveyed to Collinson in a letter that admitted, "On [making] some further Experiments, I have observ'd a Phenomenon or two that I cannot at present account for on the Principles laid down in [my earlier] Letters, and am therefore become a little diffident of my Hypothesis, and am asham'd that I have express'd myself in so positive a manner." Using as a focus the Leyden jar, he then performed experiments that, according to I. B. Cohen, reveal him as "the master experimenter."[19] The jar's power had perplexed Musschenbroek, Watson, and Nollet; its activity contradicted the predictions of the two-fluids theories, and they were unable to understand why. Franklin seems to have figured out the answer and devised his own single-fluid theory to explain what the Europeans could not.

To demonstrate it, he designed a critical series of experiments. A classical pattern for such experiments is to eliminate all other causes for a phenomenon, leaving the true one. So the Philadelphians tested many possible causes for the source of power in the Leyden jar. Pouring out the supposedly charged water into another vessel to see if it contained electricity, they found none—as Franklin had correctly predicted, because in his view water was only a conductor. The experimenters replaced the water in the jar with lead pellets and found that the jar had the same power as when it was water-filled. They similarly tested and rejected as electricity sources the cork, wire, and outer lead foil coating. Still extant was the possibility that electricity was seated in the glass of the jar; Watson thought it might be in that component. But glass, Franklin was convinced, was a non-conductor; his group's new experiments found that whatever the amount of positive charge existing on the outside coating of the jar, it was precisely equal to the negative charge on the inside. This they ascertained by attaching a wire to the outside of the jar, parallel to the wire inside, and suspending between the two wires a cork ball on a silk thread. When the apparatus was charged, the cork ball "play[ed] incessantly from one wire to another." That result conclusively demonstrated what Franklin had theorized, the equivalency of the positive charge outside and the negative one inside. There were not two fluids of electricity, there was only one.[20]

Franklin's critical experiments made it possible to understand that the Leyden Jar was not simply a storage bin, as the Europeans had believed, but a condenser of the electric charge. That was the source of its extra power. This understanding allowed Franklin's group to extend the Leyden Jar principle and obtain the same amount of electrical power from a series of glass plates interlarded with wires—a "battery," a term Franklin borrowed from the military's usage of it.

At the end of the third season's experiments, Franklin was expansive in a valedictory to Collinson:

> Chagrined a little that we have been hitherto able to produce nothing in the way of use to mankind; and the hot weather coming on, when electrical experiments are not so agreeable, it is proposed to put an end to them for the season, somewhat humourously, in a party of pleasure, on the banks of the Skuylkil. Spirits, at the same time, are to be fired by a spark sent from side to side through the river, without touching any other conductor than the water; an experiment which we some time since performed, to the amazement of many. A turkey is to be killed for our dinner by the *electrical shock,* and roasted by the *electrical jack,* before a fire kindled by the *electrical bottle:* when the healths of all the famous electricians in *England, Holland, France, and Germany,* are to be drunk in *electrified bumpers,* under the discharge of guns from the *electrical battery.*[21]

After sending off another batch of electrical letters to London in the spring of 1749, Franklin anxiously awaited word from Collinson. He took the interim to further prepare himself for life as a gentleman scientist, having already sold his printing establishment and otherwise retired from business. While waiting for word from London, he set out to publicize the electrical work. He wrote the script for and helped underwrite Kinnersley's touring lecture/demonstration, which premiered in the spring of 1749 in Annapolis.[22] As Kinnersley later put it, the lectures and demonstrations were designed "to give [the audience] more noble, more grand and exalted Ideas of the Author of Nature." Kinnersley had been ingenious in producing and directing the electric charge, inventing the stunt of sending it through the waters of the Schuylkill, and concocting the electrified image of King George II that shocked those who touched it. Other Kinnersley demonstrations were a "shower of electrified sand," the "artificial spider," an electrical horse-race, "eight musical bells run by an electrified Phial of Water," "electrified money, which few Persons will take when offered," a demonstration of "why lightning darts through the air in a crooked direction," and, as a finale, "A Battery of eleven Guns discharged by Lightning, after it has darted through ten Feet of Water."[23] The most spectacular demonstration involved the equivalency of electricity and lightning; in front of a backdrop of a church as it is being struck by lightning, Kinnersley ignited by electric charge a fire and small explosion in the model of a church, which accordingly burst into flame and disintegrated. Upon seeing this demonstration, people often went out and bought or constructed lightning rods for their homes and churches.[24] Some who came to the lectures with the preconceived notion that the demonstrations would diminish the works of the Lord emerged thinking differently; as a reviewer put it in the *New York Gazette,*

> The Truth of this Gentleman's Hypothesis appear'd in so glaring a Light, and with such undeniable Evidence, that all my former preconceiv'd Notions . . . immediately vanished . . . the Wisdom of Providence, having reserv'd the Discovery of that wonderful *Phaenomenon,* which has been a Mystery, wrapp'd up in Clouds and thick Darkness ever since its first Appearance [has yielded] to the Improvements made on the *Electric Fire,* by ingenious *Americans.*[25]

Franklin took no profit from the lecture tour, just as he had refused to profit from sales of the Franklin fireplace, feeling, as most gentlemen still did in that era, that inventions were for the benefit of mankind. Similarly, the lectures were couched in the language of self-improvement, which, historian Andrew Delbourgo suggests, reflected the "discourse of progress" that was part and parcel of the Enlightenment, especially in the colonies, where it "connoted the polishing of rough colonials into provincial cosmopolitans."[26]

COLLINSON, UPON RECEIVING Franklin's first substantive letter, had recognized that at last he had found the American genius whose appearance he had awaited. The quality of the experiments and the clarity of description were beyond the level of most other communications then being considered by the Royal Society. Knowing that if he submitted it immediately, the RS would refer it to Watson for evaluation, and perhaps fearing that Watson would find a way to trash it because Franklin's experiments disproved his theories, Collinson sought to prepare the ground so that the missives could be neither ignored nor sidetracked. For eighteen months he circulated Franklin's letters among influential friends, building a groundswell of appreciation that made it easier to introduce them into the Royal Society in the fall of 1749.

Although Franklin in his *Autobiography* recalled that his letters were received with ridicule, the printed record shows that they were respectfully discussed. Next, a private printer—with an assist from Collinson—agreed to bring them out as a pamphlet. Collinson also had the *Gentleman's Magazine* announce the forthcoming publication. In each subsequent edition of the pamphlet, its size grew as it included additional letters from Franklin, Kinnersley, Bowdoin, and others. Within a few years it became a book of several hundred pages.

Collinson had guessed well in regard to Watson. Initially, the British electrician argued that Franklin's work did little more than agree with his and demanded to know a missing detail—what amount of electricity had been needed to kill Franklin's turkey. That was supplied, and by the time the collected letters appeared in print, Watson was lauding Franklin as "able and ingenious" with "a head to conceive, and a hand to carry into execution, whatever he thinks may conduce to enlighten the subject-matter. . . . I think scarce any body is better acquainted with the subject of electricity."[27] In Watson's words was more than gracious concession, for in celebrating Franklin the British electrician articulated a respect not only for the individual but also for what American science could accomplish. This was also an acknowledgment of the democratization of the scientific polity; in the American science club, as opposed to that of the Europeans, talent and ingenuity were permitted to overcome the social obstacles of a chief experimenter not born a gentleman or having attended a college, the employment of similarly ingenious associates who were not members of the Royal Society, and a theory that did not depend on other theories previously elucidated by approved Europeans.

WHILE MUSSCHENBROEK AND OTHER European experimenters soon became Franklin supporters and acceptors of his theory of electricity, Abbé Jean-Antoine Nollet, France's leading popular lecturer on the sciences, did not, and his opinion bore weight. Voltaire—who among other achievements had translated Newton into French—wrote of Nollet, "One learns more from [his] experiments than from all the books of antiquity."[28] Nollet's anger at Franklin derived partly from old hurts involving the Comte de Buffon and Buffon's own feud with René Antoine Ferchault de Réaumur, who was Nollet's mentor. Buffon had become a champion of Franklin, having found in Franklin's letters (the bound volume sent to him by Collinson) echoes of Newton and an emphasis on non-mechanical forces that supported his own theses. He commissioned a translation.[29] Buffon's preface to the translated edition of Franklin took a swipe at Nollet by pointing out that through Franklin's "keen, reasoned, and sustained experiments . . . Nature is forced to show her secrets. . . . It is [the method] of the great Newton."[30] The French translation's introduction, commentary, and preface were so congratulatory of Franklin at the expense of Nollet—whose name was unfairly omitted from a capsule history of the field—that the abbé thought Franklin was Buffon's fictional construct. Learning that Franklin was real, Nollet wrote him a series of open letters that would eventually amount to three volumes, in which he attempted to refute Franklin's achievements.[31]

As Nollet was just beginning those letters—and before Franklin's latterly famous kite experiment—Buffon and others undertook to conduct the lightning experiment that Franklin had earlier suggested in a July 29, 1750 letter. Many electricians had noted the similarities between electricity produced in the laboratory and lightning. But no one had done an experiment to prove that lightning and electricity were the same. Franklin had suggested a critical test known as the sentry-box experiment, but he had not performed it because no spire of sufficient height then existed in

Philadelphia. However, once Franklin's laboratory experiments had been demonstrated to Louis XIV, the king expressed a wish to have the sentry-box one done. It was attempted during a storm at Marly-la-Ville, north of Paris. As Franklin had intended, a man was situated in a high sentry box accompanied by glass jars into which the lightning would be directed from rods extended to attract it. The storm arrived, lightning was drawn down, and the sentry in his wooden box, as directed, did play a bit with the charge and was not electrocuted.

The report of the Marly experiment had not reached Franklin in June 1752 when he and his son went out in a Philadelphia storm to try to capture the bolt from the blue. This was an extremely dangerous thing to do; Franklin made it less so by keeping dry the portion of the string nearest him while exposing the rest to the rain. He did not see lightning hit the kite but noticed that the kite strings were vibrating as the cork balls in his laboratory did on receiving a charge; extending his knuckle to the key, he received a mild shock. But then, as Priestley later put it, "dreading the ridicule which too commonly attends unsuccessful attempts in science," Franklin did not initially communicate his experimental results. Only after receiving reports of the Marly sentry-box success did he describe, in brief to Collinson, the lightning running down the kite to the attached key and into the phial: "From the electric fire thus obtained, spirits may be kindled, and all the other electric experiments be performed, which are usually done by the help of a rubbed glass globe or tube, and thereby the sameness of the electric matter with that of the lightning is completely demonstrated."[32]

Collinson understood that proving the equivalency of lightning and electricity was not only a triumph for Franklin, it was a disaster for Nollet. Normally a man who celebrated all scientists, Collinson turned caustic when he considered the man who was assailing his protégé: as he wrote to Franklin, Nollet was

> farr from Dealing candidly or ingeniously, the Effect of his pride who look'd upon himself as the Prince of Electricians. . . . He had erected a Machine at Paris to make your Experiments, & had gott a Sett of people about him to Vouch that they could not be verified & undoubtedly all the Citty would have sung with it. Butt [when] a Noble Man [saw] the Abbe & his Creatures putt on grave looks & shook their Heads intimating things

did not succeed—this put the Nobelman quick out of Temper & on a Nice
Inquiry and Observation found out the Juggle & Contrivance, gave them
their Due in high Language and publish'd the base & Juggling Intention all
over Paris.[33]

David Colden, son of Cadwallader, attempted to replicate experiments
said by the Frenchman to give the lie to Franklin. He could not, and, after
carefully parsing Nollet's descriptions of procedure and comparing them
to Franklin's, figured out why: Nollet had subtly changed the parame-
ters to alter his results. Cesare Beccaria of Italy did the same, comparing
experiments and explanations and preferring Franklin's, while English
physicist John Canton also duplicated the experiments and reported to
the Royal Society that one particular experiment "may be consider'd as a
kind of ocular demonstration of the truth of Mr. Franklin's hypothesis."[34]

What Franklin's work provided to the field of electricity, philosopher
of science Thomas Kuhn wrote, was revolutionary in that it created a
new paradigm to guide future research: "It suggested which experiments
would be worth performing and which . . . would not. . . . The confidence
that they were on the right track [then] encouraged scientists to undertake more precise, esoteric, and consuming sorts of work."[35] On a higher
plane, as Kuhn and sociologist of science Bruno Latour have suggested,
scientific practices that succeed in advancing a field of knowledge, especially when they create order out of what was formerly disorder, as Franklin's did, oftentimes deeply affect the world beyond the laboratory.[36] This
was Franklin's—and American science's—ultimate triumph.

Perhaps it was Franklin's sense of that wider triumph to come that
prevented him from responding to Nollet's criticisms when first made.
That stance cost him emotionally, as he revealed thirty years later in
a 1781 letter counseling a friend to shrug off a biased reception of the
friend's book on photosynthesis:

> For the present the Reputation will be given grudgingly & in as small quan-
> tity as possible, mix'd in with some mortification. One would think that
> a man so laboring disinterestedly for the Good of his Fellow-Creatures,
> could not possibly by such means make himself enemies, but there are
> Minds who cannot bear that another should distinguish himself . . . and
> tho' he demands no Profit, nor anything in Return but the Good Will of

those he is serving, they will endeavour to deprive him of that, first by dis-
puting the Truth of his Experiments, then their utility, & being defeated
there, they finally dispute his right to them, and would give the credit of
them to a man that liv'd 3000 years ago, or at 3000 leagues distance. . . .
Go on, however, and never be discouraged. Others have met with the same
Treatment before you, and will after you. And whatever some may think
& say, it is worthwhile to do Men Good, for the Satisfaction one has in the
Reflection.[37]

Back in 1683, upon the issuing of a second edition of Robert Boyle's
New Experiments and Observations Touching Cold, eighteen years after the
first edition, Boyle wrote that "some of the Particulars [in the first edi-
tion], deliver'd as Paradoxical, are now acknowledg'd for Truths by most
of the Virtuos [and] are at present come into common use among the
Curious." When first printed, Boyle's experiments had been considered
"Novelties," but "many have since thought fit to embrace the Opinions,
and make use of the Practices, there propos'd.[38]

Seventeen years elapsed between the first publication of Franklin's
letters and Priestley's 1768 book, and by then the scientific community
had similarly accepted his theory, and his experiments were being reproduced and verified by scientists in England, France, Germany, the Netherlands, Italy, and Russia, and by Americans from Boston to Savannah.
Harvard, Yale, and William & Mary awarded him honorary degrees,
for which Franklin reciprocated by donating scientific equipment that
helped train generations of students in the sciences. In the mid-1750s,
Benjamin Franklin was positioned as the icon of American scientific ingenuity in Kinnersley's popular lecture-demonstrations and in the teachings of Winthrop and Small for such students as Adams and Jefferson;
he was included for the dual purposes of understanding electricity and
celebrating the scientific achievements of an American. Franklin's success
verified that a scientific attitude toward life—eternally curious, refusing
to accept received wisdom without testing and questioning it, and insisting on the sort of proof that could be provided best by experimentation—
was the key to their individual and collective future.

FIVE

TRACKING *the* HEAVENS
from the COLONIES

EUROPEAN SCIENTISTS ACCEPTED BEN FRANKLIN as the exception proving the rule that Americans were able to offer observations of nature but were not well enough trained to significantly contribute to scientific analysis and theory-making. The desire to reverse the European community's estimate of colonial intellectual puissance became the unvoiced but palpable agenda of Franklin and the small American scientific community.

In 1752, overseas correspondents informed Franklin of a forthcoming transit of Mercury across the face of the sun to occur on May 6, 1753, a celestial event that could provide data for astronomical calculations. He had a French set of instructions for recording the transit translated and dispatched fifty copies to correspondents along the Atlantic seaboard, his ability to do so aided by his recent elevation to co-postmaster for the colonies. He also printed a detailed instructional pamphlet, derived from the *Philosophical Transactions,* in his *Pennsylvania Gazette* and provided further guidance in his annual *Poor Richard's Almanack,* packed with as much material on celestial phenomena as were college courses.

To effectively lead others into unknown territory, conditions must be ripe and followers adequately prepared. In the 1753 tracking of the Mercury transit in the American colonies, inclement weather was a factor in the failure, but the larger contributor was fumbling preparation. Yet from it Franklin, John Winthrop, and others gained experience toward readying more people to participate in observing a more important forthcoming celestial event, the transit of Venus in 1761.

Transits of Venus occur twice each century, eight years apart; the eighteenth century's pair were to be in June 1761 and 1769. Accurate measurements of the moment of penetration by Venus—a black dot on a fiery surface—time spent within the sun's face, angle of transit, and moment of exit, recorded at vantage points around the globe, would enable more accurate calculation of the distances between the sun and the planets. Currently, distances between celestial objects were understood only in relative terms. Being able to more accurately calculate them would enable the ascertaining of more exact positions on land or sea, a boon to navigation. In the late 1750s, British and French scientific institutions obtained permission from their sovereigns to put aside national rivalries so that their scientists could cooperate in a truly international scientific endeavor. For American scientists to be taken seriously, they would have to contribute credible observations to this effort.[1]

MANY STRANDS LED TOWARD better American participation in the transits of the 1760s. More Americans were being educated according to the ideas of the Scottish Enlightenment and were becoming aware of the French scientific advances, through the attention paid to the volumes of Buffon's *Histoire naturelle, générale et particulière,* the first one published in 1749 and more arriving annually. Georges-Louis Leclerc, Comte de Buffon, had studied law and mathematics and demonstrated his scientific abilities in testing more than a thousand specimens of timber for its structural qualities before being appointed as chief of the Jardin du Roi. He upgraded that institution into a research and instructional center while writing his major opus, through which he sought to become the Newton of the biological sciences, the rival to Linnaeus. "It is necessary," Buffon wrote, "to have general views, a firm glance, and reason formed more through reflection than study . . . [and] that quality of mind that permits us to grasp distant relationships, fit them together, and form a body of rational ideas." Buffon undertook to explain everything—the formation of the planets, the earth's geological history, the biology of plants and animals, and the "natural history of man," forays into physiology, psychology, and ethnology. According to Buffon, many current flora and fauna were not as they had been when God established them, and since what God had made was perfect and perfectly set in place, it was man who had wrought subsequent bad changes—through alterations in climate, epidemics, diet, and other lifestyle adaptations, which, for example, had cumulatively changed the original human species to the current population's myriad of skin colors, heights, and body features. While some critics thought Buffon more litterateur than thinker—d'Alembert called him "the great phrase-monger"—in the 1750s and 1760s, Buffon was among the most influential scientists in the world.[2]

WHILE IN THE OLD WORLD discussion of human origins as Buffon and others considered them was usually confined to the cognoscenti, in the New World it increasingly was not. To chew over just such subjects as human origins, in 1750 a protégé of Franklin's in Philadelphia replicated his 1720s Junto. Charles Thomson was orphaned at an early age, his mother having died in Ireland and his father at sea during the family's trip to America. At twenty-one, educated by a strict classicist, Thomson was considered a man of mature, serious religious and scientific interests. Franklin met him at that age, when Thomson led an outlying grammar school and Franklin, impressed, brought him to Philadelphia as a tutor at the Philadelphia Academy that Franklin had recently help to found. Friends and acquaintances often characterized Thomson as the most gentlemanly of men despite his humble origin. Among the factors recommending him to Franklin was that he had been Francis Alison's foremost student. An Edinburgh-educated Presbyterian minister, Alison was described by Franklin as "a Person of great ingenuity and learning, a catholic Divine, and what is more, an Honest Man," and by Ezra Stiles as "the finest classical scholar in America." When Alison first arrived in the mid-Atlantic colonies, he recalled, there had been no colleges or good grammar schools, "but on the other hand all that made any pretensions to learning were branded as letter learned Pharisees; and this desperate cause, of promoting learning in this Province, I undertook."[3] In 1752, Alison moved to Philadelphia to lead the Philadelphia Academy, where Thomson taught; and then he, Franklin, and Thomson worked together in several areas, among them updating the rules of the Library Company. Other "Baby Junto" members were Benjamin Franklin's son William, the son of another former old Junto member, two of John Bartram's sons (Moses and Isaac), and the brothers Biddle. They met in a tavern room to debate such topics as "What is the Difference between a Falsity and a Lye? What are the common Causes that Occasion the Downfall of an Empire? Is Light and Heat the same? Would a Public Bath be advantageous to this City?" An evening's debate celebrated the group's bond with a predecessor by drawing on Logan's groundbreaking study of maize.[4] This group was not leather-apron smart; better educated than their forebears, they discussed matters on a more sophisticated plane, symbolized by the group's renaming itself the American Society for Promoting and Propagating Useful Knowledge.

Boston had no similar organized scientific discussion group, but "the number of amateur scientists who came out of Harvard in [James] Bowdoin's generation and in the decades that followed is impressive," Bowdoin's biographers write; those who "dabbled in science" included "lawyers, pastors, businessmen, and independent gentlemen."[5] Traveling philosophic lecturers, newspaper and magazine articles, the greater availability of books on science subjects, the increased teaching of mathematics and sciences in schools, and the inclusion in almanacs of tutorials on astronomy all contributed to an enhanced climate for the appreciation and discussion of science.

But medical students were still being punished as criminals for autopsies on cadavers; serious naturalists such as John Bartram were pushed to such useless tasks as disproving that rattlesnakes could charm their prey; and many scientists remained convinced that swallows hibernated beneath iced-over ponds. The concepts of seasonal migration, extinction, and evolution remained hidden, obscured by continued adherence to the religious-based notion, reasserted by Buffon, that God had set everything in its place. That swallows could travel thousands of miles to winter in warmer climes was near heresy.

Peter Collinson tried to debunk the hibernation of swallows in what some writers label his only independent contribution to science; but even Collinson was not yet ready to accept the idea of a colonial academy of sciences when it was proposed again in the 1750s, writing to Franklin that it was "a Little to premature. Shall be glad if the Colony is come to such a Maturity as to support so Beneficial a Work." Proprietor Thomas Penn chimed in, writing that the establishment of such an academy "gives an opportunity to those fools who are always telling their fears that the Colonies will set up for themselves."[6]

Fears of American independence were increasingly reasonable for the British to entertain as some colonists agitated for more self-governance in response to Parliament's attempt to enforce colonial dependence. It was with the hope of protecting Pennsylvanians from suffering further Parliamentary inroads to their sovereignty that the General Assembly sent Franklin to London as its agent in 1757. The British government was using its taxation and commerce-controlling powers to provide financial support for the Seven Years' War then being fought between Great Britain, France, and Spain, a conflagration consuming Africa, Asia, and eastern Europe. In America, where it became known as the French and Indian War, the most severely affected British colonies were those on the northeastern and mid-Atlantic coast, whose populations were under attack from the French in Canada and their Native American allies.

The French and Indian War forced the American colonies, for the first time, to think seriously about arming themselves and taking defensive measures beyond those provided by their British protectors. It also afforded opportunities for individual development. Franklin, in London, honed his diplomatic skills and his tinkering. Attending a concert of a virtuoso playing notes on the moistened lips of wine glasses, he birthed the idea for one of his more unexpected inventions, the glass "armonica." Also, playing around with ether and a mercury thermometer, he rediscovered evaporative cooling. Washington, on the battlefield, sharpened his military abilities, mostly by learning what not to emulate in the actions of his British superiors. Adams consolidated his legal career and gained confidence in his persuasive abilities. Jefferson set the course of his life at William & Mary. The young physician John Morgan, after an apprenticeship in Philadelphia, learned a great deal about practical medicine as a surgeon with the British army on the western frontier.[7]

THE EUROPEAN SCIENTIFIC COMMUNITY, attempting to ignore the Seven Years' War for the sake of international scientific cooperation and progress, sent out expeditions to faraway places to observe the 1761 transit of Venus; most notable was that of Captain James Cook to the South Seas. Others went to St. Helena in the mid-Atlantic, to the Indian Ocean, to points within the Arctic Circle, and to South Africa's Cape of

Good Hope. The last was undertaken by neophytes Charles Mason and Jeremiah Dixon; both were escaping—Mason from a dreary seven-days-and several-nights-a-week job as the dogsbody at the Royal Observatory, and Dixon, an amateur astronomer, from the ignominy of having been expelled from his Quaker meeting for drunkenness.[8]

The 1761 transit was not predicted to be visible from the mid-Atlantic colonies, and most colonial legislatures did not consider providing funds to send observers to where it could be seen, from Hudson's Bay. But Winthrop, with the assistance of Bowdoin, obtained funds from Massachusetts and took two pupils to Newfoundland, where they recorded the transit under difficult conditions for an hour of its track. The limited observations were not of much use.

As for that, the worldwide results of the 1761 event raised as many questions as they answered due to mistaken assumptions about the timing of the piercing and exiting of the sun's umbra and inexact measuring implements. The international scientific community was grateful that there would be a second chance in 1769.

After the Treaty of Paris in 1763, which ended the Seven Years' War, preparations for that transit ramped up. In the American colonies, Franklin (who returned to Philadelphia briefly in 1764 only to be sent right back to London), Winthrop, and other American sky-gazers determined to make better use of this opportunity since the 1769 transit would be quite visible from many sites along the Atlantic Coast.

Because Americans supposedly lacked superior training and experience, the London representatives of Pennsylvania and Maryland hired Mason and Dixon, fresh from their triumph with the 1761 transit in South Africa, to be the outsiders who would settle a polite dispute that had persisted for eighty years, the exact coordinates of the Pennsylvania-Maryland mutual boundary. It took the pair from 1763 to 1768 to do the survey, and during that time they used the Library Company's reflecting telescope and trained local associates who would become integral to the American effort to record the 1769 transit of Venus. They also incorporated into their survey, without alteration or amendment, an earlier Rittenhouse survey of a twelve-mile circle on that border, which helped to certify Rittenhouse's position as a leading astronomer. Mason and Dixon also advanced science, to the delight of the Royal Society, by making an exact measure of a degree of latitude, something never before accomplished, providing a useful benchmark for navigation on land and sea.[9]

In 1761, Buffon's ninth volume of the *Histoire naturelle* became available. In it, he more adamantly asserted that the prime examples of animals and plants degenerating after being removed from their initial place were in the Americas. The tapir, llama, and jaguar of South America were smaller and inferior to their African-European counterparts, the elephant, giraffe, rhino, and lion. Lower heat and higher humidity made everything in the Americas smaller and less worthy—and that included human beings, "cold men" to go with "weak animals." Because such natives had not "restricted the torrents, or directed the rivers, or drained the swamps" for cultivation, as Europeans and all other cultivated peoples did, he considered a Native American to be of "the lowest order . . . a being without consequence, a sort of impotent automaton." The "Savage," he charged,

> has weak and small organs of generation; he has neither hair nor beard and no ardor for his female. . . . Lacking ardor for their females, and consequently love for their fellows . . . the most intimate society of all, that of the same family, only contains weak links for them; the connection of one family to another does not exist; thus, no fellowship, no republic, no social unit. The physical side of love defines their morals; their hearts are icy, their society cold and their rule hard. They look at their women only as servants at best or beasts of burden. . . . They have only a few children; and take little care of them . . . and that indifference to sex, [by] destroying the seeds of life, cuts at the same time at the root of society.[10]

To New World colonists attempting to prove that they, their continent, and their Native neighbors were the equal of anything in the Old World, Buffon's "degeneracy" attack cried out for refutation. Had the American Philosophical Society been functional, it might have amassed the scientific evidence to disprove Buffon on this point; but the APS had not yet wakened from slumber and the rival American Society was not comprised of men learned enough to take on such a sophisticated adversary.

The APS did shortly begin to stir, but in response to events that were of far greater consequence: attacks by Parliament on the colonies, the Sugar Act of 1764, and the Stamp Act of 1765. These edicts were British reactions to the Crown's continuing money problems in the wake of the Seven Years' War, exacerbated by Americans' routine evasion of other taxes. Unlike earlier indirect taxes, the Stamp Act was a direct tax on almost all printed materials, including bills of sale and conveyance. Intended to force the colonists to submit to greater British control, it produced the opposite effect, for the first time uniting colonists in opposition to London. Philadelphia's "tradesmen begin to grow clamorous for want of employment," apprentice physician Benjamin Rush wrote to a former college classmate, adding that the city was also "full of sailors who cannot procure berths, and who knows what the united resentments of these two numerous people may accomplish? An effigy of our stamp officers has been exposed to public view affixed to a gallows." Another of those men orphaned early, Rush was as prone to verbal excess as to excitability. In his missive to the classmate he labeled Benjamin Franklin a "curse to Pennsylvania and America" for not laboring hard enough in London to prevent passage of the Stamp Act.[11]

That oversight was one of Franklin's few errors of judgment, and he speedily recouped his position as hero to the colonies by testifying to Parliament for four hours on why they must repeal the Stamp Act. Franklin's biographers assign him the credit for its withdrawal, but more critical pressure on Parliament came from British merchants who were losing colonial customers. In any event, the scrapped Stamp Act was soon replaced by harsher acts that riled Americans even more.

IN THE MID-1760s some members of the dormant American Philosophical Society determined to again raise its banner even though Franklin was not there to lead it and Bartram was not inclined, having finally obtained the long-coveted post of botanist to the king. The chief revivers had personal agendas. Dr. Thomas Bond, a former member, and Dr. William Shippen Jr. were physicians seeking better recognition as scientists, and were also associated with the political group known as the Proprietary Party for its support of the Proprietor's continuing efforts to govern rather than cede decision-making to Pennsylvania's assembly. Shippen and John Morgan, his former preparatory school classmate and fellow Edinburgh medical graduate, had become Philadelphia's notable younger physicians; in the effort to resuscitate the APS, they lined up on opposite sides.

In 1762, Shippen had begun lecturing in anatomy in Philadelphia and advocating for doctors to take a more active role in obstetrics, then the province solely of midwives. Morgan had spent the mid-1760s in Edinburgh, Paris, and Leyden. Voltaire had been impressed with him and gave to him and a fellow student with whom he was traveling a note to show to other *philosophes:* "Behold two Amiable Young Men, Lovers of Truth & Inquirers into Nature. They are not satisfy'd with mear Appearances; they love Investigation & Truth, and despize Superstition. I commend You, Gentlemen—go on, love Truth & search diligently after it."[12] Returning to Philadelphia with a stellar reputation, Morgan had obtained the permission of the Proprietor to establish a medical college in Philadelphia. In a 1765 "discourse" that took two days to deliver as an oration, Morgan laid out his plans for a medical school. To professionalize practice, physicians should be neither surgeons nor "ignorant medicasters" charging patients for the medicines they prescribed; all Morgan would accept from a patient was "proper compensation for my advice and attendance as a physician." He fulminated against the lack of proper respect for physicians, who—unlike lawyers—were called upon at all hours of the night to provide their services. "Were they born slaves to the public? . . . For such a voluntary surrender of their liberty and ease as is necessary to practice conscientiously, are they to have no compensation?" Morgan allowed that Shippen Jr. might be qualified to teach a course or two in his institution, but not to have a guiding hand in it.[13] Morgan was able to establish the medical school but found himself blocked in setting up a medical society to enforce standards of practice; attributing that impasse to the Proprietary Party, he fell in with the "Anti-Proprietaries," who happened to also be members of the rival American Society for Promoting and Propagating Useful Knowledge.

Charles Thomson had progressed from schoolteacher and Franklin associate to a position as "secretary"—agent and advocate—to a Native American tribe, then to being a successful merchant, and in the mid-1760s to being a rebel leading an effort to keep British goods out of Philadelphia. As his fortunes and perspective increased, he successively broadened the American Society's concerns and its sense of the possibilities of the colonies as self-sustaining. "In the actual meetings, intellectual union went hand-in-hand with political union," Thomson's biographer notes, "so even the nonpolitical topics chosen for discussion reveal the underlying current of concern for a strengthening of those things that would unite Americans as Americans."[14]

Who was more important to Pennsylvania, the merchant or the farmer? The merchant, American Society members decided, was positioned to marshal the "genius" of the artisan and worker for the good of the many. How should they pay taxes to England? The colonies should print their own money and pay taxes only in that coin. As for "admitting women into Councils of state," they granted that "women have natural Abilities equal to the men and if improved by Education would be equally capable of advising in public Affairs [for] by their lively Imagination they would throw a Subject into new lights, whereby truth might the readier be found." But they quickly yielded to the canard that the "natural softness and delicacy of [women's] constitutions as well as the many disorders to which they are incident" precluded their taking places in the councils of state. After disposing of women's aspirations, the company switched to a discussion of electricity from a Leyden Jar. The remarkable October 18, 1766 meeting that featured all these topics concluded with Owen Biddle proposing two topics for the next meeting: (1) whether it was a good idea that "the executive powers of government over any Territory should be made hereditary and transferable in the family," a subject of vital interest in the Proprietary versus Anti-Proprietary Party dispute; and (2) whether there was communication between spirits and the living, either in dreams or visions.[15]

A few months later, American Society members listened to a paper read by new member Morgan, whose fledgling medical society he had just merged into the American Society. Members heard an abbreviated version of Morgan's Edinburgh doctoral thesis; the secretary's notes contain no discussion, as the other members were likely unable to follow the arcana of a medical treatise.[16]

Thomson articulated his largest vision in a New Year's Day 1768 oration—an address that could never have been made to an elite audience in England, for it emphasized the abilities of ordinary people. For the colonies to become less dependent upon Great Britain required innovation and application of scientific principles, Thomson acknowledged, but that could be done because "our farmers employed in cultivating the land are an intelligent, sensible set of men capable of observation, and of making experiments; our mechanics are handy and ingenious; and many of our young men, who have turned their thoughts to philosophical Enquiries, have discovered such a degree of judgment and genius as will enable them to carry their researches far into . . . Nature." "Knowledge is of little use when confined to mere Speculation," Thomson continued. "But when speculative Truths are reduced to Practice, when Theories, grounded upon Experiments, are applied to common Purposes of Life, and when, by these, Agriculture is improved, Trade enlarged, and the Arts of Living made more easy and comfortable . . . Knowledge then becomes really useful."[17]

The American Society elected men from Boston, Charleston, Newport, Halifax, Antigua, Edinburgh, and Naples and in their most brilliant stroke, probably at Thomson's instigation, elected Franklin president, in absentia and without informing him. It also published scientific articles not in expensive tomes but in newspapers, thereby honoring the society's title phrase, "useful knowledge," and quickly transmitting information to a wider public: an essay on fevers by a Carolina physician, a treatise on a new machine for cutting and polishing crystals, and a Moses Bartram paper on silkworm cultivation.[18]

NEGOTIATIONS FOR A MERGER of the American Society for Promoting and Propagating Useful Knowledge and the American Philosophical Society were already under way in August 1768 when Peter Collinson died at age seventy-six. In a late exchange, Colden had offered Collinson an insightful compliment: "I know you take pleasure in doing good where you think it deserved."[19] In one of Collinson's final papers, considered to be among his most important contributions, he provided to the Royal Society a report on the fossil bones found at Big Bone Lick, not far south of Cincinnati on the Ohio River. (Collinson had also forwarded some bones to Buffon.) The outsized bones were initially believed to have come from elephants—that is, from living creatures—because of the prevailing notion, which Collinson restated to Bartram, that it was "contrary to the Common Cause of Providence to suffer any of His creatures to be Annihilated." Collinson speculated that the bones belonged to an herbivore but went no further. More open-minded thinkers would soon address the bones' age and origin. In that sense, Collinson's passing marked the close of the notebook phase of natural history in the American colonies and the opening of a period in which analysis of results became imperative and common. In a renewed, very warm correspondence between Bartram and Franklin occasioned by Collinson's death, the Philadelphians acknowledged that transition.[20]

As the time for the June 1769 transit of Venus rapidly approached, it became obvious that the Philadelphia-based societies must put aside differences and merge. Bickering churches and competing merchants' associations were already doing so in reaction to the spur provided by the British taxation policy. After a year of false starts, the two scientific societies succumbed to the ministrations of an unlikely mediator, John Morgan, who overcame personal animosity to Thomas Bond and approached him. When the groups finally held a joint meeting under a unified banner, the collective spirit was present, but animosities simmered, and within a few months the basic APS objective—to become the equivalent of the Royal Society, focused on basic research—shouldered aside Thomsonian emphasis on the practical side as members concentrated on the proximate event.

The messages sent by the combining of the Philadelphia-based societies were unity among colonial efforts and independence from Great Britain. Ezra Stiles, attempting just then to form a northeastern scientific society, made the connection between the messages even clearer. An assiduous cultivator of the powerful, Stiles had corralled John Winthrop into his scheme. He wrote into his manifesto a requirement not needed in liberal Philadelphia but, Stiles believed, required in New England: he reserved two-thirds of his society's memberships for Presbyterians or Congregationalists, "to defeat Episcopal intrigue by which this Institution would be surreptitiously caught into an anti-American Interest."[21]

THE FIRST PAPER DELIVERED to the combined American Philosophical Society for the Promotion of Useful Knowledge, held at Philadelphia, was by David Rittenhouse, thirty-five. Already being compared to Newton, he did not like the comparison—for who could live up to that ideal?—but there were parallels. At the age of eight, Rittenhouse had constructed a wooden model of a watermill (Newton had done a windmill at that age), and at sixteen, a wooden clock (Newton had also made a water clock). Never sent to school, he educated himself by reading books, much as Franklin had. He announced in this first APS paper his plans for building an "orrery." Orreries were complicated machines used for demonstrating scientific principles—Clap had made one for Yale, Winthrop used another at Harvard, and Greenwood toured with a third—and they spread the gospel of science by making the heavens explicable to anyone watching them tick and move. Rittenhouse's orrery would limn in miniature all the planets as they orbited the machine's sun just as the real ones did our star, with their orbit lengths and times all correct for 5,000 years past and 5,000 years ahead. One face was to show Jupiter and its satellites, another Saturn, a third, earth's moon, displaying "the exact time, quantity, and duration of her eclipses—and those of the sun occasioned by her interposition. . . . Likewise, the true place of the moon in the signs, with her latitude, and the place of her apogee in the nodes; the sun's declination, equation of time &c." A British astronomer declared Rittenhouse's plans "quite wonderful," exceeding the complexity and accuracy of anything yet done. Witherspoon, the incoming president of the College of New Jersey, bought Rittenhouse's even before it was completed. Pennsylvania's college was so aghast at this plain-sight robbery by a neighboring colony that Rittenhouse had to agree to make them one as well.[22]

THE AMERICAN POPULACE being markedly more literate than those of Great Britain and Europe, reading more newspapers per capita, there was great enthusiasm for the forthcoming scientific effort to record the transit, and it produced a plethora of eager American volunteers. "It was an index of the social health and cultural vitality of the older American towns and provinces whether they did or did not take their share in the observations of 1769," writes historian Donald Fleming. Philadelphia obtained new telescopes with money from the Pennsylvania legislature, while Providence did so from private underwriting. The APS designated twenty-two such official monitoring stations. Benjamin West, a Providence almanac-maker, mathematician, and member of a mercantile family distinguished for its interest in the sciences, laid out his reasons for putting so much time and treasure into the preparations:

> We expect to discover the distance of the Earth, the Planets and Comets, from the Sun; and consequently their magnitudes and quantity of matter will be known. . . . Astronomers in future will be able . . . to discover whether the Earth and Planets approach the Sun or recede from him; and

whether the Sun be diminished by its constant expences of heat and light. From a knowledge of all these things, methinks we shall have such a demonstration of the existence of a G O D, who made and governs all things, that even the reformed atheist must tremble when he reflects on his past conduct.[23]

Providence's preparations were extraordinary and better documented than most—Stiles's report would run to 268 pages. They included a cannon fired the day before the transit, just when the sun came on the meridian, so that observers could mark a line on their windows, and sets of cotton strings connected to weights in water for synchronizing timepieces—an arrangement that proved irresistible to schoolboy tampering.[24]

From Maine to Virginia, hundreds of observers were involved. News of the impending event excited such amateurs as Adams, Jefferson, and John Page. Franklin, in Europe, cheered them all on. In London, Tom Paine became intrigued.

Rittenhouse labored mightily, constructing his own telescopes, as well as an instrument for measuring altitude, an astronomical clock, and an observatory. To triangulate, he set up posts 350 feet apart near Philadelphia. The actual transit was so exciting for him that during it the always-sickly man fainted, and it was a few minutes before he recovered and continued taking measurements, aided by his accurate timepieces.

From points in Tahiti and Baja California as well as in Sweden, Russia, and the American Colonies, came observations that allowed the calculation of the solar parallax and, derived from that, the distance from the earth to the sun, a figure put at nearly 93 million miles—within one percent of the distance as measured in the twentieth century. Rittenhouse and other Americans, not content with providing data for European analysis, did their own analyses and came up with respectable results. Franklin presented the American observations to the Royal Society. Royal astronomer Nevil Maskelyne wrote the Proprietor of Pennsylvania (who forwarded the letter to the APS), thanking the members for observations "excellent and compleat; and honour to the Gentlemen who made them."[25] Those American observations, however, had not all been made by "gentlemen"; people from many walks of life had participated directly, and a far greater number through reading about the event.

Shortly after the transit of Venus, the APS returned to more practical matters. In 1771, when the American work on the transit of Venus was printed as the main attraction in the first volume of the *Transactions of the American Philosophical Society,* it was accompanied by a preface that re-printed part of Thomson's speech to the American Society in 1768, stress-ing the need for useful knowledge, and by articles on four technological advances—William Henry's "sentinel register" for regulating the flame of a furnace, Owen Biddle's fine-cutting machine, a ship pump, and a "horizontal windmill" for raising water out of mines and wells. To convey that Americans too knew the requirements of learned scientific articles, the volume of forty-eight articles had the same dimensions as that of the Royal Society's *Transactions* and contained plates the equal of any pub-lished in that British record with a fold-out chart of Venus's path, illustra-tions of the sentinel register, and a map of proposed canal routes. Well received in London, Paris, St. Petersburg, and other capitals to which it was sent, the volume accomplished its task, in conjunction with the ob-servations on the 1769 transit of Venus, elevating the American scientific effort to the level of that of the Europeans.

Franklin, re-elected as APS president, became a more active partici-pant, sending from London communications on silk-raising and other subjects in which knowledge could aid Americans' capabilities for eco-nomic independence. Moreover, the American polity was growing: ad-ditional Americans beyond the narrow spectrum of Philadelphians and physicians were looking to the APS as the locus of scientific sustenance. On May 1, 1772, the recording secretary noted the incoming account of the travels in America of Swedish botanist Peter Kalm, two pairs of Na-tive American snowshoes and one hatchet, as well as various catalogues of American plants, animals, and insects. In 1773, the secretary recorded a haul of incoming material from a hundred sources, including a model of a bridge, a paper on the cause of sleep and dreams, a model of a dredging machine, a map of Florida rivers, a measurement of the height of the Blue Mountains, "A Shark's Jaw; a skin of the Shagreen Fish; & a Porcupine Fish," asphalt, meteorological observations, experiments on evaporation, samples of antinomy and alum bark, a letter on variations in compass readings, and a treatise on atmospheric electricity.[26]

So many "communications" arrived that they were apportioned out to committees to sort and evaluate. One group managed to reject as "doubtful" and commonplace a nicely observed letter on aurora borealis, sniffing, "In the High latitudes, one might write 50 such accounts in the year." This was unfortunate, because the letter bore the signatures of Samuel Williams, a minister who later became president of Harvard, and of nineteen-year-old Benjamin Thompson, a sometime Winthrop student. Thompson added that rejection to his stack of grudges against the American Establishment—the Society had not even noted his earlier letter about the birth of a deformed child—and became a British spy during the war, on the way to becoming the elucidator of principles about heat.[27]

Charles Thomson absented himself from these workings of the APS in the early 1770s because his attention had shifted to politics, in which he had become increasingly radical, writing screeds in support of the Boston Tea Party and organizing protests against British imports, all while courting his second wife.

An APS committee headed by Kinnersley and Rittenhouse experimented on the *gymnotus electricus,* the electric ray of Surinam.[28] Other committees reviewed demonstrations of a steam engine for draining mines—not good enough for use, they concluded—and the dredge, judged promising enough for a £100 grant from the society.[29]

There were new members, among them Benjamin Rush, who had completed his medical education in Scotland and had become a friend to Franklin. One of Rush's early investigations led to a paper on the idea that plants have nerves similar to those of animals and human beings. He sent it to Isaac Bartram, who showed it to his father, who appreciated it.[30] Returning to Philadelphia and beginning a medical practice—no easy matter in a city where nearly all physicians were Quakers—Rush presented to the APS a paper on Native medicine as it could be utilized by American physicians.

Increasingly, material came in to the Society from abroad. The Marquis de Condorcet sent in, via Franklin, queries as to whether the "calcareous" stones atop mountains contained "marine productions"; wanting to know whether the heights of those mountains occasioned changes in readings from magnetic compasses or barometers; and whether black children of "free negroes who have not mixed with whites . . . have retained the genius and character of the negroes."

The members voted to pursue these Condorcet questions, but on March 4, 1774, had to leave off such matters to approve a motion on a more pressing matter:

The Acts of the British parliament for shutting up the port of Boston, for altering the charters, and for the more impartial administration of justice, in the province of Massachusetts bay, together with the Bill for establishing popery and arbitrary power in Quebec, having alarmed the whole of the American colonies, the members of the philosophical Society partaking with their countrymen in the distress and labors brought upon their country were obliged to discontinue their meetings for some months until a mode of opposition to the said acts of parliament was established, which they hope will restore the former Harmony, and maintain a perpetual Union between Great Britain & the American colonies.[31]

SIX

"EXPRESSIONS *of the* AMERICAN MIND"

DURING THE REVOLUTIONARY WAR, WHILE American laboratory and field research was much reduced, science did not grind to a halt. Scientific thought helped frame America's initiating rhetoric of the war, and throughout the conflict innovations in medicine and disease control and in arms and armaments were integral to the American effort. This and the next two chapters deal with science-related aspects of the war, the present one with the initiating rhetoric, the next with the medical aspects, and the following chapter with technology in armament.

In the seventeenth and eighteenth centuries, Jürgen Habermas writes, the "light of reason" entered the public sphere in stages, cropping up first among the elite and in a semiprivate way before being adopted by ever wider groups. Broad public participation in debate did not take place until the "problemization of areas that had until then not been questioned," and when "the issues discussed became 'general' not merely in their significance but also in their accessibility: everyone had to be able to participate." Those stages had characterized the path of natural philosophy in the American colonies, from the initial debate in the public sphere of 1721–1722 about smallpox prevention in the Boston epidemic, increasing through the middle decades of the century and cresting in the broad participation in the recording of the 1769 transit of Venus and in the growing audience for the efforts of the renewed American Philosophical Society. The same path to acceptance was being hewed in the consideration of non-monarchical and non-church governance: the debate was moving steadily from the elite's private colloquies to publicly available written materials and thence to open assemblies. Habermas insists that the "communicative" aspects of this path were absolutely vital; in his view, the availability of newspapers able to operate beyond the day-to-day control of governing powers geometrically increased a populace's ability to engage in public argument. From 1765 on, there were increasingly sophisticated discussions in colonial newspapers of direct and indirect taxes and of an accused person's right to habeas corpus, as well as of such scientific matters as the parallax to be computed from observations of the transit of Venus. At stake in all these sort of discussions were Enlightenment ideals, particularly those of liberty, justice, and equality, enabling ordinary citizens to openly consider wresting their collective freedom from what Habermas labels the "restrictive particularism" of fealty to kings, lords, and church hierarchies.[1] In the American colonies just prior to the Revolutionary War a newly aroused sensitivity to science-related concepts intertwined with political, religious, and economic opinions. "Experimental science," philosopher David Zaret writes, "was clearly the most important for reshaping the general views of reason and public opinion that made plausible the liberal model of the public sphere," and a polity able to consider radical alterations to the status quo.[2]

Gordon Wood suggests that the ultimate aim of the Enlightenment in America was "nothing less than discovering the hidden forces in the moral world that held people together, forces that could match the great eighteenth-century scientific discoveries of the hidden forces—gravity, magnetism, electricity, and energy—that operated in the physical world;" this discovery process, Wood adds, was shared by people from many walks of life. Even if the free expression of ideas, the embrace of collaborative endeavor, and the championing of provable facts over received dogma— the core tenets of Enlightenment science—had not wholly permeated to the level of the ordinary farmer by the time of the Second Continental Congress, Daniel Boorstin argues, the delegates did generally acknowledge that "nature bound men together [and] was not to be overcome by rhetoric, chicanery or dishonesty of any kind; the winds were not to be predicted nor the poison of the rattlesnake combated, except by actual knowledge. . . . The desire to know nature was the strongest incentive to ingenuousness, and the most effective restraint against the deception of oneself or of one's neighbors." Such values, Boorstin concludes, enabled the delegates to attain to "the 'scientific' frame of mind in the best sense of the word."[3]

IN THE FALL OF 1774, as the delegates from Massachusetts—well-known radicals—were nearing the city of Philadelphia, they were met secretly by like-minded Philadelphians in the private room of a tavern in nearby Frankford, and warned, as Boston's John Adams put it, not to "utter the word independence" in the Congress or in "private conversation . . . for the idea of independence is as unpopular in Pennsylvania and in all the Middle and Southern States as the Stamp Act itself." After the secret conference, the Pennsylvanians split up so as not to be seen as a group, and each returned to Philadelphia in the coach of a Massachusetts delegate, Benjamin Rush in that of John Adams—the beginning of a long and close friendship. At that first Congress, Charles Thomson was unanimously elected its secretary despite being the leader of Philadelphia's Committee of Correspondence and a man whose radicalism was so overt that John Adams would soon label him "the Samuel Adams of Philadelphia."[4]

Philadelphia printer and publisher William Bradford warned Virginia delegate James Madison, his friend from college days, by letter that some members of the Pennsylvania, Virginia, and New York delegations were "inimical to the Liberties of America."[5] The presence of many demurrers at the First Continental Congress was indicative of there being no unanimity of political sentiment in favor of the thirteen colonies needing a new configuration of governance; nor was there unanimous support for the idea that such a new form could be established if a separation from Great Britain was attempted. Yet enough unity had developed by the time of the Second Continental Congress's effort to allow that body to culminate its effort by issuing the Declaration of Independence in July 1776.

The all-important transition from doubt to action that took place between the First and Second Congresses can be seen being prodded into existence in the science-influenced offerings of three rhetorical forebears of the Declaration—those of David Rittenhouse, Tom Paine, and Benjamin Rush.

ON FEBRUARY 24, 1775, in that year's annual address to the American Philosophical Society, Rittenhouse spoke to an audience of members, Pennsylvania's governor, and the colony's governing council. A somewhat shy and chronically frail man, the hero of the American triumph in the 1769 transit of Venus, Rittenhouse had turned forty-three, was remarried after being widowed, and had reentered the political arena after decades of reluctance to do so. His platform for political activism had been Philadelphia's Mechanics Association, whose 1,200 members had urged the calling of a Continental Congress and had used its own Committee of Correspondence to coordinate the Association's actions with the mechanics of other cities.[6]

Everyone in the audience was aware that, in the months prior to Rittenhouse's speech, the Continental Congress had sat, debated, and issued a call to King George III to settle the differences between the mother country and the colonies or suffer the consequences. Though politely worded, the petition had demanded that the king reaffirm that American colonists enjoyed the rights of all other British citizens, rights trampled by recent edicts. A full colonial boycott of all British goods was threatened should the king not agree. That boycott began at the start of 1775, after King George III's rejection of the petition out of hand became known in the colonies. It was so nearly total that British imports were on track to drop from the previous year's level by 97 percent. Accordingly, while Rittenhouse's announced subject in the February oration to the APS was astronomy, the expectations were for more than a dry recounting of the sublime science.

He began, tamely enough, with a capsule history of astronomy from antiquity through the time of Tycho Brahe, emphasizing lessons and allegorical truths: "The seven stars that now adorn our winter skies, will take their turn to shine in summer." Modern science, in the form of telescopes, he said next, had proved wrong prior assumptions about Jupiter's relative size in the universe, causing him to wonder, "How much are we then indebted to Astronomy for correcting our ideas of the visible creation; wanting its instruction, we should infallibly have supposed the earth by far the most important body in the universe." Some listeners suspected him of slyly referring to the disparity in size and import between the smaller earthly body (England) and the larger (the American colonies). They gleaned another hint from his comparison of the differing methods of ascertaining natural laws, those of the "tyrant," Aristotle, who relied on the received wisdom of the "privy council," contrasted with those of Newton, whose laws, Rittenhouse pointed out, were based on observable facts that Newton traced back to "general and simple" causes. The audience could not be wholly certain of Rittenhouse's intent, however, until he reached the shank of the speech, in which he conjured what the transporting of certain individuals to Mars—the war planet—might do for their attitudes toward the petty squabbles of the home planet:

> Take the miser from the earth, if it is possible to disengage him, he whose nightly rest has been broken by the loss of a single foot of it, useless perhaps to him, and remove him to the planet Mars. . . . Persuade the ambitious monarch to accompany him, who has sacrificed the lives of thousands of his subjects to an imaginary property in a certain small portion of the earth, now point it out to them with all its kingdoms and wealth, [no larger than] a glittering star 'close by moon' . . . Would they not turn away their disgusted sight from it, as not thinking it worth their smallest attention, and look for consolation in the gloomy regions of Mars?

After this sally—the governor's reaction to it was unrecorded—Rittenhouse returned to astronomy for a while and then glided again into fantasy, expressing the hope that the moon and outer planets were populated by peaceful, human-like beings that loved rationality and pursued scientific truths. In such places, "neither national nor moral evil have yet intruded," so that "the business of existence" could continue to be to "enjoy with gratitude and adoration the creator's bounty." He prayed that such creatures were able to govern themselves according to the dictates of their reason, and was grateful for their sake that they had thus far been denied all communication with earth's people: "We have neither corrupted you by our vices, nor injured you by our violence. None of your sons and daughters, degraded from their native dignity, have been doomed to endless slavery by us Americans, merely because their bodies may be disposed to reflect or absorb the rays of light in a manner very different from ours." Human-like beings on the moon, he continued, had been spared the hand of the "villainous Spaniard" as well as the "British thirst of gain" and the machinations of "Frederick, that tyrant of the north." Rittenhouse railed against those who, "by a vile affectation of virtues they know not, pretend at first to be the patrons of science and philosophy, but at length fail not to effectively destroy them." At length he concluded, "I am ready to wish—vain wish!—that nature raise her everlasting bars between the new and old world, and make a voyage to Europe as impractical as one to the moon."[7]

Rittenhouse's address was widely reprinted, and copies were given to each delegate to the Continental Congress when it reconvened in the spring.

SUCH DEFIANT RHETORIC was echoed by Benjamin Rush in regard to a more practical, technology-affected sphere, home manufacture. Since the passage of the Stamp Act in 1765, and its replacements in the years following, manufacturing for local consumption had been cultivated in the colonies as a way to diminish the need to import British goods. Americans were required to send their beaver furs to England to be turned into hats that would then be transported back to the colonies and sold—colonists could no longer make their own hats. Accompanying such edicts had been a pullback in British purchasing of American raw goods and resources; the combination, historian T. H. Breen suggests, fatally upset the longstanding economic reciprocity between the motherland and the colonies: "Any policy that disturbed this delicate economic structure—additional commercial taxes or the growth of consumer debt—threatened the entire balance of Atlantic trade and all the cultural and political expectations that the relationship sustained."[8] While Americans were being dunned for taxes whose revenues were earmarked to pay for troops quartered in the colonists' private homes and for judges whose task was to jail and fine those who refused to pay the new taxes, the British government also emptied British, Scottish, and Irish jails and sent their penniless prisoners to the colonies. "No taxation without representation" became the American rallying cry, and there was an allied realization that no economic parity with Great Britain was possible without the colonists' forgoing the purchase of British goods, which were equated with luxury, and instead buying American-made staples. Farmers became involved. George Washington decided to intensify his attempts to plant crops other than tobacco, in part because, as the *Virginia Gazette* put it, "The tobacco trade cannot so properly be called the trade of this colony as of Great Britain, in as much as the merchants concerned therein mostly reside there, where the profits center." Washington was one of the first to completely stop planting tobacco, ceasing on half his acres after the Stamp Act, and stopping altogether in 1769.[9] In New England, a rising fervor directed citizens to renounce the use of "foreign Superfluities." "SAVE YOUR MONEY AND YOU WILL SAVE YOUR COUNTRY," a notice read.[10] After several provincial legislatures passed do-not-buy-British resolutions, alarm at loss of business mounted in London. Voices there—including Franklin's—warned that if the new direct taxation of the colonies was not repealed, the taxes would eventually cause the colonies to explode.

The substantial overlap in the colonies between home manufactures and the activities of the science-minded became evident as scientific-inquiry institutions edged into the fray. The American Philosophical Society in Philadelphia commenced manufacturing start-ups, and the Virginia Society for Advancing Useful Knowledge, led by Jefferson's friend John Page, offered bounties to spur commercial innovations. Washington, at one of the Virginia Society's meetings, voted for a "pecuniary reward and a medal" for the inventor of an "ingenious" machine for threshing wheat.[11] Separately, Washington and his neighbor George Mason began a Virginia non-importation group pledging to make what was needed on their own plantations and to buy other necessities from Philadelphia's artisans.[12]

Rush had been in favor of domestic manufacture since his Edinburgh days. Unlike many other children of the religious revival known as the Great Awakening, Rush had never lost his deeply felt religious principles. He melded them with his burgeoning separatism in his speech accepting the presidency of the United Company of Philadelphia for Promoting American Manufactures, a group that set up a factory of 700 employees to make textiles, which was a direct slap at Great Britain's leading export. Rush laid out the rationale for the new factory in terms borrowed from John Locke: "A people who are *entirely* dependent upon foreigners for food or clothes, must always be subject to them . . . slaves." Rush did not use the term "slaves" lightly, since he was a leading abolitionist. In this instance, he explained, slavery meant that Americans would essentially "transfer unlimited obedience from our Maker to a corrupted majority in the British House of Commons." The United's factory, he said, would "erect an additional barrier against the encroachments of tyranny."[13]

Rush was not being snarky in labeling American economic dependence slavery. He was in good company: Adam Smith wrote in his 1776 *An Inquiry into the Nature and Causes of the Wealth of Nations* that British restrictions on American manufacture were to the colonists "impertinent badges of slavery imposed . . . without any sufficient reason, by the groundless jealousy of the merchants and manufacturers of the mother country. In a more advanced state, they might be really oppressive and insupportable." Since, Smith argued, the natural progression in any economy was from agriculture to manufacture for home consumption and then to manufacture for export, Great Britain's interrupting this progression in America courted rebellion and possible eclipse. America's rapidly multiplying population—Smith took his calculations from a Franklin essay—its abundant natural resources, and its consistently higher wages for labor, and higher stock prices than in Great Britain were not to be taken lightly.[14]

Modest colonial attempts at increasing manufacturing were accompanied by a more successful surge in exports. New Yorkers swore off eating lamb so that the colony's supply of wool would enlarge and improve in quality. Sawmills and gristmills proliferated. Franklin's Pennsylvania stove and lightning rod were manufactured in quantity—and relatively cheaply because Franklin took no royalties. Well before the onset of the Revolutionary War, according to historian Neil Longley York, "colonial iron operations reportedly produced more pig and bar iron than all of the forges, furnaces, and bloomeries in Wales and England combined . . . as much as one-seventh of the world's supply." Northwest Connecticut's forges were readied for a shift from making agricultural implements— themselves illegal to produce in the colonies, but often made—to cannon if need be. Such forges, and the emphasis on home manufacture, with its reliance on machinery, helped Americans to "make the mental connection between technological and political independence."[15]

The rise of American economic strength caused a ratcheting up of British anti-Americanism. As tensions increased, a controversy erupted over whether lightning rods to be installed at a British powder magazine, Purfleet, should employ Franklin's pointed ends or the rounded ones advocated by Royal Society member and electrician Benjamin Wilson; the matter was initially decided by the Royal Society in favor of Franklin's. Wilson then convinced the king—despite the monarch's training in science and his expressed appreciation of Franklin—to decree only rounded ends.[16]

Many colonists still hoped that economic accommodation by London might obviate the need to assert political independence. Some colonists even continued to believe this was possible after passage of the Coercive (or Intolerable) Acts of 1774, which punished Massachusetts for the Boston Tea Party and all of the colonies to some degree for challenging British prerogatives. The fading hope of reconciliation was reflected in the Continental Congress's plea for a "non-importation, non-consumption, and non-exportation agreement" to adequately redress the colonies' grievances, the document that was so dismissively rejected by King George III at the close of 1774.[17]

WHILE THE FIRST CONTINENTAL CONGRESS was still in its fall 1774 session, thirty-seven-year-old Thomas Paine, British sailor, teacher, corset-maker, jack-of-all-trades, and unsuccessful businessman, had arrived in Philadelphia. Although not a scientist, he had cultivated people connected to the Royal Society, and his participation in various engineering-related enterprises had given him an understanding of mechanical processes. He bore with him the most important sponsorship letter he could possibly have had, from Franklin. A chance meeting in a Philadelphia bookstore then resulted in Paine's being asked to edit a new magazine for the bookstore owner Robert Aitken; the purview of *The Pennsylvania Magazine, or, An American Monthly Museum* was to be "the whole circle of science, including politics and religion as objects of philosophical inquisition." The Paine-edited first issue, of January 24, 1775, reprinted the Congress's petition to King George III and included articles on beavers, suicide, the curing of fevers, the production of sound, mathematics, an electricity generator, and a land-surveying puzzle, as well as commodity prices, a weather diary, notations of available new books, and a poem by a "Young Lady of the City" about Christmas Day. Paine biographer John Keane concludes that many of the anonymous or pseudonymous articles on science were likely Paine's. By the second and third issues of the *Pennsylvania Magazine,* increased subscriptions had made it the most popular magazine in the colonies at a time when the colonies were saturated with printed materials.[18]

In March 1775 Paine was introduced to Benjamin Rush; a few days later, Rush read in the *Pennsylvania Journal* an article on "African Slavery in America," whose byline was "Justice and Humanity." Rush was certain that Paine had written this antislavery diatribe. It echoed Rush's own pamphlet, which had pushed Pennsylvania to set a tariff on holding slaves, an edict that helped to dismantle slaveholding in the colony. Paine's antislavery stance cemented their burgeoning friendship. Both men's radicalism soon rose substantially at the onset of hostilities—the battles at Lexington and Concord on April 19, 1775, what Ralph Waldo Emerson would later label the "shot heard 'round the world."[19] Prior to blood being shed, Paine had viewed the dispute between the colonies and London "as a kind of law-suit [and] supposed that the parties would find a way to decide or settle it. I had no thought of independence or of arms." Once the events of April 19 became known, however, "I rejected the hardened, sullen tempered Pharaoh of England for ever; and disdain the wretch, that with the pretended title of Father of his people, can unfeelingly hear of their slaughter, and composedly sleep with their blood upon his soul.[20]

OTHERS SHARED PAINE'S ANGER. John Adams wrote to a friend in June 1775:

> If We consider the Education of the Sovereign, and that the Lords the Commons, the Electors, the Army, the Navy, the officers of Excise, Customs &c., &c., have been now for many years gradually trained and disciplined by Corruption to the System of the Court, We shall be convinced that the Cancer is too deeply rooted, and too far spread to be cured by any thing short of cutting it out entire."[21]

Rush felt the same way. He considered writing a pamphlet urging that the colonies separate from Great Britain but, newly married and establishing his medical practice, he felt that the opprobrium resulting from such a publication might force him from Philadelphia; therefore he urged the task on Paine. According to Paine's biographer, the idea was Paine's. And by the summer of 1775—when Washington and the army were facing down the British in Boston—Paine and Aitken had become estranged, leaving Paine with time and energy to devote to the pamphlet. Each week's news reports of parliamentary excesses and the activities of colonial governors provided more grist for his mill. He read many sections aloud to Rush as he finished them. He rejected Rush's caution against specific mention of "independence and republicanism" but accepted Rush's most important suggestion, that he not call the pamphlet "Plain Truth," as he had intended, but instead use Rush's title, *Common Sense*.[22] That was a well-understood phrase, and "common sense" was the broader public's version of the advanced logical reasoning of the scientific laboratory and the court of law. Paine's readers might not be Newtons or Blackstones, but they were fully capable of weighing the evidence and coming to a commonsense, logical conclusion.

Of all those in Philadelphia to whom Paine might have shown the manuscript, he chose the two leading scientists, Franklin (returned from London) and David Rittenhouse, with whom he had formed a bond.[23] They suggested minor revisions, and Rush found a publisher who would not shrink from an incendiary pamphlet whose authorship was attributed to "an Englishman." The first edition, of January 10, 1776, was sold at the deliberately low price of two shillings. It appeared just as the text of King George III's annual speech to Parliament reached the colonies, with its depiction of the colonists as "deluded," of their leaders as "traitorous," of the colonists' goal as an "independent empire," and containing the king's pledge to crush rebellion by sending more troops and ships to America and by seeking foreign alliances. *Common Sense* was a defiant response to the king's arrogance. Immediately and immensely popular, in its first year it sold several hundred thousand copies in many authorized and pirated editions at a time when the usual pamphlet sold a few hundred. Although, as Gordon Wood has argued, the Revolutionary leaders generally "conceived of their audiences or readerships as restricted and aristocratic, as being made up of men essentially like themselves,"[24] the immense popularity of Paine's pamphlet suggests that he aimed for—and reached—a far wider audience. For instance, he deliberately eschewed references to the classics, as they were code for the elitist discourse that his intended audience did not like. In the mid-eighteenth century, philosopher Richard Sennett suggests, such a broad audience was always quick to respond in the negative and to do so vehemently if it did not agree with the expressed sentiments.[25]

Paine wanted the audience to do more than silently agree. He was aiming to shift his audience's paradigm from viewing the political world as a loyal subject did to viewing it as a potential rebel did. To accomplish this, he adopted the tactics of the most convincing critical science experiments. "Bring the doctrine of reconciliation to the touchstone of nature, and then tell me whether you can hereafter love, honor, and faithfully serve the power that hath carried fire and sword into your land?"[26] With such lines, Paine led Americans along a logical path to the point where they could heartily embrace his conclusion, that monarchy was an outrage against humanity, and that independence was the only way forward for America. Drawing on arguments made a century earlier by John Milton, as well as by Locke, Paine argued vehemently against monarchy in general and specifically against King George III.

Among those convinced by *Common Sense* was George Washington, who, although he had been leading the Continental Army against the British for six months, had still hoped for a negotiated compromise. Washington's letters lauded the pamphlet's "sound doctrine and unanswerable reasoning."[27] Since its authorship had not yet been revealed, many people believed *Common Sense* to be the work of Franklin. Franklin denied that but he did agree with the pamphlet and was partial to a section advocating what he had pushed for some time, the construction of a colonial navy.

Historian Bernard Bailyn, basing his study on the many pamphlets of the era, stresses that those of Paine and other Americans swayed readers by means of "arguments, not images," and were "profoundly reasonable [in their attempts] to convince their opponents, not, like the British pamphleteers of the eighteenth century, to annihilate them. . . . Communication of understanding . . . lay at the heart of the Revolutionary movement."[28] Such pamphleteers followed the path of Locke, who took as models the scientific experimentation and analyses of Newton and Boyle. Stressing the rationality of observable fact as the basis also for building political and philosophical understanding, Locke wrote that there must be "a conformity between our ideas and the reality of things," and touted his *Essay Concerning Human Understanding* and his treatises on government as scientific inquiries.[29]

The positions expressed in *Common Sense* were more radical than those previously held by many delegates to the Second Continental

Congress. The pamphlet "fueled an abrupt republican turn in 1776," historian Eric Nelson writes, "by reintroducing into Anglophone political discourse a particular kind of republican theory: one grounded in the Hebraizing conviction that it is idolatrous to assign any human being the title and dignity of a king." The pamphlet's popularity, allied to its cogent logic, helped some fence sitters jump off and consider declaring independence. Not yet ready to do so, they first approved an intermediate step, delegate John Adams's resolution for economic independence, which urged each colony to establish "a society for the improvement of agriculture arts, manufacture, and commerce . . . that the rich and numerous natural advantages of this country, for supporting its inhabitants, may not be neglected."[30]

A TUMULTUOUS SIX MONTHS after *Common Sense,* the Second Continental Congress issued a Declaration of Independence, mostly as written by Thomas Jefferson. Before Jefferson began to write, the majority of the delegates—though not of the states—were already on record as agreeing that "it is necessary that the exercise of every kind of authority under the [British] crown should be totally suppressed," the phraseology of a May 15 resolution, mostly written by John Adams, that stopped short of an actual declaring of independence. Since then, the need for such a declaration had become even more apparent, and the Congress had delegated the writing of such a document to a committee, which had in turn assigned it to committee members Jefferson and Adams. Adams had then declined in Jefferson's favor, giving him three reasons: "Reason first, you are a Virginian, and a Virginian ought to be at the head of this business. Reason second, I am obnoxious, suspected, and unpopular. You are very much otherwise. Reason third, you can write ten times better than I can."[31]

Jefferson later pointed out that the Declaration had been composed to articulate the conclusions of the committee, and that, moreover, his draft was "an expression of the American mind [whose] authority rests . . . on the harmonizing sentiments of the day, whether expressed in conversation, in letters, printed essays, or the elementary books of public right."[32] The Declaration would repeat many of the arguments of the May 15 resolution, but with important differences. While Adams's May 15 resolution uses mostly the language of lawyers, Jefferson's draft of the Declaration relies significantly on the language of scientists. As would an article in a scientific journal, the opening paragraph of Jefferson's Declaration requested peer review from a "candid world," required by a "decent respect for the opinions of mankind." Its experimental method was induction, defined as drawing a conclusion from observed facts; and therefore its promise was that it would marshal and present the facts that had led the experimenters—Congress—to their conclusion. The document promised to provide "a long train of abuses & usurpations," a series in which, Jefferson asserted, "no one fact stands in single or solitary to contradict the uniform tenor of the rest."[33]

The individual and collective rights asserted in the Declaration's preamble can be traced back to Magna Carta, but the argumentation owes an equal amount to science. Historian of ideas Gary Wills labels the Declaration's entire preamble Newtonian and parses its famous opening phrase, "When in the course of human events it becomes necessary . . ." by comparing Jefferson's use of "course," "events," and "necessary" to similar uses of those words in the scientific literature of the time. "Jefferson . . . is not saying that the separation from the English motherland is defensible, merely; preferable; or even desirable. He says it is *necessary*. Out of a sequence of observed results, a pattern emerges, and is stated as a law."[34] Jefferson adheres to what Newton advocated in his Fourth Rule: "We are to look upon propositions collected by general induction from phenomena as accurately or very nearly true, notwithstanding any contrary hypotheses that may be imagined, 'till such time as other phenomena occur, by which they may either be made more accurate, or liable to exceptions."

In Jefferson's 1825 recollection, that the document was "an expression of the American mind," he also stressed that he wrote as he had because Adams, Franklin, Roger Sherman, and Robert R. Livingston (his committee) did not want the document encountering any resistance in the Continental Congress or in the states that would have to ratify it. "There is not an idea in [the Declaration], but what had been hackneyed in Congress for two years before," Adams later asserted.[35] Jefferson, in response to this Adams comment, claimed that in composing the Declaration he had consulted no books or pamphlets and reiterated that his plan had been "not to find out new principles, or new arguments, never before thought of, not merely to say things which had never been said before;

but to place before mankind the common sense of the subject, in terms so plain and firm as to command their assent."[36]

The reason that Newtonian philosophy suffused the Declaration's ideas, Carl L. Becker asserts in his analysis, was precisely because those ideas were already accepted by a general public "indoctrinated into the new philosophy through conversation, and through popular lectures and books which humanely omitted the mathematics of the *Principia,* devoting the space thus gained to a confident and edifying amplification of its cautious conclusions . . . which made the philosophy interesting and important to the average man."[37]

The Declaration's preamble stated that the people of the new United States were assuming a station "to which the Laws of Nature and of Nature's God entitle them." These phrases have been variously interpreted. "Laws of Nature" is not the same thing as "natural law." The reference to "Laws of Nature" is to rules that have emerged from observation of nature, in specific contrast to those obtained from the divinity—those laws of nature that Galileo, Newton, Boyle, Hooke, and other scientists had been discovering. The meaning of the phrase "Nature's God" is more obscure. Some analysts ascribe it to Jefferson's need to mention God in the preamble; Pauline Maier points out that God is not evoked elsewhere in the body of Jefferson's draft. The two direct mentions of God in the finished text were added by the Continental Congress, deemed necessary to procuring ratification by traditional believers as well as by Deists and rationalists. Becker points out that by the time Jefferson wrote, God had been receding into the distance for the previous hundred years and was understood by most of Jefferson's contemporaries as no more than "the final Cause, or Great Contriver, or Prime Mover of the universe [who revealed] his will indirectly through his creation. . . . There was no longer any way to know God's will except by discovering the 'laws' of Nature, which would doubtless be the laws of 'nature's God,' as Jefferson said."[38]

John Locke, in his *Second Treatise on Civil Government,* had written, "The state of Nature has a law of Nature to govern it, which obliges everyone; and reason, which is that law, teaches all mankind . . . that being equal and independent, no one ought to harm another in his life, health, liberty, or possessions."[39] This was a lawyer's understanding. Jefferson, whether reasoning as a lawyer or as a scientist, in using these particular phrases (and no others) about nature and God, aligned his Declaration

with the assertions about nature and its imperatives made by Rittenhouse, Rush, and Paine, conflating the natural surround and the deity
rather than positing them as separate entities. For all four, "natural law"
stood in opposition to laws made by man, including the monarchial system and the codification of rule by divine right.

As for the concepts that "all men are created equal, and endowed by
their Creator with certain inalienable rights, among them life, liberty, and
the pursuit of happiness," each of these words and phrases had a basis for
which scientific verity as well as legal precedent can be claimed. Jefferson's
original draft read, "We hold these truths to be sacred & undeniable, that
all men are created equal and independent, that from that equal creation
they derive rights inherent & inalienable." As Boorstin suggests, "It is easy
to forget that the assertion of human equality . . . was not a direct statement of a moral principle, but rather of a scientific and historical fact
from which the principle [of equality] was supposed to follow."[40] Various
Europeans, including Buffon, had embraced the opposite notion, that Africans, Asians, and Native Americans had become biologically inferior to
Caucasians; Jefferson agreed with that bias in regard to Africans, but in
composing the Declaration, his term "all men are created equal" was employed mainly to underscore everyone's equality before the law. Jefferson's
view on this was echoed by his committee, with one important change,
usually ascribed to Franklin—to omit the idea that the truths held were
in any way "sacred."[41]

In asserting that all men were created equal, the Congress, which retained that phraseology in the document, was negating the notion that
any particular man could claim more direct descent from God than another, a posture that rejected the "divine right" of kings and was closely
related to other parts of the Declaration that dismissed the idea that kings
had any right to exact fealty from American colonists.

Once men were understood to have been created equal—not born
equal, but created equal by their Creator—it was logical to also believe that
they possessed certain inherent and inalienable (or unalienable) rights,
given to them when they were created, and not to be taken away by any
human being. Jefferson initially listed these rights as "the preservation of
life, & liberty, & the pursuit of happiness," later shortening the phrase.
In earlier documents, such as Locke's essay, well known to Jefferson, the
right to own property had been included among the inalienable rights. It

was also in Adams's May 15 resolution, which asserted that the American populace, and whatever government it might select for itself, had the right and the obligation to take actions "for the defence of their lives, liberties, and properties." However, the concept of property was specifically excluded from the Jefferson Declaration's preamble because—among other reasons—ownership of property was not universally shared, as were the other rights to be defended.

The rights to life and to liberty were readily understood then and are now; but in the course of the past 200 years many Americans have puzzled over the meaning of "the pursuit of happiness." In 1776, however, Jefferson's contemporaries, including the delegates to the Congress, found little to quarrel about in his use of the phrase.

"The pursuit of happiness" phrase then had several meanings. One, usually overlooked because it has no modern counterpart, was common then, and was perhaps best expressed in William Wollaston's *The Religion of Nature Delineated,* a book known to have been carefully read by Franklin and owned by Jefferson, Adams, and Washington, and that was then also being used by Yale as a teaching text. Wollaston declared that a chief aspect of "natural religion" was its ability to satisfy man's capacity for happiness. This was not happiness as sensual pleasure, as Locke had suggested. Rather, according to Wollaston, the greatest happiness lay in the discovery of truth—the design of nature as set forth by God: "There are some ends, which the nature of things and truth require us to aim at, and at which therefore if we do not aim, nature and truth are denied. If a man does not desire to prevent evils and to be happy, he denies both his own nature and the nature and definition of happiness." Happiness consisted of "abetting the cause of truth; and in being indeed so nearly allied to it, that [the two] cannot well be parted. . . . It is by the practice of truth that we aim at happiness."[42]

Another clue to Jefferson's use of the phase "pursuit of happiness" comes from a scientific concept—that of infinity. Happiness is one of several goals that the Declaration considered to be desirable but at an infinite distance—as the document also positioned two other concepts, safety and property. While individuals might endlessly aim toward possessing unimaginably vast quantities of safety, property, or happiness, individuals would never be able to achieve perfect safety, property, or happiness. Men and women, in the Declaration's assertions, had only the right to *pursue* these desiderata, but as it made no sense for the Declaration to attempt to guarantee those entities, the Declaration refused to do so—Jefferson and the Congress did not want to promise what a new government could never deliver.[43]

The Continental Congress accepted Jefferson's preamble almost entirely but deleted nearly a quarter of the remainder. They eliminated passages condemning slavery and others charging the English with complicity in subjugating the colonies, for instance, lines accusing them of giving "the last stab to agonizing affection [so that] manly spirit bids us to renounce forever these unfeeling brethren." Adams, for one, had expected such excisions and the crossing-out of ad hominem attacks on King George III—of the sort perhaps excusable in *Common Cause* and the Rittenhouse and Rush orations, but not in a communal document. Newton had wanted no superfluities of theory or irrelevancy to get in the way of "propositions collected from general induction." From an American representative body's document that similarly sought to prove a contention by induction from observed fact, and to do so as convincingly and completely as Newton had done, all harangue and side issues had to be eliminated so as not to detract from the power of the facts being presented.

SEVEN

"THIS MOST DANGEROUS ENEMY"

SMALLPOX WAS AN IMMEDIATE SEVERE THREAT to the Revolution, as it could incapacitate the army. In an era when many in the Continental Congress and in the state legislatures refused to condone, much less to promote, the use of variolation, the disease presented a significant challenge to the leadership. The Revolution was saved because the small circle of Founding Fathers, to a man, embraced variolation for smallpox, and they did so because they were convinced by the evidence of its efficacy.

IN 1721–1722, during the smallpox variolation controversy, the advocates of variolation had been few, and even after the epidemic their number remained small. By the 1740s, an improved treatment protocol for smallpox variolation had come into routine use by some medical doctors in every large city. But variolation was still not widely used and was mainly for the rich who could afford to be removed from society for about a month. Prior to being inoculated, a patient had to undergo a week or more of isolation and preparation; after inoculation, since pustules did not appear until the twelfth day, patients needed to remain isolated again until they showed, and for thirteen additional days until the infection was no longer communicable. Only then could patients safely return to society.[1]

Benjamin Franklin had not overtly taken sides during the 1721–1722 Boston variolation controversy, and the precise date on which he was inoculated is not known, but he printed articles in favor of the technique in the 1730s, and in 1736 he expressed his advocacy for the process in a public forum. That year, smallpox caused the death of his four-year-old son, Francis—"the delight of all who knew him," in the phrase Franklin inscribed on the child's gravestone. To answer rumors that Franky's death had been caused by variolation, Franklin wrote in his newspaper, "I suppose the Report could only arise from its being my known Opinion, that Inoculation was a safe and beneficial Practice," and asserted that he had not had the boy variolated because Franky had been suffering from a gastrointestinal infection and was quite weak; so the boy had then contracted smallpox "in the natural way" and died of it.[2]

Franklin transmuted his personal loss into society's gain. He became an open advocate of variolation, and in 1759, after becoming world famous, arranged with Dr. William Heberden of London to write a pamphlet of instruction that he paid to have printed and distributed free in the colonies. One cannot read Franklin's introduction to the pamphlet without being reminded of its painful personal source; the pamphlet, he wrote, revealed

> what preparations of the body should be used before the Inoculation of children, what precautions to avoid giving the infection at the same time in the common way, and how the operation is to be performed, the incisions dress'd, the patient treated. . . . [Therefore, it] might by encouraging parents to inoculate their own children, be a means of removing that objection of the expence, render the practice much more general, and thereby save the lives of thousands.[3]

But there were still difficulties in inducing Philadelphians to be variolated. Even the public championing of the technique by the respected Dr. John Redman did not bring hordes to the variolation clinics. Moreover, Redman's colleagues within the Philadelphia medical fraternity continued to oppose the practice. As one result, the 1761 epidemic in that city was particularly deadly. Forty years after Mather and Boylston had shown the way to prevent smallpox's devastations, it continued to be the colonies' leading cause of death.[4] In 1774, Franklin, Redman, Rush and other enlightened (and generally, non-Quaker) Philadelphians took the next step during yet another local epidemic of smallpox, founding a Society for Inoculating the Poor.

DURING A 1764 SMALLPOX OUTBREAK in Boston, John Adams and his brother rode into the city to undergo variolation. To enter a metropolis in the midst of an epidemic was risky, but Adams judged it riskier still not to subject himself to a medical treatment that could protect him for the rest of his life. Trying to ease his fiancée's fears, he confided in a letter to Abigail that the physicians "prepared me by a milk Diet, and a Course of Mercurial Preparations, 'til they reduced me very low," and that then he and his brother "took turns to be sick and to laugh." After the inoculations, while in isolation Adams stopped writing to Abigail for fear that the paper might be contaminated with infectious matter. Recovering, he opined, "None of the Race of Adam, ever passed the small Pox, with fewer Pains, Achs, Qualms . . . than I have done." Ten years later, upon his appointment to the Massachusetts delegation to the Continental Congress, he joked to a friend that his prime qualification was having been vaccinated and therefore being unlikely to succumb to smallpox, which was again on the rise in Philadelphia. At least four delegates from colonies that forbade or interfered with variolation, including Patrick Henry of Virginia, took the opportunity of temporary residency in Philadelphia to be inoculated.[5]

Thomas Jefferson had already done so. After passage of the Stamp Act in 1765, Jefferson put aside his grand plans for a tour of Great Britain and Europe and instead undertook a tour of the colonies, crossing innumerable rivers and streams on the way to Philadelphia. One reason for the trip was to be variolated, a treatment he had read about and heard discussed. Dr. William Shippen Jr. performed the inoculation, and Jefferson, like Adams, suffered no lasting ill effects from it.[6]

Returning to Virginia, Jefferson established his law practice. Among the hundreds of cases that he handled between 1767 and 1774, a linked pair stands out, in which he represented victims of anti-inoculation riots in Norfolk that took place in successive years, 1768 and 1769. The circumstances echoed those occurring in several other colonies: some locals objected to what they believed to be the premature release or inadequate isolation of inoculated patients, and things got out of hand. In this instance, the bad behavior of the anti-inoculators did not come from ignorant farmers but from three former mayors, who demanded that inoculated patients be sequestered in the Norfolk pesthouse; when this was not done, they attacked the doctor's home, in which the patients were being isolated, and during a driving rain herded the patients through the streets to the pesthouse. Two days later the rioters returned and burned down the doctor's house. A year after the first riot, another occurred, involving a second physician who had inoculated his slaves; his house, too, was damaged. In 1770 Jefferson handled cases for damages brought by the doctors and other victims; during the period when the cases remained undecided, his boyhood home, Shadwell, was destroyed by fire and his law records were lost. Even so, he continued with the cases, and one of his clients assured a friend, "Mr. Jefferson did us all the justice he possibly could or we expect." What with appeals and delays, the suits and countersuits dragged on and were unresolved when Jefferson turned over his practice to another lawyer in 1774. Shortly thereafter, as a member of a committee of the Virginia legislature, Jefferson, along with a few fellow members, fashioned a statute mooting a prior law that had limited the practice of variolation, substituting one that allowed the practice should the majority of a local area's citizens vote in favor of it.[7]

IN FEBRUARY 1775, prior to the Lexington and Concord battles, the Massachusetts Provincial Council had approved £500 to buy drugs and supplies from local physicians and cached the supplies to keep them from British notice. After the April 1775 battles the struggle settled into a protracted standoff, and the British learned of the caches and confiscated some.[8]

Also, at that time, a smallpox epidemic grew within Boston. Its effects could be seen through the British telescopes: the unmistakable sight of between ten and thirty funerals a day. The epidemic soon reached the Continental Army, whose losses to smallpox were large compared to those of the British army since many British soldiers had immunity from exposure to the disease in their youth, and most British officers had been inoculated. However, the British also suffered because they quartered British troops in private homes and permitted infected camp followers among them; according to one eyewitness report, the British conducted around three funerals a day.[9] The Boston outbreak was the leading edge of an epidemic that would grip most of the thirteen colonies and in the coming years would kill more than 100,000 of the 2.5 million inhabitants.

ACCORDING TO A RECENT POLL of British military historians, George Washington ranks the highest of all foes ever faced by the British, higher than Napoleon, Rommel, or Atatürk.[10] He prevailed in the Revolutionary War in large measure because he handled the American troops as a guerilla fighter might. Although Washington always rejected the notion that he was fighting in unorthodox ways, the pattern was there: he worked assiduously to ensure that even when he lost battles, his men were able to escape and not surrender, preserving them to fight again and eventually to prevail. In one of his earliest steps toward that ultimate victory, Washington forthrightly addressed the need to protect his troops from smallpox. He arrived in Cambridge on July 3, 1775, a fortnight after the British attacks on Bunker Hill and Breed's Hill, and the next day issued his first set of orders, among them directives regarding smallpox.

The majority of his troops were militiamen from rural Massachusetts, Connecticut, New Hampshire, and Rhode Island who had never been exposed to smallpox. Most of the few who were immune had acquired immunity as he had, in the "natural way," by surviving a bout with the disease. Washington first learned of variolation during the French and Indian War. By 1771 he still considered it risky: that year, when he arranged to have his stepson, Jacky, variolated, they both kept the information from Martha Washington until the lad's infection had run its course. In Cambridge in the summer of 1775, Washington judged as impractical the inoculation for smallpox of large swaths of his army, since the process would render those inoculated incapable of battle for a lengthy period, during which the army would be overly vulnerable to a British onslaught. To contain smallpox he instead ordered isolation, quarantine, strict hospital measures, and daily inspections for disease signs. On July 20, Washington wrote to John Hancock, president of the Continental Congress, that he and his staff had been "particularly attentive to the least Symptoms of the Small Pox, hitherto we have been so fortunate, as to have every Person removed so soon, as not only to prevent any Communication, but any Apprehension or Alarm it might give in the camp. We shall continue the utmost Vigilance against this most dangerous Enemy."[11]

Part of Washington's reluctance to take more aggressive action against smallpox stemmed from his relationship with the Continental Congress's Medical Committee, headed by Samuel Adams. The firebrand and his cousin John had orchestrated the selection of Washington rather than of John Hancock as commander of the rebel forces.[12] But even though Sam's son was serving as a physician in the army, the elder Adams had no knowledge to use as a basis for his decisions on medical matters. A related problem was that Congress as a body frequently played favorites, for instance, appointing as chief engineer a Bostonian whom Washington later judged not sufficiently competent, and in refusing to address the problem of medical supplies—the ample stores in the Philadelphia area were not sent to Boston, where they were sorely needed. So it was in keeping with the way Congress did business for Sam Adams to have championed an old friend as the director general of the Medical Service. Dr. Benjamin Church was competent but compromised. Adams did not then know that Church was in secret communication with the British authorities; within months, that would be learned and Church would be exposed as a spy and removed from his responsibilities. Before that exposure, however, Church served in an able but not innovative way in carrying out Washington's edict in regard to smallpox—acceding to armed guards stationed around the hospitals to prevent further infection of the patients by visitors, and visiting of those hospitals forbidden without written consent of an officer or surgeon. Upon learning that the three Massachusetts-run hospitals used by the army were not segregating patients with smallpox but allowing them to mix with and infect others, Church added three more hospitals; discovering that too many patients were being permitted to return to active duty before completely recovering from the disease, he set up a special convalescent hospital for such patients.[13]

Early in the war, Washington became irate that the physicians were not up to their tasks. To Congress he complained that many of the regimental surgeons "are very great rascals, countenancing the men in sham complaints to exempt them from duty, continually complain of each other, and bickering to the detriment of the sick."[14] So he overrode the physicians' authority by detailing a special chain of command to keep track of patients in the hospitals and by issuing standing orders on what procedures to follow if the hospital nearest the battlefield was full or if a patient required special attention. Camp barracks and streets were to be swept and food inspected daily by commanders. Washington made only one medical mistake, forbidding the presence of new cider in the camps on the mistaken assumption that it caused the bloody flux of dysentery.[15]

Disease affected Washington's battle tactics. "It has been argued," writes Mary Gillett in her official history of the army's Medical Department, "that the presence of smallpox in the city of Boston was actually to some degree responsible for Washington's reliance upon siege rather than attack on the British during the fall and winter."[16] The cold weather forced people indoors and reinvigorated smallpox among Bostonians and un-inoculated Continental troops. By the late fall, Dr. John Morgan, the best-trained physician in the colonies, had replaced the disgraced Church as medical director, but Morgan too was hampered, denied by Sam Adams's Medical Committee the power to confiscate drugs and medical supplies from private people for the benefit of the army.[17] Morgan ordered a full inventory of drugs and pharmaceutical supplies—they were barely adequate and unevenly distributed, the inventory revealed—and established a separate hospital for smallpox victims in the Boston area. Washington worried about the adequacy of such measures, writing that for the army to escape the full brunt of smallpox would be "miraculous." Morgan's measures did have what an assistant recalled as the "most happy effect" of confining the disease to a relative handful in the Continental Army. A new threat arose when Washington's opposite number, General William Howe, forced some 300 Bostonians, many ill with smallpox, to leave the city and had them transported to a location where the Continental Army would have to care for them. Washington took precautions against the likelihood of infection from the refugees. He became convinced that Howe was using smallpox as a "weapon of defense," conduct that he considered unworthy of a gentleman but not unprecedented on the part of the British military. Having served during the French and Indian War, Washington was well aware that more than one British commander had deliberately given smallpox-infested blankets to Native tribes to decimate them and thereby prevent them from aiding the enemy.[18]

In the winter of 1775–1776, as the stalemate in Boston continued, American troops under the leadership of Benedict Arnold stalled in front of Quebec, besieging the city while fighting off smallpox acquired since arriving there. John Joseph Henry, who was in that army, later wrote that the smallpox had been "introduced into our cantonments by the indecorous, yet fascinating arts of the enemy." According to the only physician there, a twenty-two-year-old, officers and soldiers frantically sought to inoculate themselves, "contrary to orders at the time." There were so many deaths from the disease, and so many men remained hospitalized in the throes of it, that a last attack ordered on Quebec could not muster enough manpower and therefore failed. Hundreds of men, including Henry, were taken prisoner, and most of those died of smallpox while incarcerated and awaiting exchange. Arnold, attempting to recoup after the debacle, remained so afraid of the infectious consequences of variolation done without adequate confinement that he forbade surgeons to administer it and threatened to cashier any officer who partook of it.[19]

Six months later, an army officer from Philadelphia who was sent north to evaluate the health of troops retreating from Quebec found 1,000 smallpox patients among a total of 3,000 men. Few of the sufferers would survive: during the first year of the Revolutionary War, from July 1775 through July 1776, more American troops perished of smallpox than were killed in the line of duty.[20]

Down in Virginia, smallpox similarly broke out in early 1776 on British ships housing large numbers of the former slaves who had left their masters in response to a proclamation by Lord Dunmore, the royal governor. Deaths among the "Ethiopian Regiment" were numerous; deserters from this plagued unit and smallpox sufferers deliberately put ashore by Dunmore thereafter spread smallpox in Virginia, seriously affecting recruitment for the Continental Army.[21]

The siege of Boston lasted until mid-March 1776. At the end of February, former bookseller Henry Knox presented Washington with cannon that he and his troops had lugged overland from Fort Ticonderoga, cannon that were then dragged up to the Dorchester Heights, where their appearance convinced General Howe to withdraw his troops and ships from Boston. Washington forbade anyone under his command to enter the city: "As the enemy with malicious assiduity, have spread the infection of the smallpox through all parts of the town, nothing but the utmost caution on our part, can prevent that fatal disease from spreading thro' the army, and country, to the infinite detriment of both," he explained.[22] Only troops whose faces bore the telltale pockmarks of having survived smallpox—as Washington's did—were in the vanguard, and among their principal tasks would be the removal of any infected inhabitants.[23] The commander was not among the first to enter the town, ceding that task to subordinates, partly as a gesture to the army and partly because Martha, who was with him, had not been inoculated and had no immunity.[24]

The American vanguard discovered that the drug supplies had been tampered with—possibly poisoned. The *Gazette* reported on April 15, "It is absolutely fact that the Doctors of the diabolical ministerial butcher when they evacuated Boston, intermixed and left 26 weight of Arsenick with the medicines which they left in the Alms House." The poison had been intermingled with precisely those drugs that were in the greatest demand. Medical director Morgan, suspecting that the claim of an adulterated stash was merely a pretext to get him to buy new supplies from local men at high prices, found plenty of unadulterated drugs in the Alms House stash and more in caches confiscated from Loyalists who had fled town when the British did—approximately twenty wagons' worth.[25] In response to Washington's instructions, Morgan divided these drugs and supplies into what the Boston area would need and what could be sent south to New York, whence there were reports that most if not all of the New York and Newark pharmacists were loyalists who would not sell their drugs to the rebel forces. Morgan brought this possibility to the attention of the Congress, which resulted in Sam Adams's reversing the prohibition against confiscation of drug supplies.[26] During the battles for New York, Washington expressed his thanks to the state's Provisional Congress for their care in preventing the spread of smallpox "by inoculation or in any other way." Washington still hoped to be able to control the disease by isolating infected soldiers and preventing the uninfected from going into areas where they might contract it.[27]

After the action had moved from Boston to New York in the fall of 1776, Massachusetts authorities finally lifted their ban on inoculation, and an orgy of variolation ensued—nearly 5,000 people in the Boston area, within a very short period of time. By winter, the disease had all but been eradicated in Boston.

WASHINGTON'S VICTORY AT BOSTON had given him an optimistic sense that he and the Continentals could prevail anywhere. That sense was contradicted by serious military losses in New York. In addition to territory and men, Washington lost large caches of arms, powder, and ammunition when the British captured the area's forts. He retreated across New Jersey to a winter redoubt. The advent of winter in 1776 helped Washington reach two realizations that thereafter shaped his strategy: that preserving his forces was more important than controlling territory, and that to properly preserve the forces might entail contradicting the wishes of the Congress—since the people's representatives had been lax in not overriding various state and military officers' orders that forbade inoculation. He tried to soften up Congress on that point by repeatedly petitioning for permission to allow troop detachments on their way to join him to skirt smallpox-prone Philadelphia. Congress acceded to these requests but did not issue an order to inoculate the troops; the idea seems not to have occurred even to the handful of physicians among the delegates.

Military victory always gives a field commander more clout with civilian overseers. Shortly after the success of Washington's shocking December 1776 raid across the Delaware River to seize Trenton, he decided in early 1777 that the moment was ripe to make inoculation for smallpox the policy of the army. "A compelling case can be made that [Washington's] swift response to the smallpox epidemic and to a policy of inoculation was the most important strategic decision of his military career," historian Joseph Ellis writes.[28]

It was not easy to accomplish. In early 1777, another complication in Washington's path toward troop immunization came from intrigue among the fraternity of physicians in Philadelphia that had led to another change in command of the medical services. Morgan's prep-school rival, William Shippen Jr., had connived to replace him as the medical service's leader on charges of poor management bordering on dereliction of duty. Washington did not like the change but accepted it and Shippen, whom he knew—he had recently inoculated Martha at Washington's request, so that she would be able to accompany him thereafter without fear of the disease—and his brothers-in-law, the Lee family of Virginia, were longtime Washington colleagues. Partly to win Shippen to his position on mass variolation, Washington informed him by letter that he would petition Congress to raise the pay of surgeons willing to travel with the troops. His main point, better expressed in a later letter to Shippen, was, "Necessity not only authorizes but seems to require the measure [inoculation against smallpox], for should the disorder infect the Army . . . and rage with its usual Virulence, we should have more to dread from it than from the sword of the enemy."[29] Shippen's initial answer on variolation was a surprising no; he objected to it on the grounds of inadequate provision for post-inoculation isolation, which would cause mass inoculation to spread rather than to limit the disease. For a few weeks Washington deferred to Shippen's caution, but when confronted by renewed outbreaks, he had to overrule it. He dictated to his aide, Alexander Hamilton, a one-page directive to inoculate all currently serving troops as well as all recruits before their units were allowed to join the army. Washington issued this order without express approval from Congress and did so deliberately, sensing that the Congress might not approve it. The inoculations were carried out secretly lest the British learn of the activity and take advantage of the vulnerability produced by having cadres of infected and isolated officers. Only small groups of Continental officers at a time were permitted to leave Washington's main camp to go to Philadelphia for the inoculation process; and physicians were dispatched to Kingston, New York, and Bethlehem, Pennsylvania, to set up facilities for inoculation, isolation, and recuperation. The isolation sites, mostly private homes and churches, were deliberately out of sight not only of British but also of prying Tory eyes. When a Continental brigadier general refused to inoculate his troops, Washington pressed him until he obeyed. He also urged Governor Patrick Henry to repeal Virginia's law against inoculation. Troops traveling north from the Carolinas were soon stopping in Virginia to be inoculated before continuing on. By the spring of 1777, the Continental Congress, acknowledging Washington's success with mass variolation, at last issued a formal inoculation order. Before the end of 1777, nearly 40,000 troops had been inoculated. In the year following the start of mass inoculation, the infection rate from smallpox in the Continental Army fell from 17 percent to 1 percent. Washington's action against smallpox effectively shielded his army from being decimated by disease until the expected foreign arms supplies could arrive and make it more possible for the tide of battle to turn in the Americans' favor.[30]

BENJAMIN RUSH, a Morgan proponent and a Shippen detractor, was a Pennsylvania delegate and became chairman of the Congress's medical committee. Not lasting long as a delegate—undone by his radical views— Rush then volunteered his services to the army. He visited the camps, treated the sick and the wounded, became appalled, and wrote an essay on how to improve the medical practices of the American forces. Unable to get his principles quickly adopted despite repeated letters to Washington and to various members of Congress, including his friend John Adams, the overly impatient Rush wrote an anonymous letter that obliquely blamed Washington for the problems and sent it to Patrick Henry. The Virginia governor was a poor choice since Henry was extremely loyal to Washington; moreover, the letter was sent during an attempt to overthrow Washington by other generals, and it seemed of a piece with missives to Congress accusing Washington of being a weak military leader. Henry forwarded the anonymous letter to Washington, who recognized Rush's handwriting, confronted him, and forced his resignation.[31]

Even so, Rush was able to get his pamphlet into print in April 1777. "To the Officers in the Army of the United States: Directions for Preserving the Health of Soldiers" maintained that an officer's duty was troop preservation, because "a greater proportion of men perish with sickness in all armies than fall by the sword." As his model Rush used some of the practices of the Roman army in Caesar's time, such as the banning of linen shirts, a diet more of vegetables than meat, the use of wheat flour instead of any other, fewer rum rations and more of vinegar with water. Above all, Rush's instructions dealt with hygiene, including directions as to where to site privies and septic fields, the instituting of frequent hand-washing, of thrice-weekly baths and shorter haircuts for the men, the washing of cooking pots after use, and the locating of animal slaughter pens away from the tents and latrine areas. General Horatio Gates was already using the Roman practice of outfitting his men in flannel rather than linen shirts. It was a measure of Washington's character that, although some of Rush's suggestions were contrary to custom and practice, and despite Washington's anger at Rush's attempts to blame him for the army's medical shortcomings, he had the army adopt many of the pamphlet's recommendations.[32] Washington went even further, later in the war, when Shippen was court-martialed (at Morgan's instigation), Rush was scheduled to testify and Washington unexpectedly invited him to dinner. During the evening, the commander refused to mention the anonymous letter. Rush was stunned by this proof of Washington's greater ability to act as a gentleman. Thereafter, he and Washington resumed cordial relations but continued to have low opinions of one another.[33]

At Washington's behest, reform of sanitation and treatment of wounded and ill soldiers were instituted in the American armies quite effectively by Baron Friedrich Wilhelm von Steuben, a former aide to Frederick II of Prussia. After joining Washington at Valley Forge in February 1778, Steuben was appointed inspector general of the forces. Taking that responsibility very seriously, he produced almost immediate gains in discipline and cleanliness and incorporated into the everyday concerns of junior and senior officers a greater sense of needing to care for the enlisted men's health and welfare. As a result of the Rush and Steuben initiatives, when the army marched out of Valley Forge to reoccupy Philadelphia in June 1778 and to do battle with the British at Monmouth, New Jersey, they were healthy and fighting fit and remained so for years.[34]

EIGHT

SEEKING *a*
TECHNOLOGICAL EDGE

AT THE OUTSET OF HOSTILITIES IN 1775, THERE
had been a sense among patriot leaders that the potentially much greater
numbers of American forces would not successfully offset British superiority in training and equipment and that a technological edge would
be necessary for victory. Yet there were few ideas as to where innovations
might arise or what they might consist of. Moreover, the leaders had to
deal immediately with related problems such as the lack of gunpowder. A
million pounds were needed to fight the British.

"The most efficacious, Sure, and infallibly conciliatory Measures We
can adopt," John Adams wrote to a friend in June 1775, "are powder and
artillery." But just then, as a later report put it, "The few powder mills
were in ruins, the manufacture of the explosive was almost a lost art, and
the country was nearly destitute of ammunition and other warlike stores."
The reasons for the dearth of powder—and of artillery—were those that
would retard American technological progress throughout the war. First,
the natural resources of the colonies had not been utilized—Native American deposits of the most important ingredient of gunpowder, saltpeter,
had not been mined because the British had found it more economical to
extract saltpeter in India and send it all over the world. Second, laws forbidding American manufacturing had kept the colonies' manufacturing

facilities and supervisory expertise to a minimum; American forges had been restricted to making only pig iron, forbidden from manufacturing such finished products as household implements—or cannon. Third, local American governments had had no authority, and therefore no experience, in organizing and encouraging manufactures.

Some gunpowder was stored in various American colonial depots, where it had lain for ten years, since the end of the French and Indian War. In December 1774, 10,000 pounds of British gunpowder was seized by the rebels from one such depot, a fort in New Hampshire. To prevent further gunpowder raids, immediately after the battles of Lexington and Concord in April 1775, the Massachusetts and Virginia colonial authorities secured their colonies' supplies for the Crown.[1]

Washington, arriving to take up his post as commander in early July 1775, found the army desperately under-provisioned with powder. "We are so exceedingly destitute," he wrote to Congress, "that our Artillery will be of little Use without a Supply both large & seasonable." By Christmas Day 1775, Washington was still pleading for gunpowder: "Our want of powder is inconceivable. A daily waste and no supply administers a gloomy prospect."[2] Congress realized that the large-scale solution to gunpowder supply lay abroad and had taken steps to purchase powder from France. Any responsible government would have done the same; but unlike European governments, the American government believed that the colonies' main resource was its people and their ingenuity; accordingly, some science-minded delegates attempted to inspire ordinary Americans to manufacture gunpowder. Here was a vote of confidence that enough Americans knew enough science and had enough mechanical ability to make a chemical compound. Gunpowder was a mixture of 75 percent saltpeter (potassium nitrate), 10 percent brimstone (sulfur), and 15 percent charcoal; any mix containing less than 75 percent saltpeter was more incendiary than explosive.[3] Adams, Franklin, Benjamin Rush, and Tom Paine exhorted colonists to make their own.

> Earth dug up from under a Stable, put into a Tub, as ashes for Lye. Filled with Water. Stand 24 Hours. Then leaked off Slowly. Then boil'd for one Hour. Then run thro another Tub full of ashes. i.e., filtrated thro the ashes a Small Quantity, not to stand. Then put into a Kettle and boiled, until it grows yellow. Then drop it on a cold stone or cold Iron, and it will

christallise for a Proof. Then set it by in Trays in cool Places. Then it will christallise. And the Salt Petre is formed. [4]

This formula, which Adams wrote out for a friend, was only one among nine published in American newspapers and magazines between 1774 and 1776. Differences among the formulae stemmed from universal ignorance of the underlying chemistry, for these efforts to make saltpeter occurred prior to its key elements being identified as nitrogen and potassium, as well as of understandings of the underlying chemical processes, oxidation and bacterial conversion of ammonium compounds into nitric acid.

Adams also corresponded with John Winthrop about saltpeter and gunpowder—Winthrop's family had operated the first chemical factory in the colonies, which had produced gunpowder; pupil and former teacher exchanged letters about an "experiment" in Providence with iron ore for manufacturing cannon and about expeditions to find sulfur. Adams directed his wife, Abigail, to manufacture saltpeter; "I have not yet attempted it," she answered in a letter, "but after making soap believe I shall make the experiment."[5]

Rush, the first chemistry teacher in America, wrote two articles on how to make saltpeter for the *Pennsylvania Magazine* that were combined into a pamphlet, issued by Congress with an introduction by Franklin, that included information gathered from his visit to a manufactory in Hanover.[6] The Pennsylvania provisional government then designated Rush to start a saltpeter factory whose products contributed to the rebel cause. APS member Owen Biddle, who assisted in the saltpeter enterprise, was drummed out of his Quaker meeting for doing so.[7]

WHEN WASHINGTON TOOK COMMAND in July 1775, the army had very few battle-seasoned American commanders, and none who were expert in military engineering. But the men whom he chose to elevate to command because of their actions in this early phase of the war were ingenious and inventive. Nathanael Greene was one of the few colonists who had overseen a sizable industrial workforce not composed of slaves—more than a hundred men at his Rhode Island forge. He first recommended himself to Washington on the strength of his command of troops in marching exercises. Henry Knox, a former bookseller, had been attached to a cannon unit, was a tinkerer, and, to Washington's approval,

was becoming widely read in military literature. Washington soon gave
Greene important commands and sent Knox on a secret mission to bring
cannon—in working order—from Fort Ticonderoga for the relief of
Boston.[8]

WAR HAD BEEN the mother of invention since the ancient Greeks, but
the American Revolutionary War was an exception. The British were so
confident in their extant armaments systems that they saw no reason to
look for new ones. The Americans generated a few interesting ideas but
were unable to implement them. Case in point: the Bushnell Turtle. In the
spring of 1775, when news spread through the colonies that shots had been
fired at Lexington and Concord, most colleges suspended classes; James
Monroe of William & Mary, Alexander Hamilton of King's College, and
Aaron Burr, a law student of Tapping Reeve in Litchfield, Connecticut
joined local militia and troop units along with many other students. The
hiatus provided extra time to the oldest undergraduate at Yale, thirty-
five-year-old David Bushnell, to devote himself exclusively to perfecting
an underwater manned submersible whose purpose was to destroy enemy
ships. He dubbed it "the Turtle," Bushnell later wrote, because it had the
shape of two connected turtle shells. An operator with a half-hour's supply of air could submerge the Turtle and move it underwater by maneuvering foot pedals so that it could attach a bomb to the subsurface hull of a
moored British ship and have enough remaining air to pedal away before
the explosion. In August 1775, through the sponsorship of Dr. Benjamin
Gale, the Turtle's potential was brought to the attention of Silas Deane,
Connecticut delegate to the Congress, and to that of Franklin. "The story
may appear Romantic, but thus far All these Experiments . . . have been
Actually made," Gale assured Franklin. Shortly, while on the way to Boston to meet with Washington, Franklin stopped in Connecticut to see
Gale. The Turtle was then undergoing repairs. He recommended more
experiments and offered a solution for the inability to see the gauges at
night, suggesting that instead of candles Bushnell use "foxfire," phospho-
rescent paint. The idea was quickly adopted. [9]

But Franklin did not do more. As the leading American scientist and
a very practical tinkerer who had himself experimented with explosive
devices, Franklin could have arranged for the government to either take
over the Turtle's production or provide adequate backing for Bushnell's

effort. He did neither, although he did ask Washington to meet with other inventors with seemingly ingenious ideas for bringing down the enemy— none of which were practical. Nor did other potential champions among the Congressional delegates help take Bushnell's idea and make it a viable weapon of war manufactured in quantity. Bushnell's was the most promising device to provide the American forces with a significant technological edge. The failure to exploit it and similar inventions, historian Neil York suggests, reflected the colonies' lack of the institutional infrastructure able to produce weapons in quantity and of the trained military managers to oversee production.[10]

Short of money, Bushnell was unable to complete repairs to the submersible before freezing weather rendered subsurface navigation impossible. He resumed development in February 1776 after receiving Connecticut money to pay some of his back bills, and by the following summer the Turtle was ready. Transported to New York harbor, it was deployed against the British flagship. Unfortunately, the submersible's most skilled pilot, David Bushnell's brother, Ezra, was ill, and the substitute pilot, while able to maneuver on the night of September 6, was unable to properly attach the explosives to the target. As General Washington, Bushnell, and others watched, the "torpedo" floated to mid-harbor and exploded harmlessly, although throwing up a "prodigious column of water, resembling a great water spout, attended with a report like thunder," as an observer later noted.[11] Washington would later recall for Jefferson that Bushnell's was "an effort of genius; but that a combination of too many things were requisite to expect much success from the enterprise against an enemy who are always upon guard."[12] After a second aborted attempt, a British salvo sank the barge on which the Turtle was being transported. Bushnell then gave up the Turtle idea.

FRANKLIN'S NOSE for the key factor failed him in regard to the Bushnell Turtle, but it did not in making the effort to fill another of Washington's desperate needs, for properly trained military engineers. "I can hardly express the Disappointment I have experienced on this Subject," Washington had written to Congress in July 1775. "The Skill of those [engineers] we have, being very imperfect & confined to the mere manual Exercise of Cannon. Whereas—the War in which we are engaged requires a Knowledge comprehending the Duties of the Field and Fortification."

Washington was dismissive of Richard Gridley, who had been forced on him as chief engineer but whose expertise was limited. At the end of 1775, Washington was complaining of the Congress's poor judgment in not paying engineers sufficiently well: "The pay of the Assistant Engineers is So very Small, that we Cannot expect men of Science will engage in it."[13] By then, Congress had authorized Franklin and Silas Deane, who were in Paris, to negotiate to borrow two French army engineers.

While Washington was waiting for them, he had to solve an immediate engineering problem: evicting the British from Boston before they were reinforced and could overwhelm his army. In March 1776, to prevent the British from storming American lines, Washington needed a defensive breastworks for Dorchester Heights. Fortunately for the American effort, an ingenious and experienced surveyor found in a British textbook, itself a translation of a French book, a design for "chandeliers," heavy wood frames for use as the backbone of such a breastworks. The chandeliers helped to ensure that the battle of Dorchester Heights became Washington's first military victory. Placed behind such redoubts, a few Continentals were able to hold off much larger British forces.[14]

The roundabout route through which a French fortification notion had saved the day reinforced Washington's belief that he needed scientifically trained, experienced field engineers from Europe. Franklin had gone to Paris in part to obtain them. Mystery had attended Franklin's arrival there, generating speculation that he had come for his health or was having a fight with his countrymen, confusion that allowed Franklin to better accomplish his tasks.[15] His and Deane's arrangement with the king to borrow engineers was kept quiet so that the British would not learn of it. The Americans made deals with engineers selected by Phillipe Charles du Coudray, an artillery expert who successfully passed himself off as more than that. Coudray's picks included Louis Lebègue Duportail, thirty-four, a graduate of the Mézières engineering school. Coudray and his colleagues agreed to come to America in exchange for being elevated in rank in the American forces, paid more than equivalent-ranked American officers, and having their travel expenses reimbursed.

While the French engineers were in transit, Thaddeus Kosciuszko, trained in Warsaw and through five years of advanced courses in Paris, arrived in Philadelphia at the end of August 1776. Congress, by then confronted with a flood of foreign military seeking commissions, not all of whom were qualified, initially hesitated to commission the Pole. But the Pennsylvania Council of Safety, led by David Rittenhouse, utilized him as a volunteer to design and build fortifications at Billingsport on the New Jersey side of the Delaware to block the British from sailing up the river and taking Philadelphia. The plan of these fortifications, although never completed, so impressed Congress that Kosciuszko received his commission and became the engineer for American General Horatio Gates.[16]

In April 1777, *Amphitrite,* the first supply ship from France, arrived in Portsmouth, New Hampshire, with "52 Pieces of Brass Cannon with all the Apparatus, 6132 Stand of Arms, 255,000 Gun Flints, 925 Tents, 21 Bales and one Case Cloths, Serges, Linnens &c. Five Bales Blankets, 62 Packages of Tin Plates, a large Quantity of Iron and Lead Balls, Intrenching Tools, Granadoes, 1029 bls. of Powder, &c." accompanied by repairmen. Similar ships eased the American forces' supply problems.[17] But when the engineers Coudray, Duportail, and associates arrived a bit later in the year, Congress had come under even more pressure from American officers not to allow them to be outranked by awarding to foreigners the commissions overpromised by Deane, who had since been recalled for arrogance. Although the French engineers were not awarded the pay and ranks that they had negotiated, they decided to stay and work for the Revolution; Duportail later estimated that he had laid out from his own funds twice what he eventually received from America.

Washington was happy to welcome these well-trained, practical-minded foreigners. More so than most commanders—especially those still in the British system—Washington judged officers by their deeds rather than by their connections. When the nineteen-year-old Marquis de Lafayette, previously untested in battle, had valiantly proved his worth on the battlefield, Washington instructed aides to care for the wounded young man as if he were his son. Coudray proved corrosive immediately on his arrival. He complained to Washington, "If his Excellency intends that [my officers and I] should not be useless, and that an invincible disgust should not succeed the most ardent zeal, it is absolutely necessary to cause a change in the conduct . . . and to accelerate the slowness of the Civil and Military administration."[18] When Coudray fell off his horse into the Schuylkill River and died, Washington did not grieve. But Duportail quickly proved his mettle through superb military judgment based on his engineering expertise. His memoranda to Washington in November and December 1777 specifically opposed other advisors' recommendation of attacks to oust the British from Philadelphia. "To attack the Enemy in their Lines appears to me a difficult and dangerous Project," the first memo began; "It has especially this very considerable inconvenience, the exposing our Army, in case it does not succeed, to a total Defeat.... *Does it become [this army] to stake the fate of America on a single Action?* I think not." To Washington, whose main task was preserving the army until the French officially entered the war on the American side, Duportail's logic was irrefutable. Upon choosing Valley Forge as the site of the winter encampment, Washington asked the Frenchman to fortify it against possible assault. The resulting fortifications were never tested because, among other reasons, they were formidable enough to add to the British reluctance to attack.[19]

While in Valley Forge, Duportail repeatedly importuned Washington to designate and upgrade the engineer corps so that when he and the other Europeans left, American-born men would be qualified to take over. Richard Gridley's questionable activities had previously sapped Washington's enthusiasm for a dedicated corps. But two years further into the war, and coming from a man who had earned Washington's trust, the recommendation was better received. Washington urged Congress to approve Duportail's formal request for three corps of "sappers," directed by engineers. Congress agreed, and in 1779 Duportail was appointed chief of the engineer corps.[20]

THE ATTEMPT TO PREVENT the British from sailing up the Delaware River and attacking Philadelphia occasioned some of the most advanced American military engineering work. Kosciuszko's designs for Billingsport were only one part of it. Various members of the APS presented plans for underwater obstacles to sink in the main channel, for chains and other impediments across the river, and other devices. The main machine used, known as a cheval-de-frise, was a thirty-foot-square sunken "chandelier" bristling with steel-tipped logs that could spear the undersides of a passing vessel. Put into the river bottom, the chevaux produced a false sense of security that, in turn, resulted in too-leisurely construction of forts downstream.[21]

In any event, the British bypassed some of those downriver forts, as well as Philadelphia's underwater defenses, by debarking their forces in

Chesapeake Bay. Traveling overland, they trounced Washington's men in a pitched formal battle at Brandywine Creek. The war might have ended in an American defeat at Brandywine but for an escape of the forces organized by Lafayette. Another narrow escape for the Revolution came from Washington's use of the engineers to make works that would delay the British from too quickly traversing the twenty-six miles between Brandywine and Philadelphia. Washington warned the engineers that "the whole of [the works] should be rather calculated for dispatch than any unnecessary Decorations or Regularity which Engineer's are frequently too fond of."[22] The works provided time for the successful evacuation of important people and objects from Philadelphia. During the ensuing months, the British, secure in the city, removed many of the marine obstacles emplaced in the bed of the Delaware River.

WHILE THE BRITISH occupied Philadelphia, the American capital was shunted from place to place. During its time in York, Pennsylvania, Rittenhouse, Paine, and a third friend were quartered in the Lancaster home of William Henry, a gunsmith, tinkerer and inventor—Henry's sentinel register for regulating the flame in a furnace had been featured in the bound volume of the APS *Transactions*. Henry and his boarders discussed designs for canals—there were none in America, but Rittenhouse and Henry had met when surveying for one—an auger screw that Henry was perfecting, and a model steamboat. Henry also went over these with his twelve-year-old neighbor, Robert Fulton, already the creator of many mechanical devices, who used so much mercury in his works that he was known as "Quicksilver Bob."[23]

Rittenhouse, in collaboration with painter Charles Willson Peale, another Philadelphia exile, tried to improve rifles by attaching a telescope to provide longer-distance accuracy; the duo only stopped because they almost blinded themselves in the attempt. They also tried to construct a better breach box cut into the stock but gave that up as well. Paine's idea of setting fire to British ships from shore with flaming steel arrows shot by a steel crossbow had merit, people agreed, but no one knew how to make such a steel crossbow.

Lancaster, Pennsylvania—the largest inland colonial city, though its populations was only 2,000—had become a center for making and repairing guns as successive generations of immigrants from Germany and other arms-manufacturing states arrived. The latest models, known as Kentucky rifles for the legendary scout Daniel Boone, were more efficient, able to be loaded and fired in a quarter of the time it took for prior models, the efficiency due to a greased textile patch rammed into the barrel prior to inserting the bullet and to a slightly smaller bullet. The rifles were also several inches longer, which gave them greater range. Problems of repair were quite serious, for each rifle contained between forty-four and fifty parts.[24]

American recruits, largely from farms, had been hunting since childhood and were more proficient than British recruits in the use of guns. Washington therefore wanted sharpshooters for his army and tried to encourage their esprit de corps by the issue of 10,000 hunting shirts, which, he told Congress, "would have a happy Tendency to unite the men, and abolish those Provincial distinctions that lead to Jealousy and Dissatisfaction."[25] The more critical distinction to overcome was the troops' near-universal dislike of rifles—a friend of John Adams from Virginia who was now on the front lines wrote to him, "We are badly off for Musquets, I fear we shall have to use rifles."[26] Most Continental troops used firelock muskets. Easier than rifles to aim, the muskets were able to use coarser powder and were more readily repaired. Washington too became leery of rifles, refusing in July 1776 to send any rifles to another general unless he could vouch for having adequate numbers of soldiers under his command who already knew how to use them. Moreover, despite Washington's admiration for hunters, he was wedded to the European style of battle in which bodies of troops marched across fields in lines and shot muskets until they were close enough to fix bayonets. The spotty use of rifles was another instance of an available technological edge not being used by Americans, and of a leadership that professed enthusiasm but would not put adequate bureaucratic resources into its manufacture, distribution, and training. Washington did not object when, at Valley Forge in the winter of 1777, Steuben preached against the use of rifles and forbade the men to carry them in order to standardize both the troops and the weapons they used. Thereafter, while American corps of "riflemen" were employed here and there, the rifles proved most useful to the American effort in fighting small-scale contingents of British Loyalists through guerilla actions.[27]

ENGINEER KOSCIUSZKO'S POSITIONING and fortifications advice to the northern army was initially less well heeded by that army's chieftains than was Duportail's advice to Washington's main force; as a result, the initial battles at Fort Ticonderoga were lost. However, the Pole's later technological efforts—constructing roadblocks, destroying bridges, and damming streams—to prevent American troops from being wiped out as they fled south gave the rebels time to make a stand at Saratoga, where his fortifications at Bemis Heights were considered crucial in General Horatio Gates's victory in October 1777. Kosciuszko's subsequent work in defenses at West Point (where he clashed with a Duportail colleague) was similarly effective in preventing British forces from sailing down the Hudson and dividing New England from the South.[28]

THE BRITISH STILL HELD Philadelphia on January 6, 1778, when David Bushnell and a carpenter associate floated gunpowder-filled kegs aimed at the British fleet down the Delaware. But the British, to prevent their ships being iced in, had moored them close to the bank; the mines hit only one barge, killing several soldiers. Awakened by that explosion, the British then fired on every floating piece of wood in the river, occasioning Francis Hopkinson's writing of a Revolutionary ditty, "The Battle of the Kegs," which satirized the British over-reaction to the floating mines.

Duportail's prediction to Washington regarding the tenuousness of the British occupation of Philadelphia, made in December 1777, was proved correct in the spring of 1778: when the British generals learned that France had become an American ally, and that King George III had declared war on France, they became fearful of a French attack on their ships in the Delaware, and in June 1778 they quit the American capital. It was the turning point of the war.

NINE

SCIENCE RESURFACES

AMID THE FRAY, SOME AMERICANS MANAGED TO entertain thoughts of scientific endeavor. "Though much of my time is employed in the councils of America," Jefferson informed a correspondent in 1778, "I have yet a little leisure to indulge my fondness for philosophical studies . . . for instance, of the true power of our climate as discoverable from the Thermometer, from the force and direction of the winds, the quantity of rain, the plants which grow without shelter in the winter, &c." Accordingly, he told his friend, he made meteorological observations "as early as possible in the morning and again about 4 o'clock in the afternoon."[1]

John Adams, arriving in Paris to replace the recalled Silas Deane, spent some of his non-working time visiting scientific displays and a bit of it discussing electricity and other matters with Franklin.

In Philadelphia, David Rittenhouse was fully engaged in supervising the defenses of Pennsylvania as president of its Council of Safety—so much so that his wife had to take over the household accounting—when he expressed a plaintive wish to John Page to take observations alongside him during the forthcoming total eclipse of the sun on June 24, 1778. It would be the first total eclipse in America, and the astronomer was eager to use the results to calculate the exact latitude of the city, never before accurately ascertained. Rittenhouse's war duties kept him from traveling to Virginia, but he and Owen Biddle did observe the eclipse in Philadelphia.

In Virginia, during the four minutes of solar eclipse, clouds mostly obscured the view, so neither Page in Williamsburg nor Jefferson at Monticello could do much more than marvel at midday darkness. Never one to waste a crisis, Jefferson took the muddied eclipse observations as opportunity to complain to Rittenhouse about his lack of an adequate timepiece; Rittenhouse had promised him one, and Jefferson hinted that the promise could now be more readily fulfilled since the British had vacated Philadelphia. Lauding Rittenhouse's orrery as an "amazing" creation that by accurately limning the heavens had reversed the biblical "inhibition" against making graven images, Jefferson exhorted its maker to eschew governmental affairs and "fulfill the highest purposes of your creation by employing yourself in the highest breach of that inhibition," i.e., by crafting that timepiece. "Are those powers then, which being intended for the erudition of the world are, like air and light, the world's common property, to be taken from their proper pursuit to do the commonplace drudgery of governing a single state, a work which may be executed by men of an ordinary stature?"[2]

Rittenhouse rejected Jefferson's suggestion that scientific geniuses were too important to waste on ordinary affairs. And when similar flattery was tried with Franklin, the elder statesman would have none of it, long ago having set out the rationale for scientists' eschewing research in wartime: "Had Newton been pilot but of a single common Ship, the finest of his Discoveries would scarce have excus'd, or aton'd for his abandoning the Helm one Hour in Time of Danger; how much less if she carried the Fate of the Commonwealth."[3]

Jefferson, taking office as governor of Virginia in June 1779, introduced two bills to the Virginia legislature, one to create a system of public lower schools and a second to elevate the College of William & Mary to national-university status. Neither passed, but with the aid of the college's new president, the Reverend James Madison, the changes to the college were made, among them eliminating the divinity school and restructuring the curriculum to emphasize science. Notes from Madison's later lectures show him leading students through physics, chemistry, hydrostatics, electricity, magnetism, and astronomy.

Magnetism and meteors were in the thoughts of several compatriots. Page wrote to Rittenhouse in December 1779, "I have amused myself with supposing that magnetism is only a species of electricity, whose matter is as yet not discovered by human sight; as that of electricity was, when a few years ago, it was perceivable only by its effects in attracting or repelling light bodies, as magnetism now is in attracting or repelling iron." Page's notion anticipated the studies of Michael Faraday on electricity and magnetism. His letter to Rittenhouse also contained his observations on a falling meteor. In response, Rittenhouse offered a theory of meteor origin (not from this earth) and luminosity (from friction as it passed through the atmosphere) that was also well ahead of its time:

> May not these shooting stars be bodies altogether foreign to the earth and its atmosphere, accidentally meeting with it as they are swiftly traversing the great void of space? And may they not, either electrically or by some other means, excite a luminous appearance on entering our atmosphere? I am inclined to this opinion for the following reasons: 1st. It is not probable that meteors should be generated in the air at the height of 50 or 60 miles, on account of its extreme rareness. . . . 2dly. Their motions cannot be owing to gravity, for they descend in all directions, and but seldom perpendicularly to the horizon. Besides, their velocities are much too great.[4]

Rittenhouse entered a controversy between adherents of Newton, who had proposed a corpuscular theory of light, and those of Christian Huygens, whose wave theory had been dismissed by Newtonians. Newton's corpuscles could not explain the phenomenon of interference, but Rittenhouse made a plane diffraction grating—a device capable of splitting light into its colors—whose actions supported Huygens's theory. The American's conclusions were not taken seriously in London, partially because they were offered when America was Great Britain's enemy, and chiefly because they contradicted Newton—but they would later be proved astute.[5]

Rittenhouse and Reverend Madison continued to be in touch, thrown together at Jefferson's behest as fellow surveyors when Pennsylvania and Virginia jointly looked into settling their boundary dispute. Rittenhouse took along his nephew, Benjamin Smith Barton, on his first field trip; Barton later wrote that the trip "fostered my love and zeal for natural history." At the conclusion of the surveying, Rittenhouse wrote that while Pennsylvania technically had title to certain lands along the Potomac, the residents had assumed they were Virginians and obeyed Virginia law, so "for the sake of peace, and to manifest our earnest desire of adjusting the dispute on amicable terms," Pennsylvania would cede the area.[6]

IN 1779 THE AMERICAN PHILOSOPHICAL SOCIETY resumed meetings, and the Philadelphia Academy and the College of Philadelphia merged to become the University of Pennsylvania. During the winter of 1779, the coldest that anyone could recall, the APS hired a laborer to dig down to reveal the depth of frozen earth, circulated a request to other cities for similar information, and compared them. Reverend Madison, who transmitted some of his and Jefferson's meteorological data, also sent a letter taking issue with Franklin's contention that the aurora borealis was an electrical phenomenon.[7]

In Paris, there had been a spectacular display of the northern lights, and in a paper presented to the Académie des Sciences Franklin opined that a concentration of colder, denser air in the northern regions usually kept the aurora's excess of electricity from descending to earth. An interesting and logical guess celebrated by Paris as was everything related to Franklin, it was off the mark. Franklin's days of superb scientific insight were over, although in France he burnished his scientific reputation, spent time with Buffon, Antoine Lavoisier, and Voltaire, was inducted into the Académie—which was much more selective than its British counterpart—and was lionized and immortalized. Sketches and paintings limned him as the godlike creature who brought lightning down from the heavens and with it smote the British. His scientific reputation did not suffer even as Alessandro Volta successfully challenged an aspect of his theory of electricity and British electricians attacked his configuration of the lightning rod.

In a letter to Dr. Benjamin Waterhouse, Adams recalled some of his own questions to Franklin about electricity that demonstrated Adams's keen interest in current scientific affairs: "Pray, where is there Evidence of the Existence of a subtle Electrical fluid which pervades the Universe? And if that fact were proved, where is your Authority for saying that such an Electrick fluid is the Cause of Life? Why may it not as well be Magnetism? or Steam, or Nitre? or fixed Air? These are all tremendous Forces in nature." Another such Adams-Franklin discussion revolved around the question of how animal life sustained itself: "It has long appeared to me astonishing, that it should be impossible to discover, what it is, which the

Air conveys into our Lungs and leaves behind it, in the Body when we breathe." Adams was convinced that such a substance ought to be discoverable by microscope.[8]

Returning briefly to America in mid-1779, Adams took two actions in support of science. Designated by fellow Massachusetts constitutional committee members to draft a state constitution, he did so brilliantly and included in it support of science. His state constitution did as much to assert individual and collective rights to worship, bear arms, assemble peacefully, speak freely, be secure against unreasonable search, and other items later featured in the United States' Bill of Rights, as it did to lay out the duties of legislatures, courts, and office-holders. A then-unique provision, included by Adams, was that regular public support for science and the arts was an obligation of government.[9] Biographer David McCullough traces this tenet to Adams's early embrace of Cicero as a model: "To be good, the country must be taught from its infancy to use knowledge and the measured moral reasoning of wisdom and virtue. The resemblance of these beliefs to positions passed down through the Ciceronian tradition is unmistakable, particularly the union of arts and sciences with a growth in wisdom and virtue."[10] Adams later recalled for Waterhouse that he did not think this portion would pass the state legislature; rather, he "expected it would be attack'd . . . from all quarters, on the Score of Affectation, Pedantry, Hypocrisy, and above all Oeconomy," because delegates "had rather starve their Souls than draw upon their purses to pay for nourishment for them." Nonetheless, the provision passed, which pleased him.[11]

Just prior to Adams's constitution writing, during an August 1779 meeting in Cambridge in the Harvard room in which he had been taught by John Winthrop—who had died two months earlier—Adams proposed an American Académy for Arts and Sciences to serve the Boston area as the American Philosophical Society did Philadelphia. A state charter for it was included in the legislation for the Massachusetts constitution but ran into difficulties when John Hancock objected to his name being placed in a less prominent position than Adams's. An alphabetical relisting cooled Hancock's pique and the American Academy was chartered in 1780 with James Bowdoin selected as its first president. Around the same time, the APS, newly rechartered by Pennsylvania as a public instead of a private institution, elected to membership General Washington,

Governor Jefferson, and other public officials.[12] Later, Adams would rank the establishing of the American Academy as one of his proudest achievements, just as Jefferson would list the establishment of the University of Virginia as one of his and would cherish his membership in and eventual presidency of the American Philosophical Society.

Friendly chroniclers characterize the early memoirs and papers of the American Academy as like the "communications to the Royal Society more than a century before, with the papers of Boyle, Newton, and Hooke omitted"; yet the sheer number of letters received testified to deep public interest in scientific affairs, engendering "a kind of scientific patriotism."[13]

That was reinforced in Philadelphia as Owen Biddle gave the 1781 annual oration to the APS on March 2. Offering a history of science and technology to date, Biddle began with Tubal Cain, ironworker of the Bible, and proceeded through several thousand years of "those capital inventions and discoveries, which had led to all the subsequent improvements in useful knowledge." He conceded that after Newton most people believed there was little left to discover, but "there was reserved! And with confidence I assert it,—there is yet in reserve! a vast fund to gratify the utmost ambition of the inquisitive sons of America, it only requires the same predominant affection for science,—the same ardour, and the same assiduity, directed by a liberal education, and new instances will occur." The future objective was for science to help us live "in a state of improved ease, dignity, and opulence."[14]

EUROPEANS DOUBTED THE LIKELIHOOD of American progress. Their attitude was neatly encapsulated in Abbé Guillaume Raynal's charge that "America has not produced . . . one able mathematician, one man of genius in a single art or a single science." To this canard, Jefferson would make the most appropriate response:

> When we shall have existed as a people as long as the Greeks did before they produced a Homer, the Romans a Virgil, the French a Racine and Voltaire, the English a Shakespeare and Milton, should this reproach be still true, we will enquire from what unfriendly causes it has proceeded. . . . In war we have produced a Washington, whose memory will be adored while liberty shall have votaries. . . . In physics we have produced a Franklin, than whom no one of the present age has made more important discoveries,

nor has enriched philosophy with more, or more ingenious solutions of the phaenomena of nature.[15]

Jefferson's retort to Raynal was part of his response to a set of queries that came to him from the French government in 1780. François Barbé-Marbois, secretary of the French delegation in Philadelphia, at the behest of official circles in Paris sent out sets of queries to all thirteen states, seeking information on their lands, laws, populations, natural resources, histories, and cultures. For Jefferson, the twenty-two Marbois queries provided a "mysterious obligation for making me much better acquainted with my own country than I ever was before." He began the gathering process while governor, but writing and full compilation had to wait until he completed his term—and had escaped from the British, who narrowly missed capturing him but occupied Monticello and drank up its fabled wine cellar.[16]

Just then, Washington and some American troops were encamped north of West Point, watching the British in New York, which the Crown's forces had reoccupied, while other American armies were fighting in Virginia and the Carolinas. Learning of a discovery of fossilized bones on a Hudson Valley farm not far from his encampment, Washington and several officers rode over to see them, and the general remarked that the huge molars found at the site resembled one that he had at Mount Vernon, which came from Big Bone Lick in Kentucky.

Shortly, the assessments by Henry Knox and Louis Lebègue Duportail of what it would take to dislodge the British from New York and win a war-ending victory—an array of forces and an amount of powder that Washington did not have—tipped the balance and dissuaded him and the Comte de Rochambeau from such an attack. Instead, they would head south and hope to battle the forces of General Charles Cornwallis somewhere in Virginia. Tricking the British land and sea forces to remain in New York, the combined Continental and French armies rapidly moved down the seaboard. It was the moment to do so, British historian Andrew Jackson O'Shaughnessy writes, because "Britain was trying to win the war in America with fewer troops and a smaller navy than it had deployed in America in 1776." By 1780, British forces and supply lines were overextended to twenty-seven garrisons in the American colonies, not counting those in the Canadian colonies, and more in the West Indies, Africa, and

India, while British naval vessels were overwhelmingly engaged in protecting commerce on four oceans, and the London government was also keeping troops in reserve to counter a potential Irish revolt.[17]

Sieges were then considered the province of military engineers, and since 1778 it had been the engineers' expertise that permitted American forces in the South to continue the war and that in 1781 effectively bottled up Cornwallis on the Yorktown peninsula. But the British were well protected with what amounted to a natural moat and strong fortifications; one report noted "redoubts, bristling with stages and palisaded, and surrounded by an abbatis," a dense brush bramble with lots of thorns. Under another French engineer and siege expert, Marshal Sébastien le Prestre de Vauban, a three-week siege was begun in stages, with lines of circumvallation and countervallation, strategic raids on individual British redoubts, and regular intervals of cannon fire.[18]

The arrival of the French fleet effectively made it impossible for the British forces to evacuate by sea. Faced with starvation, military defeat, or surrender, on October 19, 1781, Cornwallis chose the last. During the ceremony of yielding, the British band played the tune, "The World Turned Upside Down."

WHILE THE BATTLE OF YORKTOWN was taking place, a hundred miles further inland Jefferson began to write *Notes of the State of Virginia*, a work that combined natural history information, ranging from statistics on bones to observations on Native burial mounds, with commentaries on law and on human nature. He had gathered the data from many sources, among them Reverend Madison and several members of the American Philosophical Society, particularly Charles Thomson, former stalwart of the American Society for Useful Knowledge. Thomson wrote an extended commentary to Jefferson's draft, a paper that Jefferson excerpted and used as an attributed appendix to the *Notes*. Among its more notable passages was an attack on Buffon, who "has indeed given an afflicting picture of human nature in his description of the [Red] man of America. But I am sure there never was a picture more unlike the original." Coming from Thomson, who had worked for Native tribes and remained on good terms with them, the comment was an important one. Thomson also urged Jefferson to excavate certain Native American mounds to determine their age, content, and purpose.

On several matters the religiously devout Philadelphian disagreed with Jefferson, including what natural forces had shaped Virginia's "natural bridge," whose site Jefferson had purchased. Thomson's more important demurral, however, was political: he begged Jefferson to "expunge" his paragraphs on the racial inferiority of blacks and its relationship to slavery. Even though in the book Jefferson decried slavery per se, the references to racial inferiority, Thomson pleaded, would cause Jefferson no end of trouble were they to be published. Jefferson left them in, to his eventual chagrin.[19]

For many years it was believed that Jefferson's main source of information for the book had been his own notes, gathered over the course of previous decades; more recent scholarship suggests that the composition was based on information collected in the early 1780s from correspondents and neighbors and from perusal of documents.[20] Among his correspondents was the Chevalier de Chastellux, who had served with distinction at Yorktown and then undertook an extensive tour of America. Chastellux and Jefferson became good friends. Staying at Monticello, Chastellux marveled at Jefferson's familiarity with and easy discourse on natural philosophy, politics, and the arts: "It seems indeed as though, ever since his youth, he had placed his mind, like his house, on a lofty height, whence he might contemplate the whole universe."[21]

Jefferson characterized his *Notes on Virginia* as a mirror of the country and added that, since America was "Nature's nation," the obligation of all Americans was to study nature. His own conception of nature was constrained by his hewing to antiquated canons, as in his assertion, "It is by the assistance of heat and moisture that vegetables are elaborated from the elements of earth, air, water, and fire." Such Aristotelian formulations were fast disappearing from the writings of leading scientists. Jefferson did reach beyond biblical understandings in his guesses as to why and when geological features had come into being. Formerly a believer in the six-day timeline of the earth's origin in the book of Genesis, he now questioned how long it might have taken to create the earth, and whether the Noachian deluge could explain the fossilized seashells found atop the Blue Ridge Mountains. His skepticism did not extend to all of Genesis, for he still clung to the tenet that all men and women were descendants of Adam and Eve, even though he had difficulty reconciling that notion with the differences he perceived among the races.

Jefferson directed most of his fire in the scientific sections of the book to a highly detailed refutation of Buffon's assertion about the "degeneracy" of American flora, fauna, and civilization. Jefferson even reorganized the contents of the book to better attack Buffon, whose work on other aspects of nature Jefferson admired. Noting that Buffon's conclusions on American matters were not based on first-hand observations but on the reports of travelers, Jefferson asked: "Who were those travelers? . . . Was natural history the object of their travels? Did they measure or weigh the animals they speak of? Or did they not judge them by sight or perhaps even from report only?" Seeking support, Jefferson polled many people, among them a neighbor and former William & Mary classmate to whom he sent the part of the manuscript dealing with Buffon, commenting, "I would wish to have [it] very correct in matters of fact," and asking him to supply tables of the weights of mammalian animals, "from the mouse to the mammoth," with special emphasis on the moose.[22]

Jefferson then tackled the allied Buffon contention that American Natives were themselves "degenerate," addressing Buffon's statements about the Natives' stature, size of "organs of generation," absence of hair, and lack of ardor for women. Jefferson had dealt with Natives for some time, believed himself to be a serious student of them, and had a high opinion of them; he included in the *Notes on Virginia,* as an example of their eloquence, the text of a speech by a Mingo tribe chief.

Buffon was also wrong on other subjects dealing with America, Jefferson insisted, among these the quality of the soil, which Buffon considered incapable of being improved. American soil was as lush and improvable as that of any other nation, Jefferson asserted. Benjamin Cohen, in his history of the American soil, suggests that in making such statements in the *Notes,* Jefferson had a far larger objective, that he "premised his argument for a great nation on assumptions of composition and soil identity made evident by science."[23] Jefferson, to buttress his argument against Buffon, wrote about the mammoth, "or big buffalo," which he labeled the largest of American land animals, although it had never been seen by a white man or, for that matter, by a living Native. But it existed in Native lore:

> Their tradition is, that he was carnivorous, and still exists in the northern parts of America. A delegation of warriors from the Delaware tribe having visited the governor of Virginia . . . the governor asked them . . . what

they knew of the animal whose bones were found at the Saltlicks, on the Ohio. Their chief speaker . . . informed him that . . ."in antient times a herd of these tremendous animals came to the Big-bone licks, and began an universal destruction of the bear, deer, elks, buffaloes, and other animals, which had been created for the use of the Indians: that the Great Man above . . . was so enraged that he seized his lightning, descended on the earth . . . and hurled his bolts among them till the whole were slaughtered, except the big bull, who . . . bounded over the Ohio, over the Wabash, the Illinois, and finally over the great lakes, where he is living at this day." It is well known that on the Ohio, and in many parts of America further north, tusks, grinders, and skeletons of unparalleled magnitude, are found in great numbers, some lying on the surface of the earth, and some a little below it. . . . From the accounts published in Europe . . . these are of the same kind with those found in Siberia.

Highly curious to Jefferson was that the tusks found at Big Bone Lick had been ascribed to an elephant-like animal but the teeth to a hippopotamus-like one. Since tusks and teeth were found together, Jefferson reasoned, they must have belonged to the same animal, and it must be neither elephant nor hippo. He calculated that had the land where the bones been found ever been tropical, it would have to have been 250,000 years into the past—a figure dangerous to use, contradicting Bishop Ussher's contention that the earth had been created in 4004 BC. Jefferson wrote that even if his age calculations were in error, the past if not present existence of this creature from Big Bone Lick should "have stifled, in its birth, the opinion of a writer, the most learned . . . of all the others in the science of animal history," Buffon. It therefore could not be true, as Buffon asserted, that on the American side of the Atlantic, "nature is less active, less energetic," as though "both sides were not warmed by the same genial sun [and fed by] soil of the same composition." Buffon's entire theory of degeneracy was poppycock, Jefferson concluded. "The truth is that a Pigmy and a Patagonian, a Mouse and a Mammoth, derive their dimensions from the same nutritive juices."[24]

Jefferson owned fossils from Big Bone Lick, acquired more, and would display them at Monticello. For his book he systematically compared the weights and sizes of those fossils, as well as of skeletons of currently living species, to show that American animals were frequently larger than their

European counterparts. *Notes on the State of Virginia* remained incomplete while Jefferson sought more information and was unpublished as he sailed for France, where he would complete it and first have it issued.

IN THE SPRING OF 1783, negotiations for a peace treaty were still ongoing and the Continental Army was unsettled, having been denied back pay and subjected to other indignities. Washington, feeling old, asked Rittenhouse to obtain for him a pair of reading glasses. They were sent immediately, and Washington acknowledged them with thanks and a confession that while without the glasses the lettering on missives was "a mist blended together and confused," with them on he could read perfectly.[25] Washington used the spectacles to great effect during the Newburgh Conspiracy, when officers sought to rebel and march the army away for lack of congressional action on back pay. At a crucial moment in his address to those officers, in attempting to read a letter from a representative who promised to push for Congress for the allocation, Washington paused to put on his spectacles. "Gentlemen, you must pardon me," he said as he did. "I have grown gray in your service, and now I find myself going blind, as well." The conspiracy dissolved.

After news arrived that the peace treaty had been signed, Washington resigned as general of the American armies and retired to Mount Vernon; his action astonished the British and the French, whose history books bulged with tales of military commanders who had initially served others but then crowned themselves. His refusal to even consider becoming a king certified him as a true, disinterested gentleman patriot and ratified the American Revolution as substantively different from past revolts in Great Britain and on the Continent.

THE NEGOTIATIONS TO REACH the war's end by treaty had been difficult. The British had attempted to retain what they could of the Americas, and the French tried to reacquire Canada before settling for increased ownership in the Caribbean. Franklin and Adams had been the main negotiators in the drawn-out process. Adams, idled for much of the time, spent a winter teaching his son, John Quincy, mathematics, geometry, and algebra before—as he wrote to Waterhouse, who had lived with the Adamses in Europe for a time—he "attempted a sublime Flight and endeavoured to give him some Idea of the Differential Method of

Calculation of the Marquis de L'Hospital and the Method of Fluxions and infinite Series of Sir Isaac Newton." Adams worried that he had not taught his son very well but hoped his tutelage was sufficient to prevent Quincy's embarrassing both of them when he entered Harvard. As time would prove, his tutelage had been not only sufficient for that purpose, it had also pointed John Quincy Adams toward becoming one of America's most scientific-minded presidents.[26]

Adams also wrote to Waterhouse that he and Franklin had been in the audience when the Montgolfier brothers made their historic balloon ascent and told of the wonder of Franklin's takedown of Anton Mesmer, then all the rage in Paris for his "animal magnetism." Mesmer's notions had even been presented favorably by Lafayette in a lecture to the American Philosophical Society prior to Louis XVI's appointing four members of the medical society and five from the Académie des Sciences, including Franklin and chemist Antoine Lavoisier, to look into the phenomenon. Such tasks were usual for French academicians, who as civil servants were required now and then to evaluate matters ranging from street lighting to perpetual motion machines.[27]

Mesmer had written of a universal fluid that could be "magnetized" to affect its direction and effects: "It is a fluid universally diffused; the vehicle of mutual influence between the celestial bodies, the earth, and the bodies of animated beings. . . . The animal body is subject to the effects of this agent; and these effects are immediately produced by the agent insinuating itself into the substance of the nerves." Lavoisier took the lead in the inquiry and was more upset about Mesmer's challenge to scientific authority than Franklin was. Spurred by Mesmer, Franklin wrote some "loose thoughts" on a universal fluid composed mainly of light and heat that, among other feats, controlled growth in plants and health in human beings and, as with so many things he thought about, sought equilibrium.[28] The commissioners studiously observed Mesmer's work, even subjecting themselves to his powers, which were considerable on other people—convulsions, spitting up blood and water, uncontrollable shaking—although most of the commissioners remained unmoved. They commented:

Nothing can be more astonishing than the sight of these convulsions; he that has not had it can have no idea of it; and in beholding it, a man is not less struck with the profound repose of one class of patients than with the violence which agitates another. . . . They are entirely under the government of the person who distributes the magnetic virtue: in vain they may be appear to be in a state of the extremest drowsiness, his voice, a look, a sign from him, rouses them.[29]

The commissioners chose seven fairly ill people and had them assemble at Franklin's villa one day and found that Mesmer's chief experimenter was able to palliate the pain of several, but not all. The commissioners concluded that mesmerism, "the dominion of the imagination," worked best with the uneducated and the poor: "There is so intimate a connection . . . between the volitions of the soul and the motions of the body, that it is not easy to prescribe limits to the influence of attention, which appears to be nothing more than a train of volitions, directed constantly, and without interruption, to the same object."[30] They recommended against the government's supporting Mesmer's methods because even when effective, they were temporary and accompanied by deleterious sensations in the patients. Their report curtailed the enthusiasm among the cognoscenti for Mesmer and his "cures." Nonetheless, Adams wrote to Waterhouse, who had become one of the three professors at Harvard's recently inaugurated medical school, that he hoped American doctors would investigate that unknown territory in which the brain was able to exert the sort of mastery of the body so artfully demonstrated by Mesmer. Jefferson, arriving in Paris in time for the controversy, sent a copy of the Franklin committee's report to Charles Thomson and wrote to another friend that for "reasonable men" the Franklin-Lavoisier report had laid the doctrine of Mesmerism to rest, but unfortunately, the "largest part of mankind" was the unreasonable.[31]

THE MEDICAL COMMITTEE'S SEPARATE REPORT on Mesmerism began with the observation that the fad was first "embraced" during a period "when suppositions were admitted to hold the place of facts; and this hypothesis vanished, together with many others, when experimental philosophy began to dissipate the impostures of the imagination." That dissipation, happening principally on the Continent, involved serious upending of prior understandings of the natural world. Lavoisier and his associates were compiling a new chemistry text that specifically refuted the Aristotelian-Aquinan four-elements concept by pointing out that at least a dozen new elements—parts of Air and Water—had already been chemically separated and identified, including oxygen, which Lavoisier had recently named, and nitrogen. Similarly, many parts of Earth, such as copper and sulfur, had also been separated and were now believed to be irreducible—the very definition of an element. Some writers on science divided "simple" earth into five types, calcareous (pure quicklime), ponderous, magnefia, argillaceous (pure clay), and siliceous. "These earths have never yet been decomposed," according to William Nicholson's *Introduction to Natural Philosophy*, first published in 1781.[32]

In geology, the discussion was shifting from the unscientific speculations about earth's origin and toward the understanding that the globe was neither uniform nor particularly solid and was continuing to change. In all the sciences, new formulations had not yet entirely effaced the old; an outdated one—the invisible, weightless substance called phlogiston, supposedly involved when anything burned—generated increasingly intemperate discussions. Joseph Priestley and Lavoisier clashed over whether the newly discovered elements of oxygen and nitrogen were evidence for or against the existence of phlogiston. Lavoisier dismissed the notion while Priestley made phlogiston's reality the centerpiece of his chemistry. The last of the four elements that still stood as indivisible and primary was fire, but after Franklin's revelations it was under further attack in a battle that pitted Alessandro Volta against Luigi Galvani in regard to whether or not a "spark of life" manifested itself in the "animal electricity" that Galvani thought produced spasms in dead frogs in his laboratory.

In this scientifically volatile atmosphere, Jefferson arrived in Paris to do battle with Buffon; John Adams went to Great Britain to take up his post as ambassador to the Court of St. James's and to find time for visits to astronomer William Herschel and the Royal Observatory; and Benjamin Franklin, now seventy-nine, sailed for home for the last time to reinvigorate the American Philosophical Society, whose leadership he had held in absentia for so many years.

TEN

MIDCOURSE CORRECTIONS

THE WAR WAS ONLY THE "FIRST ACT" OF AN
American Revolution, Benjamin Rush reminded his countrymen: "It
remains yet to establish and perfect our new forms of government, and
to prepare the principles, morals, and manners of our citizens for these
forms." While the Founders had not formally articulated a hypothesis
underlying the governance of the new United States of America, one
was nevertheless generally understood: that a confederation of former
colonies whose interests overlapped at times, but only at times, could be
governed in a democratic way, without a monarch or a powerful parliament, and could remain stable in the face of exterior or interior attacks.
George Washington's 1783 "Circular to the States," sent after receiving the
news of the peace treaty's signing, expressed well the circumstances under
which the hypothesis had been formed:

> When we consider the magnitude of the prize we contended for, the
> doubtful nature of the contest, and the favorable manner in which it has
> terminated, we shall find the greatest possible reason for gratitude and re-
> joicing. . . . The foundation of our Empire was not laid in the gloomy age
> of Ignorance and Superstition, but at an Epocha when the rights of man-
> kind were better understood and more clearly defined, than at any former
> period, the researches of the human mind, after social happiness, have
> been carried to a great extent, the Treasures of knowledge, acquired by the

labours of Philosophers, Sages and Legislatures . . . are laid open for our use, and their collected wisdom may be happily applied in the Establishment of our forms of Government .[1]

Scientific hypotheses, to be considered valid, must explain all the extant facts. The Founders' governing configuration did so by showing that all prior, authoritarian forms of governance had proved inadequate to governing a free people, and by configuring a democracy that was designed to ameliorate the wrongs of those authoritarian forms; but a good hypothesis must also be able to encompass facts not yet in evidence. For the Founders, that second requirement was quite palpable after the war, as was its corollary demand, that if the current governmental configuration proved unable to meet new challenges resulting from independence, the hypothesis merited adjustment, to be accomplished in ways that did not compromise that government's democratic integrity and power.

In Jürgen Habermas's terms, at the close of the Revolutionary War, Americans existed within new "frames of reference": they were now fellow citizens rather than fellow subjects, sovereign actors in a society in which distinctions of inherited class no longer officially obtained, and they were being served by elected leaders rather than dictated to by royal appointees. The new configurations were part of a predictable upheaval attendant on what Gordon Wood characterizes as a radical reordering of the whole of American society. As St. John de Crèvecoeur wrote in 1782, "What is an American? The American is a new man, who acts on new principles; he must therefore entertain new ideas, and form new opinions."[2] Many among America's three million people shared sensations relating to these changed frames of reference: of newness all around, of enabling and encouraging further exploration, and of an awareness of setting an example for the world to judge—feelings that fulfill Foucault's definition of modernity as a sense of dealing with reality that "marks a relation of belonging and presents itself as a task."

Washington also addressed that task in his 1783 circular: "The Citizens of America, placed in the most enviable condition, as the sole Lords and Proprietors of a vast Tract of Continent . . . are now . . . acknowledged to be possessed of absolute freedom and Independency; They are, from this period, to be considered as the Actors on a most conspicuous Theatre . . . surrounded with every thing which can contribute to the

completion of private and domestic enjoyment, [including] a fairer op-
pertunity for political happiness, than any other Nation has ever been
favored with." The populace, he added, was in the midst of "political
probation." That trial of the experimental entity lasted throughout the
interregnum between the Peace of Paris in 1783 and Washington's inauguration as president in 1789. As Alexander Hamilton would state boldly
toward the end of the period, "It seems to have been reserved to the people
of this country, by their conduct and example, to decide the important
question, whether societies of men are really capable or not, of establishing good government from reflection and choice."[3]

TO SUPPORT THE NEW NATION required new structures and
institutions. One was a national language, whose delineation and form was
spearheaded by Noah Webster through his series of spellers, grammars,
and readers, which began publication in 1783. These texts crystallized past
experience as a bridge to the future. Webster had no doubt as to their foun-
dations: "Next to the sacred writings, those books which teach us the principles of science and lay the basis on which all our future improvements
must be made, best deserve the patronage of the public."[4]

Webster concurrently pursued a restructuring of the patent system,
starting with that of his home state, Connecticut, to better protect inventors; his activities in this regard were part of the widespread American
realization that true independence from Great Britain would require getting beyond dependence in ways other than the political. The new country's economy was still too much like that of a servile colony, its people
continuing to buy most of their manufactured goods from Great Britain
and to sell (often to the same British middlemen who represented the
manufacturers) their crops and natural resources. The British flooded
America with lower-priced manufactured goods and generous credit. A
Virginia lawyer imagined their reasoning for doing so: "If . . . we can
continue to monopolize [American] trade as heretofore, Britain can suffer no injury whatsoever from the American revolution.—If the profits of
her trade center not in her own states, America will ever be indigent and
contemptible, while the nation which engrosses her trade will increase in
wealth and power proportionate to [America's] poverty."[5]

In the war's wake the new nation was enmeshed in financial depres-
sion. Wages in cities dropped by a third, and on farms were down to 40

cents a day. Credit collapsed, and when it "burst," writes historian Richard B. Morris, "a combination of indebtedness and unemployment resulted, and to a degree of severity Americans had never previously experienced." Tench Coxe, a Philadelphia merchant, wrote, "As long as we remained in our colonial situation, our progress was very slow, and indeed the necessity of manufacture was not so urgent, as it has become since our assuming an independent station." For Coxe, manufacturing was the key to a more robust national economy as well as being essential to national defense.[6] But he experienced difficulties in prodding the loosely configured, not very powerful confederacy government to support manufacturing. Doing so state by state also proved unsatisfactory.

ACCORDINGLY, AS THOMAS JEFFERSON HEADED to Paris on behalf of the Confederation, his principal brief was shoring up America's economic ties with France, Spain, and other continental powers. Among the various paths to accomplishing his mission he focused on one that he could immediately address: dispelling pseudoscientific notions of American inferiority that if left in place would rationalize Europeans' refusal to treat the new nation as an equal. Some European intellectuals had already adopted Buffon's degeneracy thesis—Immanuel Kant, in a 1775 essay, described Native Americans as a race "not yet properly formed, or half-degenerate."[7]

With Lafayette and Chastellux making introductions to the leading thinkers, Jefferson was soon able to report to Secretary of State John Jay quite a bit of news of scientific interest, along with diplomatic initiatives. To dispel the scientific myths, Jefferson had brought along a Florida panther pelt; he sent it to Buffon, who had argued that American "cougars" were less formidable than their Afro-European counterparts. Some months later Jefferson received an invitation to dine with Buffon. He excitedly wrote to Chastellux that Franklin, his colleague in Paris, had provided him with first-hand observations proving "the air of London and of Paris to be more humid than that of Philadelphia," which would help him refute Buffon's ancillary contention that excess humidity in America was a main cause of the degeneracy. During the Buffon-Jefferson dinner party, the host graciously recanted his claims about the lesser stature of the panther but did not do so for his general claim of American degeneracy. However, he did confess to being "unacquainted" with the moose, which Jefferson described as so large that reindeer (similarly antlered European creatures) could run beneath its belly. In letters to Washington, Adams, and Monroe—all hunters—Jefferson asked repeatedly for such a specimen, whose "acquisition," he wrote to an old friend, now governor of New Hampshire, would in Paris be "more precious than you can imagine." After a series of adventures and mishaps, the governor managed to transport to Jefferson a seven-foot-high, large-antlered moose skeleton, which Jefferson had delivered to Buffon. The Frenchman promised to take the moose into account in his next volume, but when Buffon died six months after the moose arrived, that volume remained incomplete.[8]

Many of the thousands of letters that Jefferson wrote during his four years in France concerned scientific matters. He reported to Reverend James Madison, David Rittenhouse, Francis Hopkinson, Ezra Stiles, and a dozen others on such new French scientific developments as a fulminating powder, an etching material, and Pierre Simon Laplace's refining of the understanding of the sun's effect on the movements of the moon and the increase or decrease of the earth's orbit. He also continued colloquies on subjects that he and his correspondents had earlier begun to discuss, such as with Stiles on whether pre-contact Natives in the Americas had been capable of using iron or bricks in their construction. Initially, Jefferson did not correspond with Charles Thomson while he was in France; their prior discussions of the early history of the planet had uncovered the deep divide in their beliefs, with Thomson clinging to the Noachian deluge as the shaper when Jefferson no longer believed in that notion. But while traveling abroad, Jefferson found a congenial subject to discuss with Thomson—steam engines—and they resumed correspondence, especially after a Jefferson visit to Matthew Boulton in England, where he saw some steam machinery at work and conveyed to Thomson his enthusiasm for steam's potential in America.[9]

With Reverend Madison, Jefferson chewed over the discovery of "Herschel's planet," Uranus, and the mechanism of an "optical screw" that might work for balloons in air as well as with boats in water—he confided to Hugh Williamson, another scientific correspondent, that he thought Bushnell's Turtle had operated on that principle. He checked his impressions of the Turtle with Washington, who provided some insight into the Bushnell failure. To Rittenhouse, Jefferson touted an Icelandic crystal that polarized light. But Jefferson was perplexed by the science making the most important strides, chemistry, in the work of Antoine Lavoisier. Like Buffon, Jefferson was not fond of chemistry, asserting that while it could be "the most useful of sciences, and big with future discoveries," at present its experiments were "contradictory," subject to varying explanations as to what had caused the results. The battles of Priestley and Lavoisier over oxygen's function in the world and over whether there existed such an intangible fluid as phlogiston were evidence to Jefferson that little hope of certainty obtained in chemistry. Moreover, the science did not meet his standard of utility—he could not yet see, he wrote, how chemistry's principles applied to beer-brewing or cheese- or soap-making. Nonetheless, Jefferson purchased Lavoisier's *Méthode de nomenclature chimique* and signed up for his textbook in preparation, *Traité élémentaire de chimie.*[10]

On trips to southern France, Italy, Holland, and Germany, Jefferson obtained and surreptitiously sent home Italian rice, whose exportation was forbidden, studied wine-making processes, looked into the building of canals and was intrigued by mass manufacturing of gun parts in a factory, a breakthrough that he recognized as significant and reported on to John Jay for the edification of Congress. He also spent freely on scientific instruments, including an "air pump"—vacuum apparatus—and hygrometers that he had modified so he could distribute them to American friends for the purpose of making comparative observations. He would read of a particular device in a book such as *Philosophica Britania,* which described an author's course of lectures; he would then find such an instrument, either in a manufacturer's catalog or shop, and order it or have a new one made, often with modifications to meet his measurement needs. His excessive spending on these instruments contributed substantially to his fiscal bankruptcy.[11]

On a seven-week garden tour of Great Britain with Adams, Jefferson became a convert to the "georgic" ethic. Based on Virgil's poem about agriculture, and popularized by the British writer Arthur Young, the georgic ethic, according to historian of agriculture Benjamin Cohen, was an "agrarian and environmental ethic combining cultural and material values. . . . The georgic approach emphasized the dual development of intellectual work and physical work as another way to treat moral and material pursuits as of a piece." American versions of the georgic ethic existed in such books as *Practical Farmer, Being a New and Compendious System of Husbandry, Adapted to the Different Soils and Climates of America,* and *The New England Farmer, or Georgical Dictionary.* Washington and Jefferson owned multiple copies of those titles and gave them as instruction to their farm supervisors.[12]

UPON HIS RETURN to Mount Vernon in 1783 after an absence of six years, Washington was appalled at the degree to which his farms and holdings had been neglected during the war and determined to make them more modern and profitable. "The bed of the Potomac before my door, contains an inexhaustable fund of manure . . . if I could adopt an easy, simple, and expeditious method of raising, and taking it to the Land,"[13] he wrote. He thought he'd found a way in "the Hippopotamus," a special dredge developed with a grant from the APS. When Washington could not obtain that machine, he borrowed a scow and had mud raised from the riverbed and carefully placed on one field, to do what Arthur Young had recommended in a letter, "make a full experiment on a small scale." Washington was so obsessed with manure that he tried many such experiments and looked to hire the sort of farm manger, as he wrote to Young, who could "convert everything he touches into manure, as the first transmutation into Gold."[14]

"The spectacle of a great commander retiring . . . from the head of a victorious army to the amusements of agriculture," Young wrote back, "calls all the feelings of my bosom into play & gives me the strongest inclination . . . to contribute to the success of so laudable a pleasure. . . . Your expression concerning manure being the first transmutation towards gold, is good, and shews that you may be as great a farmer as a general." They commenced a correspondence so extensive that after Washington's death the British agriculturalist would print it as a separate volume.[15] Washington found Young's works to be so valuable that he copied portions into his notes and diaries as instructions for better farming. After the British "bailiff"—farm manager—reached Mount Vernon and started work, the general remained in close touch with farming, production, and experiment on his substantial holdings. He invented a device to aid in sowing seeds, which he labeled a "drill plow." A barrel containing seeds was attached to a plow and rotated when the plow was driven forward; as the barrel turned, seeds dropped from it through pipes into the plowed ground. A typical diary entry reveals Washington covering his

usual twenty miles a day on horseback, stopping to see his fishing operation, three of his plantation's five farms, observing work with the "drill
plow," the growth stages of oats, barley, and wheat, having an extended
conversation with a neighbor on how to grow potatoes, and agreeing to
sell to a visitor several thousand acres of his Pennsylvania holdings.[16] "Every experiment is a treasure," he wrote to an old friend. Accordingly, he
designed a sixteen-sided barn with an internal threshing floor.

ONCE JEFFERSON WAS SETTLED in Paris, Benjamin Franklin
returned home. On the voyage, he wrote two scientific essays, one on heat
flow in chimneys and the other on how the Atlantic's water flows affected
navigation, and he started formulating a third on applying steam power
to navigation. Although nearly eighty, he was selected as president of
Pennsylvania, and his presence reinvigorated the American Philosophical
Society.

The Philadelphia scientific community was changing. Will Bartram
had assumed the mantle of chief botanist while a brother ran the import-
export business; Will's drawings were sought after, and he readied for
publication his major work, the account of his travels in Georgia and the
Floridas. He began to have disciples, among them Benjamin Smith Barton, a Rittenhouse nephew. Rittenhouse, in an article for the *Columbian
Magazine* in 1786, demonstrated that the scientific purview of the Philadelphia scientific community was expanding beyond astronomy: "The
several ranges of earths, stones, and minerals, as we now observe them
in [Pennsylvania], I have long since thought by far too irregular to be the
same in which they were originally formed." He now believed that the
earth was "once in fluid state" and had then settled, shaped by gravity. As
evidence he cited layers of stones extruding at angles. "I have long since
considered these prodigious ranges of hills . . . as the edges of huge cakes
thrown aloft; whilst far the greater part of the cake sunk down into the
interior fluid."[17]

Benjamin Rush, despite his fidelity to biblical ideals of morality and
conduct, now agreed with Rittenhouse on geological matters and was expanding his outlook in other ways. Having distanced himself from the
Calvinistic predetermination that he had embraced since childhood, in
the postwar ferment he spread an inclusionary gospel, in part by founding colleges. To complete the revolutionary process, he believed, required

the turning of ordinary uneducated farmers into literate aware citizens trained to make good decisions. As Rush's former student, physician and historian David Ramsay, was warning him just then, "The Revolution has introduced so much anarchy that it will take half a century to eradicate the licentiousness of the people."[18] To counter it, Rush worked hard to establish Dickinson College in Carlisle and, to a lesser degree, the college that became Franklin and Marshall. In his plan for Dickinson, Rush observed:

> Europe in its present state of political torpor affords no scope for the activity of a benevolent mind. Here everything is in a plastic state. . . . Human nature here (unsubdued by the tyranny of European habits and customs) yields to reason, justice, and common sense. . . . America seems destined by heaven to exhibit to the world the perfection which the mind of man is capable of receiving from the combined operations of liberty, learning, and the gospel upon it.

Among his innovations were the elimination of the study of Greek and Latin, the banishing of alcoholic spirits, and studying the sciences in conjunction with Christian ethics: "Religion is necessary to correct the effects of learning. Without religion I believe learning does real mischief to the morals and principles of mankind; a mode of worship is necessary to support religion; and education is the surest way of producing a preference and constant attachment to a mode of worship."[19]

The impulse to have educational institutions teach the natural sciences also animated the university in Providence that was to be upgraded and renamed as Brown; the first five professors hired were all scientists, among them the young physician Benjamin Waterhouse. One of his colleagues, Peres Fobes, argued that the college's board must spend freely to acquire natural philosophy apparatus and accompanying books—or continue to lose the most promising students to Harvard: "The popularity of Cambridge College, especially on account of its Apparatus, operated as an Insuperable Objection against procuring schollars for providence college, nor cod I devise any other method of removing the objection, but by providing an Apparatus, by which all the experiments in natural Philosophy done at Cambridge, cod be exhibited to the schollars at R. I. college."[20]

IN HIS YOUTH, Charles Willson Peale had been a saddler and a watchrepairer and had dabbled in other manual trades before his talent as a painter was recognized and he was sent to England to burnish it. Returning to Philadelphia as an accomplished portraitist, during the Revolution he completed portraits of many of its leaders and served in the army. He greeted the war's official end with a paper, wood, and painted Arch of Triumph. In the postwar era, he too began to alter his ways in the direction of scientific and technological endeavor. As the new owner of a downtown property vacated by a Tory, he used it to display portraits of American heroes and expanded his presentations to include sketches of Dr. Morgan's collection of fossil bones from Big Bone Lick. Those had been commissioned by a German collector who wanted images to take home. Along with the sketches and the bones, when they were in temporary residence, Peale offered a four-foot-long "paddlefish" donated by mathematician Robert Patterson. To this mix he then added "moving pictures," transparencies that with a switch in lighting from one to another appeared to move, and charged 25¢ admission. From these displays, mounted with increasing theatricality, it was just a short leap to dioramas of stuffed wild animals in their "natural" contexts—and the beginnings of America's first natural history museum.[21]

The Revolutionary War–era leader whose life was the most uprooted by peace was Tom Paine. In dire financial straits, suffering inordinate difficulties in claiming recompense for service during the Revolution, he turned his mind to invention. He collaborated with Rittenhouse to determine whether the air emitted by a combustible substance was flammable, even in a vacuum. It was. The pair exploded various substances, including sawdust. Inventing a smokeless candle, Paine sent some to Franklin, accompanied by a letter that mused, "I have often observed that by lending words for my Thoughts I understand my thoughts the better—that they are a kind of mental smoke which requires words to illuminate them." Puns on "smoke" and "smokeless" reflected Paine's insider understanding of how best to get Franklin to pay attention. Six months later, Paine dispatched to him wooden and cast-iron models of a several-hundred-foot-span iron bridge, to be made with a metal arch that would stretch farther than any then made of wood or stone. "It would, I believe, be the most extensive arch in the world, and the longest bridge without piers. I should therefore wish to see it undertaken and performed during your Presidency [of Pennsylvania]." American rivers often froze over during winter, which precluded adopting designs of bridges with piers, which worked well in the warmer climate of Europe. Paine continued to refine the idea, delivering a third, larger iron model to Franklin's home that was soon put on public display in the statehouse. However, during the postwar economic downturn, Pennsylvania exhibited no official appetite for such an expensive experiment.[22]

Shortly, Paine took the design and models to France, where he and Jefferson worked on them, the Virginian liking the "Catenarian arch," a rare architectural form. Jefferson was unable to convince the French government to build the bridge and suggested Paine might do better in Great Britain. Hesitant to return to the land of his birth, he nonetheless did, and continued to trade letters with Jefferson about it. "You mention that instead of arranging your tubes and bolts as ordinates to the cord of the arch, you had reverted to your first idea, of arranging them in the direction of the radii," Jefferson wrote. "I am sure it will gain, both in beauty and strength. It is true that the divergence of those radii recurs as a difficulty, in getting the rails on upon the bolts; but I thought this fully removed by the answer you first gave me . . . that you should place the rails first, and drive the bolts through them, and not, as I had imagined, place the bolts first, and put the rails on them."[23] When Paine returned to France, the bridge had not yet been built.

"HE THAT STUDIES and writes on the improvements of the arts and sciences labours to benefit generations yet unborn, for it is not probable that his contemporaries will pay any attention to him." That was the story of his life, Oliver Evans believed, and would enshrine the bitter lesson on the last bank page of his final book, *The Abortion of the Young Steam Engineer's Guide*. Prior to the war, when we was in his early twenties, Evans had invented a way of making fine wire, and from it card teeth for manufacturing machines. He had not sought patents for the process, believing then that it was immoral to benefit from inventions—Franklin's credo, and also Jefferson's. But others profited from Evans's ingenuity and so, during the interregnum, when he designed a way to use steam power to move machinery, he obtained a patent from Maryland. By then he had already made preliminary designs and paper models for his most technologically complex invention, a fully mechanized, integrated grist-mill. Its five machines, he wrote, "perform every necessary movement of the grain, and meal, from one part of the mill to another, or from one machine to another, through all the various operations from the time the grain is emptied from the wagoner's bag . . . until it be completely manufactured into flour . . . without the aid of manual labour." He operated such a mill at Red Clay Creek in Delaware while applying for patents from Pennsylvania and Delaware. Those in hand, he took a trip of a thousand miles along the Atlantic Coast, but did not receive a single order. His problem, in part, was the inadequacy of patent protection, which was obtained on a state-by-state basis and only for limited duration; another part was the absence of enforcement provisions, which permitted illegal copying of inventions without punishment or compensation for the inventor or licensee. In time, however, Evans's automated flour mill would catch on and revolutionize the production of flour.[24]

IN THE FALL OF 1784, Washington felt comfortable enough to leave Mount Vernon for an extended trip west along the Potomac to visit the thousands of acres he owned in Pennsylvania and Western Virginia, and to scout—as he had in his youth as a surveyor, and again on his trip to join the British forces—the possibilities for a through route to Pittsburgh. The headwaters of the Potomac and the Ohio were not far separated and might be connectable by canal. He sought "to facilitate . . . the Inland Navigation of the Potomack," and wrote to Lafayette of his vision of proceeding from Pittsburgh up into Canada and down to New Orleans: "A great tour this, you will say, probably it will take place no where but in imagination." He also discussed it at length with Jefferson, who enthusiastically agreed with the objective of uniting the geographical sectors and connecting the inland ones to the ocean. To Madison, Washington insisted that Virginia must soon start the canal project to beat out a competing canal route planned by Pennsylvania, to connect Philadelphia with the Susquehanna River, for which the two states had been quoted what Washington considered a moderate price. Canals were the key, he was convinced.[25]

Washington visited the town of Bath, Virginia, where he owned property, and happened to stay overnight at an inn owned by inventor James Rumsey, who showed him a working model of a paddle-propelled boat that could make headway against the currents. Washington leapt at the idea. As he recorded in his diary, Rumsey not only displayed the model, but "the principles of this [mechanism] were . . . exhibited in practice in privacy under the injunction of secrecy [until a patent could be obtained]. . . . The model . . . not only convinced me of what I before thought next to, if not quite impracticable, but that it might be to the greatest possible utility in inland navigation."[26]

As was true of nearly all of the important inventors in this era, Rumsey had grown up on a farm. When Washington encountered him, he was forty-one, had acquired a mill as well as an interest in an ironworks, and had become a mechanical engineering genius—the greatest in America, Jefferson would later argue. His boat model worked with poles attached to paddles. Washington hired Rumsey to build a house and stable on his property, gave him a recommendation, and filled him in on his project to make the Potomac navigable into its far upstream reaches.[27]

In early 1785, the James River and Potomac Canal Company was formed, and the Virginia Assembly, knowing of Washington's interest in the subject, sought to present him with 150 shares. As Wood writes, this offer "led him into temptation . . . and it was agony. . . . Few decisions in Washington's career caused him more distress." To accept the shares, Washington reasoned, would be tantamount to taking pay for services rendered, which he had sworn not to do and had never done—but he was a passionate enthusiast for the project. Jefferson and Madison's advice provided a way through the dilemma; Washington accepted the shares but immediately donated them to a college that became Washington and Lee.[28] He then threw himself into the Potomac project, becoming president of the canal companies and hiring Rumsey to oversee the work of clearing rocks from the river near Harpers Ferry. While doing so, both hoped, Rumsey would also have the opportunity to test his boat. During a very difficult year on the job, directing a hundred laborers, Rumsey quickly realized that his initial design for the boat was too limited and determined to use steam power to move the poles. He soon abandoned poles altogether as they caused the boat to veer off-center in fast waters, but he could not quite get right the use of water to fuel the steam boiler.

From Paris, Jefferson wrote to a medical doctor in North Carolina who sought his commitment to a canal in the Dismal Swamp area, "It is the only speculation in my life I have decidedly wished to be engaged in. The uniting the navigation of Chesapeak and the Sound renders the enterprize so interesting to the public as well as the adventurers that the embarking in it can never admit a reproach. Whenever it shall be concluded I will pointedly answer your draught for the price . . . I trust that neither [state legislature] will hesitate to give just privileges to the adventurers."[29]

Not long after Washington had given his blessing to Rumsey's steam-powered boat, the general was approached by another inventor, John Fitch, with a somewhat similar scheme. Washington turned him down, citing his extant promise to Rumsey. It may have mattered to Washington, writes Andrea Sutcliffe in her history of the American steamboat, "that Rumsey was a well-dressed, well-mannered southern gentleman, while Fitch was a straight-talking New Englander in threadbare clothes." In Philadelphia, Fitch visited Franklin, who put him off with vague compliments, saying he was preparing to deliver his own paper on steamboats and hadn't yet made up his mind exactly which mechanism he would recommend; and in Lancaster Fitch was shrugged off by William Henry, inventor of the screw auger, who dismissed Fitch's ideas as reminiscent of the "nonsensical" ones of Paine and Rittenhouse when they had stayed with him during the war. Petitioning the Continental Congress, then sitting in New York, Fitch made another error, telling some members his boat would be of use in conquering the Mississippi River, too far away to be of interest to them. Unable to obtain a Boulton-Watt steam engine, whose export was forbidden by the British government, Fitch nonetheless found a way to build a similar engine and tried to use it to power a boat.[30]

IN EUROPE, JOHN ADAMS HAD BEEN an assiduous visitor to science displays, and when posted to London he took in the British Museum, which included among the 71,000 items some that had been sent by John Bartram and other Americans to Sir Hans Sloane, whose collections formed the nucleus of the museum. As ambassador to the Court of St. James's, Adams was repeatedly subjected to shabby treatment. His dolor was momentarily relieved by a scientist whose work he had admired, Royal Astronomer William Herschel, whose recent books on double stars and the configuration of the Milky Way Adams had bought. Herschel received Adams with the respect due a student of John Winthrop. Adams's daughter, Nabby, wrote in her diary that the visit was deeply satisfying for her father. And Adams, in a "ramble" of a letter to his physician cousin expressed his frustration with London as well as his admiration for Herschel and science in general:

> Neither History nor Poetry, or any Thing but Painting and Musick, Balls
> and Spectacles, are in vogue. . . . Philosophy itself has become a Fop gam-
> bolling in a Balloon. . . . Herschell indeed with his new Glass, has discov-
> ered the most magnificent Spectacle that ever was seen or imagined, and I
> suppose it is chiefly as a Spectacle that his Discovery is admired. If all those
> Single double, tripple quadruple Worlds are peopled as fully as every leaf
> and drop is in this, what a merry Company there is of Us, in the Universe?
> All fellow Creatures Insects Animalcules and all. . . . fancy We shall know
> each other better, and shall see that even . . . dancing Dogs, learned Piggs,
> scientific Birds &c are not so despicable Things as We . . . sometimes think
> them. The Bishop of Landaff, has made the Trees, not walk, but feel and
> think, and why should We not at once settle it that every Attom, thinks
> and feels?[31]

In 1785, the American scientific society that Adams had helped bring into existence, the American Academy, issued its first volume of *Memoirs,* a 600-page tome introduced by an essay touting its practical tone, apologizing if any of the articles "contain deep speculation," and assuring readers that the criterion for choosing papers was to present those that "may eventually tend to the security and welfare" of Americans, as well as to "the extension of . . . commerce and the improvement of those arts which adorn and embellish life." The speculations included James Bowdoin's theory of the origin of light—even more dismissible than Cadwallader Colden's theory of gravity had been—and very good essays on botany and on the chemical composition of the water in Boston's harbor.

SIMULTANEOUSLY WITH THESE EVENTS, evidence had been mounting that a loose confederation of states was inadequate to the task of governing a fast-growing country. Meetings of the Confederation's deliberative body were sporadic and often unproductive, as nothing could be done unless nine of the thirteen state delegations showed up, which they seldom did. Shays' Rebellion (1786–1787), in which Revolutionary War veterans whose farms had been seized for non-payment of taxes made an uprising that roiled western Massachusetts and adjoining parts of New York and Vermont, was difficult to quell because of state rivalries. Such matters highlighted the need for adjustments to the hypothesis. The configuration would still be a democracy, but a stronger central authority would be able to cross state lines to protect against internal dissident groups, to regulate interstate commerce, and to issue a standard currency—Virginia's pound then contained 10 percent more silver than Pennsylvania's. The evidence had shown an allied need for a strong chief executive—not for a king, but for the people's supreme representative. The Revolution's basic hypothesis, that men were capable of self-government, had certainly been affirmed; but there had been enough difficulties attendant on the current configuration of that governance to warrant a midcourse correction. To codify it, a Constitutional Convention was scheduled for 1787.

The problems of the confederate configuration spurred Adams, principal author of an acknowledged better governing instrument, the Massachusetts constitution, to hastily write a three-volume *Defence of the Constitutions* while he was in Great Britain. Based on his studies of state constitutions, it specifically refuted the ideas for changes in governance being put forth by French and British writers and by Franklin and Paine. In important ways, Adams's *Defence,* like Jefferson's Declaration, was the product of scientific conceptions, analogies, and evaluation strategies. Viewing the problem to be solved as how men should be governed, Adams researched prior monarchic, oligarchic, and democratic societies, derived lessons from their successes and failures, and constructed a revised theory of democratic governance. It included a federal government that could overrule those of the states, a moderately powerful federal chief executive, a bicameral national legislature, an independent courts system, and—above all—a balance of power among these three branches as the best guarantor that the rights and needs of the general public would be continually and helpfully served.

Many readers of Adams's *Defence* thought the balance of power idea was scientific in nature. I. B. Cohen points out that Adams's understanding of Newton was in error and that his notions drew more on hazy student perceptions of the field of "statics"—on mere mechanical principles rather than on Newton's celestial ones.[32] But Adams had not set out to echo Newton in political form; rather, his *Defence* consciously drew on what laymen believed that Newton had achieved, the promulgation of a set of "laws" that perfectly explained and properly governed the physical behavior of the universe. That understanding affected Adams's description of a perhaps unachievable ideal government, "brought to as great a degree of perfection [and] as near to the character of governments of laws and not of men" as was humanly possible, in part through a "knowledge of the principles and construction" that underlay those laws. Adams argued that the establishing of an independent United States of America had already provided evidence that a government could be successfully "erected on the simple principles of nature [and] contrived merely by the use of reason and the senses, as Copley painted Chatham . . . as Dwight, Barlow, Trumbull and Humphreys composed their verse . . . as Godfrey invented his quadrant, and Rittenhouse his planetarium, as Boylston practiced inoculation, and Franklin electricity; as Paine exposed the mistakes of Raynal, and Jefferson those of Buffon." He continued: "A prospect into futurity in America is like contemplating the heavens through the telescopes of Herschel. Objects stupendous in their magnitudes and motions strike us from all quarters and fill us with amazement." At various other junctures in the *Defence,* Adams used scientific analogies, for instance in writing that if executive power was left to a democratic assembly instead of being vested in an executive, "it will corrupt the legislature as necessarily as rust corrupts iron, or as arsenic poisons the human body." His stated aims in writing his *Defence* were the same as those of scientists in designing critical experiments—to dispel "artifice, imposture, hypocrisy, and superstition," in his case, of the sort of falsities that had too often been used to legitimatize forms of government other than a balance-of-forces democracy.[33]

Adams was particularly incensed by the inadequacies of proposals then in vogue, those of Franklin, Paine, and French economist Jacques Turgot, which called for unicameral legislatures and weak chief executives. Adams insisted that executive, legislative, and judicial branches must have nearly equal shares of power so that each could counter another's potential bad decisions. As David McCullough observes, Adams used the English constitution as his model, "knowing he would be taken to task for it" but embracing its balance of forces.[34] Jefferson in Paris, to whom Adams sent the book, and Madison and Rush in Philadelphia, where the Constitutional Convention was gathering in the summer of 1787, praised Adams's *Defence* and wrote of its salutary effects on the deliberations of the delegates who had come to the capital to replace the outdated Articles of Confederation.

IT WAS TIME FOR THE FOUNDERS to refine the governing hypothesis by incorporating the lessons of experience. Central to that process were a most extensive set of researches, the products of an investigation conducted by James Madison over the course of two years to identify the "vices" of the Confederation and the precedents in "virtue" in the operations of prior governments in history. Madison's research became the basis of many proposed clauses in the Constitution.[35]

The delegates to the Convention worked on a relaxed schedule that afforded time for viewing and hearing the many demonstrations, such as the Fitch and Rumsey steamboat models, and an entire textile manufactory just begun by Tench Coxe's Pennsylvania Society for the Encouragement of Manufactures and the Useful Arts (PSEUMA). Coxe spoke to a group—the Society for Political Inquiries—at Franklin's home and repeated his speech, at Rush's request, to the PSEMUA on August 9, 1787, while the Convention met across town. "You have exhibited to the world a spectacle of magnanimity in war; suffer not yourselves to be pointed at for imbecility in peace," which imbecility, Coxe explained, meant continuing their "bias" against manufacturing. To support the legislators, he asserted, all private citizens had to make "corresponding exertions . . . reject the use of all foreign manufactures which are superfluous; and employ your own people as much as possible in making those which are necessary." Coxe suggested premiums for inventions and "liberal rewards in land" for those who set up factories and in other ways helped the economy along.[36] Historian Leo Marx argues that Coxe was articulating "a prophetic vision of machine technology as the fulcrum of national power" and that he saw the "peculiar affinities between the machine and the New World setting in its entirety: geographical, political, social, and . . . cultural."[37]

Washington had been persuaded to chair the convention, which he had not wanted to attend, out of a concern that some delegates would construe his absence as reason not to replace the Confederation with a better governing structure. He contributed to Constitution-building in other ways, his exhorting of Maryland, Virginia, and Pennsylvania to cooperate across state borders, essential to his plan for conquering and exploiting the Potomac, pointing the way toward the key constitutional principle, interstate cooperation for the benefit of the whole nation.

Several of the proposed provisions of the new Constitution directly involved science—those regarding coinage, weights and measures, and the census—whose supervision required expertise in mathematics and metallurgy and future experimentation to determine the exact ratios of metals for each coin denomination. The most significant debate regarding science and technology involved attempts to have the new federal government provide protection to inventors, superseding the state-by-state patent or license practice. Franklin, present at the convention but mostly silent, and Jefferson, still in Paris, had articulated the position that there should be no patents because inventions ought to be for the benefit of mankind. But in recent years Jefferson had softened his opposition, having been led to understand that inventors who were not, as he was, men of wealth, needed such protections to raise money to have their inventions manufactured and be of use to society. Madison now advanced that revised viewpoint in discussing his own proposal and one by Charles Pinckney of South Carolina. He and Pinckney were frequently at odds, but on this matter they agreed. The lack of nationwide patent protection was among the "vices" of the Confederation in Madison's painstaking research. He put forward a plan to "encourage by premiums and provisions, the advancement of useful knowledge and discoveries." Pinckney's original plan had included governmentally supported "seminaries" to advance science and the arts and "to establish public institutions rewards and immunities for the promotion of agriculture, commerce, trades, and manufactures."

The advocacy of Pinckney and Madison went too far in the estimate of Roger Sherman of Connecticut and others who feared federal encroachment on state prerogatives—the issue on which the delegates had the most difficulty in achieving consensus.[38] As a result of this overarching debate, and the need to achieve consensus, the national university idea went by the boards, as did specific provisions for premiums. As eventually agreed to, a clause in Article I, Section VIII, known as the "commerce clause," stated that Congress had the power "to promote the Progress of Science and useful Arts, by securing for limited Times to Authors and Inventors the exclusive Right to their respective Writings and Discoveries." The word "patent" was deliberately avoided as it implied a connection with the British patent system, a royal prerogative that had been used to advance the interests of monopolies and corporate entities rather than those of inventors.[39]

In the race to demonstrate a steamboat, Fitch won, putting *Persever-ance,* a working model, into the Delaware for this most important audience. The boat worked by means of steam-powered banks of oars and was no small affair, able to carry passengers. He invited all delegates to ride in it, and some did, while many more lined the banks and watched the successful demonstration. Fitch's steamboat thus beat out Rumsey's, which had been delayed for technical reasons.

In mid-July the Convention deadlocked over rival plans for a new government. A trip to Bartram's Gardens had been scheduled for the delegates, and nearly a dozen, including Hamilton and Madison, took carriages and a ferry to Will Bartram's. They were charmed and amazed by a garden that transcended regional boundaries in its grand collection of plants and whose crowning glory was the plant that John Bartram had named for Franklin, too ill that day to accompany the delegates. Upon their return to the Convention, these attendees at Bartram's were the ones who brokered the compromise that ended the deadlock. Franklin rose from his sickbed to give the convention's final speech, urging that the Constitution be adopted unanimously so that it would have greater weight with the citizenry. In a possibly apocryphal incident reported to have taken place on a Philadelphia street after the convention's close, Franklin was asked by a woman what sort of government the new country would have, a monarchy or a republic, and responded, "A republic, if you can keep it."

WASHINGTON EXPLAINED to a learned friend: "Should the proposed government be generally and harmoniously adopted, it will be a new phenomenon in the political & moral world; and an astonishing victory gained by enlightened reason over brute force."[40] But its ratification was far from assured and hung fire in several states. One factor in its eventual acceptance were the eighty-five essays of the *Federalist Papers,* written mostly by Hamilton and Madison, that appeared in newspapers between October 1787 and August 1788. Numbers 11 and 51 deal specifically with aspects of science, the first drawing on still-extant populist anger against the slurs of Buffon, Raynal, and others; and the second using the John

Adams way of referencing Newtonian and other physics ideas to champion the naturalness of the proposed new system of checks and balances for governmental structures. Historian Pauline Maier argues that the *Federalist Papers* did not make much of an impact beyond New York. The deciding factors were the understanding that the needs and imperatives of the people as a whole, rather than those of the citizens of any particular state, should control the destiny of all—and the unwavering support of ratification by George Washington.[41]

Nine of the thirteen states had to officially ratify the Constitution before it could take effect, and in each state that did so, there were celebratory events, culminating in "Federal Processions" in Charleston, Baltimore, New York, Boston, and Portsmouth. While Virginia and New York had endured tremendous debates in which the outcome remained in doubt for some time, Pennsylvania had not, and by the time Pennsylvania ratified, nine other states had assured adoption, and so Pennsylvania held the grandest celebration of all—on July 4, 1788. Historian Laura Rigal suggests that it was an astonishing projection of a desired American future, emphasizing that artisanship, science, and manufacturing were as basic to the country as political freedom and independence. Rush wrote a long report of it in an anonymous letter published in the *American Museum*. He billed the occasion as a way "to celebrate a triumph of knowledge over ignorance, of virtue over vice, and of liberty over slavery." Forty-five different crafts marched, many with floats displaying artisanry in action—cordwainers cobbling shoes, sailmakers darning, blacksmiths clanging horseshoes—as well as working cotton-spinning and -manufacturing machines. Above a textile-manufacturing float was a banner, "May the Union Government Protect the Manufacturers of America." The presence of a large fraction of the population, between 10,000 marchers (and 17,000 onlookers) from a city of 28,000, demonstrated not only freedom and republicanism but also, Rush wrote, America as a classless society. "The Grand Federal Edifice or *The New Roof*" was an actual structure supported by thirteen columns—ten finished (representing the ten ratifications) and three unfinished, with a cupola supporting the goddess Plenty and her cornucopia.[42]

The evidence-based spirit in which the Constitution had been constructed, the debates over its adoption, and the symbolism accompanying its acceptance all emphasized the process by which the old hypothesis about how the best government ought to work had been tested, the positive and negative results of experience incorporated into a revised theory, and that theory newly codified and promulgated. In the future, should the Constitution, that embodiment of the theory, not prove able to best govern the country, it would be similarly refined to take into account new facts—that was the way science proceeded, and it was to be the American way.

ELEVEN

PATENTS, INNOVATIONS,
and FIRST STEPS

FREED FROM THE RESTRAINTS OF WAR AND STATE
agendas and enabled by a new Constitution, the government of the United
States of America took important structural steps to enhance growth.
During the administrations of George Washington and John Adams,
the number of post offices increased twelve-fold, the amount of mail per
capita five-fold. "Critical to extending trade by transmitting business
correspondence and bills of exchange, the [postal] system also transmitted technological knowledge," writes a historian of technology. Further
impetus came from having a standard coinage and standardized weights
and measures and from utilizing the information from the first census
(1790).[1]

The United States possessed three distinct advantages over Great Britain and European rivals. First, businesses in America operated with fewer
constricting circumstances—no religious and other kinds of persecution,
no high rates of conscription, no confiscation of assets, no excessive rents.
Second, the United States was richer in natural resources, such as its endless forests, rivers and falls, ample arable land, and significant deposits of
iron ore and other minerals. The third resource was that large fraction
of the American populace possessing an ingrained competence in dealing with machinery, "whittling boys" who had learned on the farm to

handle many rudimentary technologies and grown up to be what St. John de Crèvecouer called "universal fabricator[s] . . . skilful enough to use [tools] with some dexterity in mending and making whatever is wanted." They were supplemented in the factories by a flood of craftsmen from Europe, already knowledgeable in the use of manufacturing machinery, most of it British and frequently obtained illicitly since the British embargoed the export of both such men and such machinery. Samuel Slater, after an apprenticeship in an Arkwright frame mill, came to the United States in 1789—in the guise of a farmer so he would not be stopped—having memorized the workings of the mill so that he could reproduce its machinery. George and Isaac Hodgson of Manchester disguised their tools as fruit trees to make their way to Brandywine Creek, near Wilmington, where some 500 people in twenty-six different occupations already worked in a cluster of two dozen small manufactures for paper, flour, lumber, gunpowder, tobacco, and textiles. The Hodgsons located a tool-making factory there. Because of the availability of such workmen, E. I. DuPont would also establish there his gunpowder-making facility.[2]

IN THE MONTHS before George Washington was due to take office as president he was engaged, he wrote Jefferson, in pursuing what he gleaned from the populace to be utmost in its mind, "manufactures & inland navigation." Washington touted his forthcoming visit to a glassworks that could end America's need to import glass, wonderful new surveys from which canal routes and highways could be fashioned, and the enhancement of cotton production through new agricultural techniques.[3]

At his inauguration on April 30, 1789, Washington reiterated his belief that "the preservation of the sacred fire of liberty, and the destiny of the Republican model of Government, are justly considered as deeply, perhaps as finally staked, on the experiment entrusted to the hands of the American people."

In Paris, Jefferson still had not made up his mind whether or not to accept the post of secretary of state. A revolution was brewing in France; the Estates-General were gathering for the first time since 1614 to alter the government in the direction already taken by the American experiment in democracy. While awaiting events, Jefferson requested of painter John Trumbull a triple portrait of Bacon, Newton, and Locke, "the three

greatest men that ever lived . . . having laid the foundation of those super-
structures which have been raised in the Physical and Moral sciences."
Thanking the president of Harvard for an honorary degree—"this notice
from so eminent a seat of science is very precious to me"—Jefferson cited
American science-based accomplishments to date, the not-yet-completed
but marvelously designed Paine's bridge, and Rumsey's steamboat, then
nearing a European trial, the product of "the most original and the greatest mechanical genius I have ever seen," as prelude to touting the sciences
as the route to the future:

> What a field have we at our doors to signalize ourselves in! The botany of
> America is far from being exhausted: it's Mineralogy is untouched, and it's
> Natural history or Zoology totally mistaken and misrepresented. . . . It is
> the work to which the young men, whom you are forming, should lay their
> hands. We have spent the prime of our lives in procuring them the precious
> blessing of liberty. Let them spend theirs in shewing that it is the great par-
> ent of science and of virtue; and that a nation will be great in both always
> in proportion as it is free.[4]

The first nine months of Washington's administration were consumed
with establishing administrative offices and readying legislation, including a patent law, to be introduced at the forthcoming winter session of
Congress. On January 8, 1790, Washington previewed its rationale in the
first state of the union message:

> I cannot forbear intimating to you the expedience of giving effectual en-
> couragement . . . to the introduction of new and useful inventions from
> abroad, as to the exertions of skill and genius in producing them at
> home. . . . There is nothing that can better deserve your patronage, than the
> promotion of science and literature. Knowledge is in every country the sur-
> est basis of publick happiness. In one, in which the measures of government
> receive their impressions so immediately from the sense of the community,
> as in ours, it is proportionately essential.[5]

The dawn of the age in which science's practical side predominated in
America coincided with the passing of the Founder who had most advocated it, Benjamin Franklin. His death in 1790 occasioned pageantry as

well as mourning, but also a sense that Franklin, as ever, had good timing in his exit—when his ideas had become so much a part of public life that they were no longer attributed to him.

To evaluate all patent applications, the legislation established a Cabinet-level Committee for the Promotion of Useful Arts—the secretary of state, the secretary of war, and the attorney general; two votes were required to award a patent. Jefferson and Secretary of War Henry Knox were knowledgeable about technology, and Attorney General Edmund Randolph had learned basic science at William & Mary. For them to consider a machine for a patent, it had to be broadly useful, Jefferson later recalled; the right of any man to use it "ought not to be taken from him and given to a monopolist," nor could a patent be obtained merely by changing the material used from a previous version.[6] The examination process differentiated the American from the European patent processes, which had no examinations and therefore, according to historian of intellectual property B. Zorina Khan, were tilted toward the elite. "Instead," Khan writes, "the United States consciously created patent and copyright institutions that were intended to function as the keystone of a democratic society."[7]

While the three Cabinet officers had no problem issuing the first patent, for a process for manufacturing potash, the committee refused many applications, granting just three in its first year and only fifty-seven in the three years until the law was revised. Most were for eminently practical innovations—punches for typesetting, improvements in distilling liquor and in sinking piles for bridges, the "breaking and swingling" of hemp, a machine for raising the nap on cloth, and improvements in paper molding, sail cloths, and fire retardants.[8]

One early application that gave Jefferson pause was a chemical mixture for the desalination of seawater. He asked the American Philosophical Society to help him evaluate the process. "There is something sublime and pathetic," writes historian A. Hunter Dupree, "in the spectacle of the secretary of state and a battery of professors from the University of Pennsylvania gathered around a distilling apparatus in the secretary's office to test the efficiency of a mixture supposed to help make salt water fresh." The application was rejected since better, lower-cost desalination methods existed. Nonetheless, out of this application came something salutary: Jefferson had the government issue a pamphlet, to be given to all American ships, containing diagrams of how to set up shipboard de-salination machinery.[9]

The most consequential patent considered by the commissioners involved the steamboat. By 1790, Fitch's full-sized *Perseverance II* was regularly ferrying passengers between Philadelphia and Trenton on the Delaware River at about eight miles per hour, fast but not fast enough to make many potential customers choose the boat over the stagecoach for that journey. David Rittenhouse and mathematician Robert Patterson, who had decried an earlier Fitch boat, took passage on the new one and became fans. While Jefferson had been in Europe, he had championed Rumsey's boat to the French government; in America, Rumsey had the backing of a Rumseian Society, many members of which, including Franklin before his death, were also members of the APS.

Fitch's boat was superior to Rumsey's and to those of two other inventors who submitted designs, models, and attestations of worth. However, Jefferson's secretary told them all that the commissioners, considering all of the applications unsatisfactory, would judge them together. After an acrimonious hearing, Jefferson convinced the other committee members that the only fair procedure was to issue patents to all four applicants, dated the same day. As Andrea Sutcliffe writes, "Jefferson's unwillingness to choose one man over the other helped ruin both [Fitch and Rumsey]." Rumsey died shortly thereafter, in December 1792, the day before his *Columbian Maid* was scheduled for a trial in Great Britain; Fitch, mired in financial and legal difficulties, went into a desperate downward spiral and died in 1798 without ever realizing his dream.[10]

WHEN ADAMS AND JEFFERSON first read the Constitution, both were aghast at the absence of safeguards to individual rights. Nothing demonstrates better the willingness of the Founders to make midcourse corrections to their hypothesis of optimal governance than the attempt to add to the Constitution a Bill of Rights. Madison did not initially think such a revision necessary; in the Federalist Papers, he had taken to task Jefferson's notion that governments should be subject to relatively easy repeal and reconsideration, arguing that such ease would lead to insta-bility. Jefferson had famously replied, "No society can make a perpetual constitution, even a perpetual law. The earth belongs always to the living generation."[11] Several years later, Madison had moved toward Jefferson's viewpoint and, over the objections of Hamilton and other Federalists, championed amending legislation. When there was not enough congressional enthusiasm for altering the Constitution piece by piece, Madison proposed a single list of twelve amendments. Washington approved of it in a letter that Madison showed to legislators whose minds had not been made up. In debate, the number of amendments was cut to ten. Congress then passed the Bill of Rights.

To take effect, it still had to be ratified by the states, whose assent was not a given. During this process, and after the government had transferred from New York to Philadelphia in 1791 for an expected decade until the District of Columbia was ready, scientific pursuits came more to the fore. Washington discussed agricultural improvements with experts, worked to establish facilities for manufacturing arms and, when convinced by calculations of the need to include some silver in the nation's first coinage, provided some from his own stash. Rittenhouse, director of the mint for the new government, had also been selected as successor to Franklin as head of the APS; in that position he quickly became more active than Franklin had been in his final years. Jefferson spent time socializing with Rittenhouse and other APS members. He breakfasted occasionally with Rush and read to him an excerpt from his scientific forays in Europe on the cultivation of olive and peach trees in southern France. Rush had become a professor at the University of Pennsylvania's medical school, giving a course of lectures that encompassed his work in mental as well as in physical diseases, and was pressing ahead with crusades for prison reform, abolition of slavery, and temperance. With Charles Willson Peale, Jefferson discussed transforming the artist's museum into more of a national facility and agreed to join its board of visitors.

Jefferson used the APS to investigate science matters that were not considered the business of the federal government, such as farmers' fear of the encroaching Hessian fly. Harmless in its adult form, in larval form it destroyed wheat and, to a lesser extent, barley and rye. "Unless means are discovered to prevent its progress, the whole continent will be overrun— a calamity more to be dreaded than the ravages of war," the *American Museum* warned in 1787. The British refused to buy American wheat out of the worry that the Hessian fly might leap the Atlantic and ravage their crops. An APS committee investigated the pest, and Jefferson, a member, urged the work on: "I long to be free for pursuits of this kind instead of the detestable ones in which I am now labouring without pleasure to myself, or profit to others." He also asked his son-in-law, to whom he had delegated the task of investigating a similar pest, the grain weevil, to try to grow and understand the Hessian fly. Receiving specimen insects in various stages from several correspondents, Jefferson incubated and examined the pest himself.[12]

Jefferson and Madison, with the brief of gathering evidence on the Hessian fly, among other matters, took a one-month tour of the Hudson Valley and New England environs after the close of the congressional session in the spring of 1791. At Jefferson's urging, Madison was now keeping meteorological observations and data on when various vegetables and fruits were ready for the table, crops planted, and various birds first sighted in his fields. Their scientific journey was partly political, stumping for ratification of the Bill of Rights. The Virginians toured farms and forests, lakes and rivers, including the Hudson and Connecticut Rivers and Lakes George and Champlain. Jefferson took notes on types of fish and on the making of maple sap in Vermont; he bought sugar maple trees in several varieties and purchased many other plants for Monticello. He and Madison also interviewed farmers on the Hessian fly, and Jefferson sat with members of the Unquachog tribe, seeking information for his study of Native American languages.[13]

Shortly after Jefferson's return, he received from Benjamin Banneker an "ephemerides" forecasting the positions of all the known elements of the heavens for 1792. Banneker was a freeborn black, a self-taught astronomer employed as a surveyor in laying out the District of Columbia along with his mentor, Andrew Ellicott. He also argued in his August 19, 1791, letter that his calculations (and his use of language) demonstrated conclusively that—contrary to Jefferson's opinion in the *Notes on Virginia*—blacks had as much brainpower as any other race:

> Sir, I suppose that your knowledge of the situation of my brethren is too extensive to need a recital here; neither shall I presume to prescribe methods by which they may be relieved; otherwise than by recommending to you and all others, to wean yourselves from these narrow prejudices which you have imbibed with respect to them, and as Job proposed to his friends "Put your Souls in their Souls stead," thus shall your hearts be enlarged with kindness and benevolence toward them.

Jefferson was impressed. He wrote Banneker a note saying so and forwarded the manuscript to the Marquis de Condorcet in Paris so that he, too, could be impressed.[14]

Condorcet was too busy with the Revolution to reply; he was attempting to incorporate into a new constitution such advanced principles as women's suffrage and opposing the execution of Louis XVI on the grounds that it would be better to enslave him on a galley ship. In hiding to forestall his own beheading, Condorcet wrote a *Sketch for a Historical Picture of the Progress of the Human Spirit,* equating progress with the advance of scientific knowledge and justice. Across the Channel, initial elation at the French Revolution had turned to dismay at the savagery that would culminate in the elevation of a tyrannical Directoire in 1795. Edmund Burke, who had supported the American Revolution, wrote a harsh critique, *Reflections on the Revolution in France.* Thomas Paine responded with a defense of it, the *Rights of Man.* Their debates and the events in France continued to affect the US governmental climate during Washington's first term, underscoring the need to consolidate America's Revolution by building an economy that could sustain political independence and democracy.

AMONG THE EARLIEST PATENTS awarded was that to Oliver Evans for his highly mechanized flour mill; Evans's mills were so efficient that both Washington and Jefferson ordered them, as did a hundred other mill owners. In the ensuing decades nearly all newly built mills incorporated Evans's design improvements and labor-saving devices, and flour-milling became the country's leading industry in terms of the dollar value of goods produced—although not in terms of people employed, for the highly automated mills needed few people to tend them. Evans invented or improved evaporators, steam engines, solar boilers, a hot-air heating system, a machine gun, and a vapor-compression refrigeration machine but made very little money until his book *The Young Mill-wright's Guide* became a bestseller.[15]

Not all inventors attempted to patent their notions; Paine, for instance, simply corresponded with Jefferson about a "geometrical wheelbarrow"—he had seen one advertised and had an idea for a better one—as well as a design to move a wheeled vehicle by explosions of gunpowder more efficiently than by steam.[16]

One of the first literary works copyrighted was William Bartram's *Travels through North and South Carolina, Georgia, East and West Florida.* He had become known to the Natives as "puc puggee," the flower hunter, and his descriptions of native life and customs, as well as of their natural surroundings were so lyrical that they would furnish inspiration to Wordsworth and other Romantic poets. Increasingly confined by ailments, Bartram mentored the next generation of naturalists: Rittenhouse's nephew Benjamin Barton, Bartram's nephew Thomas Say, Henry Muhlenberg, the British illustrator Alexander Wilson, and the French botanist André Michaux. He also wrote an unpublished essay, "The Dignity of Human Nature," arguing against the idea that man is the only animal that can know God: if "divine intelligence . . . penetrates and animates the Univers" and was "the immortal soul of Nature, of living moving beings," then "I cannot be so impious, Nay my Soul revolts, is destroyed, by such conjectures as to desire or imagen, that Man who is guilty of more mischief & Wickedness than all the other Animal together in this World, should be exclusively endued with the knowledge of the Creator."[17]

In May 1790 Alexander Hamilton fired his assistant secretary of the treasury and hired Tench Coxe for that position. The two then collaborated on important enterprises. The Society for Establishing Useful Manufactures, later called "the most ambitious industrial experiment in early American history," aimed at creating an entire manufacturing town—Paterson, New Jersey—and hired a superintendent who had made his reputation stealing British manufacturing secrets and processes and workers who were British artisan refugees. Their second project, based on Coxe's research and earlier papers, was the *Report on Manufactures,* sent to Congress in late 1791. It was the third plant in Hamilton's economic program that included the federal government's assumption of the states' debts from the Revolutionary War and the establishment of a Bank of the United States. His relatively brief *Report on Manufactures* used as its rationale the need to build American capacity to make guns and gunpowder but ranged far beyond that. During the research and writing, Hamilton queried American manufacturers, traders, tax collectors and others whose fingers were on the economy's pulse. He submitted his *Report* accompanied by samples of manufactured goods collected from many different states.[18] The *Report* was a capitalist manifesto, a call for American nationalism, a blueprint for economic progress, and a paean to the possibilities inherent in technology. Hamilton contended that although farming would continue to be the American economy's backbone, to assure independence and economic viability, manufacturing must be more firmly established. His prime example was Slater's technologically advanced textile mill. Hamilton sought to award "bounties"—subsidies—to such enterprises, to punish incoming manufactured goods by prohibitive tariffs, and to build roads and canals to facilitate movement of goods to market. A side benefit to the heightened manufacturing, Hamilton asserted, would be increased numbers of available jobs, many for women and children who were otherwise not contributing to the economy.[19]

The Democrat-Republicans opposed Hamilton's *Report* on multiple grounds, foremost among them the fear of increased federal power over the economy. They also cited social-welfare problems—manufacturing was so overly intertwined with urban crowding and poverty that it seemed to cause them. Moreover, while Jefferson admired the spinning jennies and Evans's mill because they liberated workers from overly laborious tasks, he decried the factory system as the equivalent of feudal serfdom. During the Constitutional Convention, Madison had proposed subsidies for inventors, but he now argued that Hamilton's subsidies would mainly benefit manufacturers and investors, not inventors. The controversy over the *Report* was so severe that the House of Representatives shelved it. Even so, it created a positive climate for the encouragement of manufacturing based on technological processes.

THE PATENT ACT REVISION was signed into law in February 1793, to take effect at the end of the calendar year. Newly hired bureaucrats, with presumably greater expertise than that of Cabinet members, would now process applications—and fewer would be rejected because the revised bill eliminated the requirements that an invention be "sufficiently useful and important" as well as closely examined prior to issuing a patent. "The [new] registration system permitted any inventor to obtain a patent regardless of the fact that he might not have been the original inventor or that his contrivance might not have been useful or novel," the patent office's official history states. "The power of revision and rejection previously exercised . . . was destroyed, [causing] questions of originality, duplication, frivolousness of patent applications. . . . The courts became overwhelmed with patent litigation." Among the frequent litigants was Oliver Evans, who felt that his patents were continuously being impinged upon.[20]

In 1793, Jefferson asked the APS for institutional sponsorship of an ambitious expedition to explore the West. Accordingly, the institution offered a £1000 prize to whoever could travel over land and rivers to the Pacific and return, conveying "information he shall have acquired of the geography of said country, its inhabitants, soil, climate, animals, vegetables, minerals, and other circumstances of note," that would be "interesting to curiosity, to science, and to the future prospects of mankind." André Michaux, who had worked with Bartram and established botanical gardens in South Carolina and New Jersey, was designated to lead the effort. Jefferson had sought such an expedition since 1783, when he discussed it with George Rogers Clark, the highest-ranked army officer in the northwest territories. In 1793, Jefferson turned down the application of Meriwether Lewis, then eighteen, as too inexperienced. But for Michaux he corralled a stellar list of underwriters, led by President Washington ($100), Vice President Adams ($20), himself ($50), Secretary of the Treasury Hamilton ($50), Representative Madison ($20), David Rittenhouse ($50), and John Page ($20).[21]

It was soon learned that Michaux was being manipulated by the French diplomat "Citizen" Edmond-Charles Genêt, who had raised an American fleet, enlisted a battalion of would-be American revolutionaries for France, and descended with them on Philadelphia to pressure the Washington administration into joining France in its war with Great Britain—a position that neither the president nor anyone else in the government, including the Francophile Jefferson, wanted to adopt. Support for Michaux was withdrawn. The expedition floundered. But the notion of sending explorers to examine the West for population expansion and for scientific knowledge of its flora and fauna remained a Jefferson goal.

ELI WHITNEY WORKED CLOSELY with Jefferson before both men left Philadelphia in the summer of 1793, exchanging drafts of design specs and models of Whitney's cotton-cleaning machine in his quest for a patent. After that patent was granted in 1794, the first under the revised law, Whitney's cotton gin became the first transformative product of the government's support of invention. It revolutionized agriculture, making the

South into one of the world's most important cotton-growing areas, and making possible extensive US manufacture of cotton goods.

Born in 1765, Whitney was among the scientific sons of the Revolution who came of age in the 1780s and 1790s. He had attended Yale when Ezra Stiles was the college's dominant force and had studied "Mechanical Powers, Laws of simple and compound motion, Hydrostatics and Hydraulics, Central Forces, Optics, electricity, Chemistry." The Yale laboratory's device of most future use to him was a micrometer, by which he was able to adjust the gauges of his gin. The best cotton, a green-seed variety, was hard to grow and clean—one person could only clean a pound a day. On the Savannah plantation that had been awarded to Revolutionary War General Nathanael Greene, Whitney, befriended by Greene's young widow, Catherine, perfected a mechanical reaper-cleaner. It used sets of teeth on cylinders to separate the seeds from the cotton and a rotating brush to sweep the cotton from the teethed cylinders. With it, as Whitney later wrote, "One man and a horse will do more [in a day] than fifty men with the old machines. It makes the labour fifty times less, without throwing any class of People out of business." Whitney, although poor, was so enthusiastic about its potential that he refused Mrs. Greene's buyout offer of a hundred guineas. He readily found investors who were attracted to the machine's potential not only by the machinery but because the promise of federal tariffs against imported cotton goods enhanced the machine's potential. Jefferson bought a machine as soon as it was manufactured.

Previously, the United States had exported only 138,000 pounds of cotton annually. A year after the Whitney gin patent was awarded, the 1795 treaty with Great Britain, as negotiated by John Jay in London, contained a clause preventing US ships from carrying cotton. But when the Senate took up the treaty, the formerly secret existence of the Whitney machine had become known, and the Senators struck the cotton-carrying provision from the treaty. Whitney's gin did not have many sales in the United States; many farmers refused to pay the high price set for the machine, which included a percentage of the farmer's income from the harvested cotton, and instead bought lower-priced knock-offs and paid no royalties. Like Evans, Fitch, and Rumsey, Whitney never realized much income from his best-known invention.

By a decade after the introduction of the cotton gin, the United States was producing nearly 50 million pounds of cotton a year. Unlike Evans's automated flour mill, which enhanced the flour industry but utilized fewer people to run the machinery, Whitney's invention accelerated the number of people needed to operate the cotton-harvesting industry as growers added to their acreage by cultivating previously unusable fields or buying additional land. To work the added acres, the number of slaves had to be increased.[22]

THE WORST DISEASE OUTBREAK ever to occur in the new nation, the yellow fever epidemic of 1793, began in Philadelphia as July yielded to August. Congress and the president had left town, but most of the 50,000 residents were still there. A prolonged dry spell had exposed mud flats along the Delaware and the Schuylkill, with piles of dead fish, garbage, and huge clouds of insects. A stench on the docks was traced to a rotting sack of coffee beans from Santo Domingo. The first case of fever was reported on August 3, but its exact nature and origin remained unknown. An early victim was Polly Lear, wife of Washington's secretary, Tobias Lear, who lived with the president in Philadelphia. Understanding better than his fellow physicians the gravity of the situation, Benjamin Rush sent his family to the suburbs while he remained to service his patients.

The yellow fever epidemics—for that of 1793 was only one among those impacting the new nation in its first decades—were troubling not only because they caused so many casualties, writes historian Thomas Apel, but also because they spread discord, "and discord to the body politic threatened death to the republic." Annual visitations of disease brought commerce to a halt, produced "burdensome quarantine regulations," the near-total cessation of government operations, "and fostered resentment amongst lower classes, whose impoverishment all but forced them to remain in the diseased environments."[23]

Over the objections of his fellow physicians, on August 29, 1793, Rush made several import assertions in the *American Daily Advertiser:* that there was an epidemic, and not a minor one that might quickly pass or be easily confined; that it was "bilious remitting yellow fever"; and that—contrary to his earlier opinion—its source was not the rotting coffee but the area's own marshes and their "miasmas." Rush's fellow founders of the medical college, as well as the Quaker establishment, thought the scourge might be the plague. The Quakers called it God's punishment for their members having forsaken modest clothing for the fashions worn by many

Congressmen—lace, ruffles, and jeweled shoe buckles; other clergymen saw Philadelphians' refusal to obey God's laws as reason for the divine punishment.

As smoke was the usual tool to ward off miasmas, many people took to chain-smoking cigars while others put their faith in garlic, chewed regularly or inserted into their shoes, or whitewashed their walls and spread vinegar on their floors. Rush did not think such treatments as effective as better hygiene, fresh breezes in infected homes, frequent changes of bed linens, and draining the swamps. It would only be understood decades later that the disease was mosquito-borne—but had the city followed Rush's suggestion to drain swampy areas, there would have been fewer mosquitoes and fewer cases of yellow fever.

The eventual total was 4,044 dead. Infected houses were marked by a small red flag, and blocks of homes were shuttered and empty, their residents dead or having fled. During the epidemic, Rush and his wife exchanged daily letters, Julia reporting the "hard-hearted" measures taken by outlying towns that prevented refugees from the city from finding succor. Rush believed that God preserved him for his purposes, referred to himself in these letters as the equivalent of various biblical personages, and seemed to relish his martyr-like suffering and abuse. "The most offensive thing I did to my brethren was to refuse to consult with them. . . . The sick . . . are always the sufferers or sacrifices by consultations between physicians of opposite principles and practice." Forced to resign from the faculty of the medical school, he sent in his resignation accompanied by a copy of Thomas Sydenham's book, on which he had relied for his identification of the epidemic as of local origin.[24]

THOMAS JEFFERSON, in retirement at Monticello, turned his energies to farming and was soon so engaged, he told Washington, that like a farmer he answered letters only on rainy days. He modified a threshing machine, made more refinements to his moldboard plough, considered and rejected starting a potash-making business, and began a "nailery," utilizing his underage male slaves as the workforce. He traded astronomical and meteorological data with Madison of William and Mary, who had recently been elevated to bishop, and asked him to conduct an experiment on a magnetized instrument for readings of the heavens. Upset about the political shifts in Europe resulting from the upheaval in France, he opined to the bishop, "We had before all our chemistry to learn over again, and also our calendaring time revolutionized. We have now to learn a new system of geography, if the partition of Europe in the papers of the day be authentic. . . . [We] ourselves had set the example of reformation in the principles of politics."

Jefferson's major scientific project was preparing materials on American fossils for a tour d'horizon. In the midst of composing the paper, a correspondent sent him parts of an unusual fossil found beneath the floor of a Virginia limestone cave; Jefferson was certain that the bones were like those of lions and tigers, although considerably larger, and named this *incognitum* the Megalonyx. Then he read an article by the French zoologist and anatomist Georges Cuvier, which presented a skeleton that Jefferson thought was similar but that Cuvier labeled a Megatherium; Jefferson yielded to the better-trained Cuvier's judgment and inserted into the later, printed version of his article a note that the Megalonyx was probably a version of the Megatherium. But Jefferson continued to believe (as Cuvier did not) that this *incognitum* had living relatives somewhere in the West, because "the movements of nature are in a never-ending cycle. The animal species which have once [been] put into a train of motion, is still probably moving in that train. For, if one link in nature's chain might be broken, another and another might be lost, till the whole system of things should vanish by piecemeal."[25]

Jefferson's former colleague Charles Thomson might have agreed with that last thought. He too had retired, but not by choice. The first Congress chartered under the Constitution refused to continue him in office in the new government. Unlike Jefferson, Thomson in retirement gave up his former aspirations in science to devote his energies to religious matters, focusing on translating into English a Greek version of the Old and New Testaments.[26]

Caspar Wistar was inspired by Jefferson's Megalonyx to do a comparison of its bones with those of every other sort of animal fossil and with possible living relatives. This was the basis for his 1799 paper in the *APS Transactions,* the first serious American technical paper in the field of vertebrate paleontology.

PUBLIC UNDERSTANDING OF SCIENTIFIC MATTERS just then was neatly encapsulated in a brief, anonymously written primer for grammar school use, "A Compendious View of Natural Philosophy: For the Use of Both Sexes," published in Boston in 1796. To teach such science to girls was itself new, and so were the pamphlet's conclusions. While contemporary textbooks such as William Nicholson's *An Introduction to Natural Philosophy,* widely used in colleges, still had difficulty in letting go of the Aristotelian-Aquinan contentions, the thirty-six-page text for younger children did not. Describing the earth as a ball surrounded by an atmosphere and circumnavigating the sun in the course of a year, it explained why we see only one face of the moon and opined that there might be planets, moons, and comets not yet discovered by telescopes. While Nicholson assigned the cause of earthquakes to electricity, the pamphlet forthrightly attributed them to the shifting of molten materials and volcanic activity beneath the earth's surface. Science, the pamphlet summed up,

> extends our views of the universe, of its various phenomena, and of the principles and powers by which they are produced; it invigorates and improves our mental faculties, and enlarges our dominion over nature; it tends to confirm the truth of natural religion; it contributes to the necessities, conveniences, and enjoyments of life; it humanizes the manners, and cherishes and promotes the amiable affections.[27]

Until the middle 1790s, Henry F. May asserts in his study of the American enlightenment, American science was far too cautious in its explorations; but then it was reinvigorated by an influx of immigrants, more than 10,000 Britons each year and, as the French Revolution became increasingly bloody, thousands of French. The scientific-minded among the British included Benjamin and John Vaughan, who became important facilitators for the APS; Scottish botanist and illustrator Alexander Wilson; geologist William Maclure; barrister and chemist Thomas Cooper; and Joseph Priestley. In Great Britain, Priestley had become the leading antiestablishment divine and enthusiast for revolutions, and one of the leading scientists, the discoverer of oxygen, the chronicler of the field of electricity, a contributor to the understanding of photosynthesis and of the role of blood in respiration, and an integral member of the Lunar Circle that had helped improve the steam engine. A correspondent of Franklin, Adams, and Jefferson, Priestley had encouraged them and been inspired by them. He was sixty-one in 1794, and although France had granted citizenship to him and to one of his sons, both considered France too dangerous for establishing new lives after persecution, arson, and a bombing attack at home had made it impossible to continue in Great Britain.[28]

In Philadelphia, Priestley began a friendship with Benjamin Rush, with whom he shared a reverence for the works of David Hartley, the physician founder of the "associationist" school of psychology. "Both Priestley and Rush," Walter Woodward writes, "were intensely religious men, who believed they lived in a time of great spiritual importance, a time that might herald the onset of the millennium. . . . Both were chemical researchers who believed unflaggingly in the compatibility of the new sciences and scripture [and] both were early, ardent public proponents of the abolition of slavery." Priestley lectured to the APS and considered settling in Philadelphia permanently. Jefferson and Madison tried to lure him to Virginia with promises of a professorship and good intellectual company—Jefferson, now isolated, particularly craved this for himself—but Priestley decided to colonize a tract in mid-Pennsylvania, intending to make a model community in Northumberland. He reestablished his laboratory, which became the finest in the Americas. It featured a "burning glass" that focused the sun's rays to make intense heat, a larger one than he had used in discovering oxygen, and a eudiometer for volumetric measuring of gases. In this laboratory he would conduct more experiments than he had ever done before, including a series that culminated in his identifying carbon monoxide.[29]

Priestley did not come to America without scientific baggage. Even though Lavoisier had conclusively demonstrated that oxygen adequately explained burning, Priestley clung to the notion of phlogiston as the key to combustion, an error that led him to misinterpretations, for instance in his 1796 lecture to the APS on phlogiston and in reports of his own experiments to the first-ever American medical magazine, the *Medical Repository*, which Priestley's articles helped to legitimate. Priestley stimulated American chemistry, but his opposition to Lavoisier also delayed the acceptance of Lavoisier's principles in America.

TOM PAINE HAD FOLLOWED his *Rights of Man* to France, where he had been awarded honorary citizenship. Embroiled in the Revolution, elected to its parliament despite not being able to speak French, he ran afoul of the authorities for suggesting they exile rather than execute the king, and was sent to prison. Paine used his jail time to write the *Age of Reason,* part of whose argument for the ascendancy of reason over religion was based on scientific findings; he wrote, for instance, that the sort of calculations that had predicted the details of the 1761 and 1769 transits of Venus showed that man's reason was astute enough to figure out such things as the plan of the solar system, and therefore there was no need for a religious explanation of it.

Paine narrowly missed being guillotined and was eventually sprung from prison by the timely intercession of American ambassador James Monroe (who similarly interceded for Mme. Lafayette). Paine then returned briefly to Great Britain—judged guilty in a British libel suit, he was a fugitive—and in 1796 managed to have his iron-span bridge constructed over the Wear River, near Newcastle-upon-Tyne. The longest metal bridge of the time, it served as a model, its arch and innovative construction allowing the spanning of portions of rivers previously considered too broad to traverse.

IN THE FIRST CONTESTED presidential election, that of 1796, John Adams was selected over the candidate with the second-largest electoral college total, Thomas Jefferson, who became vice president. In Philadelphia, David Rittenhouse had died; and after Priestley declined the presidency of the American Philosophical Society on the grounds that an American should hold that position, Jefferson became its new president. He opined to Madison that Washington had been "fortunate to get off just as the bubble is bursting, leaving others to hold the bag," and that difficulties would ensue.

Indeed, John Adams's one-term presidency was marked by acrimony. Although Washington in a farewell address had fulminated about "the baneful effects of the spirit of party," there was no stopping that trend There are hints that Adams might have liked to turn some of his attention as president to scientific matters, but during his four years in that office he was perpetually enmeshed in domestic and foreign skirmishes. The Federalists, led by Hamilton even after he was forced to retire because of the exposure of a scandalous extramarital affair, and the Democrat-Republicans, led by Jefferson and Madison, drew further apart in their beliefs in what policies the government should adopt. The most difficult clashes were over dealings with France. Under the Directoire, and still at war with Great Britain, France interpreted the Jay Treaty as a British-American re-alliance and authorized the capture of American ships at sea. To meet the threat of war, in 1798 Adams recalled Washington to the army; the former president accepted but turned over most of the work to his deputy, Hamilton. Adams also tried to hasten the modernization of Harpers Ferry. The need to equip the military, aided by the new canons of patentability and the availability of federal funds through a first direct tax on landowners, gave rise to innovation, some products eventually finding their way into civilian manufacturing, among them improved designs for ships' keels.

Because of the imminence of war and the presence in the United States of French and "wild Irish," in 1798 Congress passed an Alien and Sedition Act so broad that it spawned the prosecution of more than a few whose speeches and writings fell far short of treason. This spawned many prosecutions and private suits. Among these suits was that brought by Benjamin Rush who, after chafing for years under harsh criticism, sued his most frequent attackers, the publishers of the *Gazette of the United States* and of *Porcupine's Gazette,* who had repeatedly vilified him for excessive bloodletting, dubbing him "Dr. Vampire." The same papers had also called on Adams to deport Priestley. Adams admired Priestley and Thomas Cooper, who both, to Jefferson's delight, became strident critics of Adams and the Federalists. But it was only when Cooper attacked Adams personally that he was put on trial under the Sedition Act, convicted, fined, and jailed for six months.[30]

IN 1796, COUNT RUMFORD, the former Benjamin Thompson of Massachusetts—a one-time student of John Winthrop at Harvard—having become one of the world's most acclaimed scientists for his studies of heat, proposed to the American Academy and to the Royal Society to personally underwrite $5,000 annual prizes to be awarded to "the Author of the most Important Discovery or useful Improvement . . . on Heat or on Light." He wanted the first award given to him. The Royal Society agreed. The American Academy did not immediately accept the donation; for various reasons, most of them having to do with Rumford's personal history. In 1781, Rumford had bought the lieutenant colonelcy of a regiment of British dragoons, and with them wreaked havoc on the American countryside—and some Americans would not forget. But Adams was impressed enough by Rumford's credentials to offer him the posts of superintendent of the new Military Academy at West Point and inspector general of the armed forces. Rumford declined. Instead, he turned his energies to the creation of the Royal Institution, which, unlike the Royal Society, was open to a broader membership and aimed to educate the public in matters of science—more in the manner of the American Philosophical Society.[31]

Hamilton had been inspired by the idea of an American national military academy and proposed an ambitious plan, a two-year fundamentals course in mathematics and military, after which a student would enter a higher two-year school featuring courses of interest to engineers, cavalry, infantry, or navy. The final Congress of the Adams presidency adjourned with the plan not yet voted on.

IN 1798, DR. BENJAMIN WATERHOUSE received from London a copy of Dr. Edward Jenner's "An Inquiry into the Causes and Effects of the Variolae Vaccinae, a Disease Discovered in Some of the Western Counties of England, Particularly Gloucestershire, and known by the name of The Cow Pox." Knowing that milkmaids had acquired immunity to smallpox, Jenner traced the source to a bovine form of the disease, cultivated the pus from infected cows and with it vaccinated humans. The technique protected them with far less trauma than earlier variolations. Excited at the new technique, Waterhouse alerted John Adams. The president had recently signed into law the Act for the Relief of Sick and Disabled Seamen and was favorably inclined to extending coverage to all men on active service. Adams thought a vaccine against smallpox an important breakthrough, but he was fearful of trying to push the idea through Congress, many of whose members still thought of smallpox as a scourge from God.

Moreover, Adams had to focus his energies on the undeclared war with France. In February 1799, in what is regarded as his most important action, he convinced the Senate to send a message to France that, after the breakup of the Directoire, allowed both countries to avoid further hostilities.

Ten months after that message was sent, on December 14, 1799, George Washington, aged sixty-seven, died after a brief battle with a septic sore throat. His last letter was to Hamilton, commending him on the design for the military academy at West Point. Washington's death was hastened by a series of bloodlettings—which he initially approved—that drained nearly half of the blood from his body. The only physician among the three attending who did not approve of the extent of this bleeding was the one trained by Benjamin Rush.[32]

TWELVE

The SCIENCE-MINDED PRESIDENCY

VITRIOLIC AD HOMINEM ATTACKS BY ADAMS partisans on Jefferson, and reciprocal ones on Adams by Jefferson partisans characterized the contentious election of 1800. Jefferson was accused of being too much the scientist, his interests in insects and astronomical phenomena construed as evidence of the absence of the sort of leadership qualities required of a president. When he was also assailed for being an atheist, Madison, who knew him to be a Deist, begged him to respond. Jefferson replied, "It is impossible to contradict all their lies, that I have determined to contradict none, for while I should be engaged with one, they would publish twenty new ones."[1]

A tie in the Electoral College forced the election into the House of Representatives. Although controlled by Federalists, that body did not want Adams, its own presidential candidate, and for thirty-five ballots there was no decision, the Federalist members backing Aaron Burr despite pressure from Alexander Hamilton, who thought Jefferson would be less detrimental for the country. Only after Jefferson secretly agreed not to fire all the Federalist government employees did enough representatives change their votes to elect him. The outcome so angered Adams that when he and the Speaker of the House, Theodore Sedgwick, a close Hamilton ally, left town for Massachusetts in the same coach, they did not exchange a word on the long journey, each blaming the other for the Federalists' losses.

JEFFERSON BECAME PRESIDENT at a threshold moment for the country and for science itself. The old four-elements conception of the universe had been dealt a final blow in 1800 by Alessandro Volta's electric battery. Able to separate water into its components oxygen and hydrogen, and to generate electricity without friction, the battery enabled new understandings of chemistry and physics to go along with similar advances in geology. As for the United States, it was a moment when the federal government was steady enough to entertain the possibility of governmental support of science and technology for building the nation. Scientific training had been regularized on the university level and was also being taught to younger students. In the private sector, technological innovation was accepted as a route to profits and to less backbreaking manual labor. Moreover, the new president was an avid amateur scientist and technological innovator, the leader of the American Philosophical Society, and a man who for many years had kept in close touch with leading European scientists. "All the members of Jefferson's circle, at home or abroad," regardless of political, religious, or regional differences, Keith Thomson notes, "shared one characteristic above all.... [They] were convinced that for any well-educated man who wanted to achieve greatness for himself and for his country through the application of the intellect, science was a central necessity."[2] As president, Jefferson was more willing than Adams or Washington had been to harness the resources of the federal government to scientific projects other than military ones; two such projects began within months of his inauguration.

Longtime Jefferson friend Charles Willson Peale learned that near West Point, close to where George Washington had been intrigued by the fossils from the cliffs above the Hudson, were unmistakable signs that an entire, intact mammoth skeleton was buried in a peat bog. In 1800, Jefferson, in concert with anatomist Caspar Wistar of the APS and Robert Livingston, then chancellor of New York, had tried to obtain some bones but were stymied by locals who were attempting to dig them up themselves. As soon as Jefferson was inaugurated, Peale tried to take over the project. Rushing to the Hudson's banks, he found many already excavated bones on the floor of the barn at John Masters's farm in a pattern resembling that of an elephant. He bought them all on the spot for $200 and then tried to raise money and official support for further diggings and removals. He easily convinced Jefferson that to properly exhume the remaining fossils and ready them for educational display at his museum in Philadelphia required the government's technological resources as well as money.

To Jefferson, such a mammoth would show that America was indeed the home of gigantic rather than of "degenerate" animal forms; for although Buffon had been dead for fifteen years, his bad ideas survived him and continued to rankle. Jefferson directed that ample resources be made available to Peale. The results were spectacular: the excavation of three partial skeletons. Many sections were brought up by Peale in what historian Laura Rigal labels an early manufacturing enterprise, with teams of bailers, riggers, and carpenters working with mechanical equipment, some designed by Peale, to drain the bog and raise the bones. A waterwheel powered by three men walking inside removed 1,440 gallons of water per hour; any slower rate would have allowed the water table to refill the ditch and hamper the excavation.[3]

Back in Philadelphia, Peale combined two sets of bones plus wooden and papier-mâché replacements for missing parts into a single impressive skeleton that was installed in his museum along with a large painting of the excavation with himself at its center, and an explanatory pamphlet about the "exhumation" by one of his sons. Because of Peale's incomplete knowledge of the beast, the mammoth's tusks were pointed up, like an elephant's. Similarly, the sketches of the supposed environment of the mammoth when alive made it a raging meat-eating beast—similar to what Native Americans had described to Jefferson twenty years earlier—rather than the stolid vegetarian that later scientific study showed it to have been.[4]

Georges Cuvier had recently named twenty-three species that he was certain had become extinct, the mammoth among them, and Dr. Samuel L. Mitchill's *Medical Repository* repeated that claim in articles describing the discoveries at John Masters's farm. Jefferson's hope that a living specimen of the mammoth could be found somewhere on the American continent faded, although it was not yet extinguished.

THE JENNER COWPOX VACCINE for smallpox was "the most important medical discovery ever made since the world began," Dr. Benjamin Waterhouse believed; he had been incensed when his longtime friend

John Adams did not champion universal vaccination during his presidency. The Massachusetts medical society also opposed the technique even though Waterhouse was the star of the Harvard Medical School faculty. To provide a dramatic demonstration of the vaccine, Waterhouse inoculated his own children, maids, and neighbors with cowpox "matter" received from Great Britain and then tested the children's immunity by having them deliberately infected at a smallpox hospital. They recovered, as did nineteen boys inoculated by the Massachusetts Board of Health—and two who were not inoculated died. This successful "experiment," he wrote, was "worth a thousand arguments." He sent copies of his study to high federal officials, including Jefferson, in December 1800.[5]

Jefferson responded the very next day, and after his inauguration as president, Waterhouse worked with him, through physicians nearer to Monticello, to inoculate Jefferson's household. Because the "matter" did not travel well, not all of the samples sent by Waterhouse retained their potency. Jefferson offered suggestions on improving the transport procedure; these ideas helped, but it took several shipments before the matter could be used before it deteriorated. Among the advantages of the new vaccine was that inoculated people did not need isolation afterwards. The president sent the cowpox matter to, and corresponded with, physicians in Virginia, Washington, and Philadelphia. These efforts were not always successful, he wrote to Waterhouse, as "Avarice, rivalship, and mistrust have accompanied its incipient practice in most parts of the Eastern States."[6]

Jefferson explained to Little Turtle, chief of the Miami tribe, during a delegation's visit to the capital, that the "Great Spirit had lately made a precious donation to the enlightened white men over the great water." During the previous centuries, more Native Americans than European settlers and their offspring had been killed by the disease—estimates as high as 90 percent of the indigenous population. Little Turtle agreed to have himself and ten accompanying warriors vaccinated, and the delegation was provided with materials and instructions for vaccinating the rest of the tribe. Jefferson's championing of the Jenner vaccine was trumpeted in medical and popular journals, contributing substantially to its acceptance in America.[7]

DURING THE JEFFERSON PRESIDENCY, the generation of the sons of the Revolution reached maturity and came to the fore.

Dr. Caspar Wistar (born 1761), Philadelphia professor of anatomy, advised Jefferson on the likely anatomical position and purpose of fossil bones. On winter Sunday evenings at his home Wistar served cakes and wine to a scientific and literary salon, soon dubbed a "Wistar party," that featured such distinguished guests as Alexander von Humboldt.

Benjamin Smith Barton (born 1766), student of Will Bartram and nephew and protégé of David Rittenhouse, seized the leadership of the American naturalist community in 1797 by skewering a hoary notion in his *Memoir Concerning the Fascinating Faculty Which Has been Ascribed to the Rattle-Snake.* He became the leading American linguist with his texts on the etymology of Native words, endearing himself to Jefferson, whose study of Native languages had led him to some of the same conclusions. Barton's claims to scientific fame were augmented by his 1803 *Elements of Botany, or Outlines of the Natural History of Vegetables.* Priestley, upon reading fragments of the *Elements* prior to publication, wrote to Barton that, had he been younger, "I would apply to Natural History, and should rejoice to have such a guide, and an example as you have set."[8]

Nathaniel Bowditch (born 1773) benefited in an interesting way from the Revolution: in 1780, an American privateer had captured a British ship containing the entire library of Dr. Richard Kirwan, a noted Scottish geologist and chemist; and to prevent the pages from being used as wrapping paper, the materials were bought for the library in Salem, Massachusetts, where Bowditch lived. The Kirwan cache constituted the finest collection of scientific books outside of Philadelphia. When Bowditch, son of a sea captain, showed promise as a mathematician, he was given library privileges to educate himself from that collection. At fourteen, he had conquered algebra, Latin, and French, read the *Principia,* constructed a barometer, and compiled a new astronomical almanac whose predictions covered the next third of a century. Then he went to sea and learned navigation. On Christmas Day 1795, he wrote in his journal, "Thought of a method of making a lunar observation which to me is new & in some respects I think it preferable to any method hitherto published." With it, on his next voyage he found errors in the standard navigational text, *The Practical Navigator.* He found 8,000 mistakes, many made by authorities such as Nevil Maskelyne. The publisher accepted Bowditch's changes and in 1802 published Bowditch's own navigator, which then became the standard.[9]

Also coming of age was New York physician David Hosack (born 1769). Seeing that botany was progressing in Philadelphia under Barton, various New York City professors, including Mitchill, sought to have their city's colleges and state authorities establish a botanical garden for teaching and research purposes; they chose Hosack, who had trained under British botanists, to begin the Elgin Botanical Garden on the campus of Columbia College. The land was acquired and the garden begun in 1801. One of Hosack's earlier students, DeWitt Clinton, was rising to political power and helped provide state funds for the enterprise. As a family physician, Hosack had an elite list of client families, including that of Alexander Hamilton.[10]

Studying in Philadelphia just then was Benjamin Silliman (born 1779), who after being convinced by Yale's president to give up his legal studies for science, was cramming in Philadelphia to prepare to become the first chemistry professor at Yale. To accept his professorship, Silliman had to swear an oath that his word, given before God, was inviolate. Devout, he did so willingly; but in Philadelphia, his devoutness occasioned a clash with the equally devout Benjamin Rush, who referred to his lancet as *"magnum donum Dei,"* God's greatest gift. Silliman found that offensive and also detested another professor as an absent-minded dolt. In reaction, Silliman invented an alter ego, a Hindu philosopher, Shahcoolen, who wrote letters from Philadelphia to a friend in Delhi about the absurdities of American philosophers who sought to be free of everything. "Republicanism has made a glorious progress in America," Shahcoolen observed, and "a philosopher and philanthropist is in the chair of supreme magistracy." Attacking Americans for not being properly respectful of their elders, for equating freedom with licentiousness, and for overly admiring the feminism of Mary Wollstonecraft and the pompous poetry of Joel Barlow, Shahcoolen became a popular sensation when the letters were published.[11]

AS EVERY SUCCESSFUL PRESIDENT MUST, Jefferson cultivated people in order to utilize their talents for the benefit of the country. Dr. Samuel Mitchill would later say, "If [Jefferson] sought information, no one knew better the art of listening and inquiring than he. . . . That which he did not instantly call to mind he knew where to go and find."[12] Jefferson consulted with such men as architect Benjamin Latrobe, surveyor

Andrew Ellicott, and mathematician Robert Patterson. He persuaded Latrobe, the first classically trained architect to practice in the United States, to take over work on the US Capitol, but was initially unable to convince Ellicott, with whom he had worked to lay out the designs for the District of Columbia, to become the country's surveyor general. The Adams administration had refused to pay Ellicott for previous work and he had become disillusioned with federal government assignments. Patterson was vice president of the APS and the best mathematician in the country. He and Jefferson shared a passion for cryptography, and during the Revolutionary War Patterson had worked on a Jefferson-invented system for coding. In 1802 Patterson created a new coding system that the president judged "more convenient in practice than my wheel cylinder."[13] Jefferson appointed as the superintendent of West Point Jonathan Williams, a grandnephew of Benjamin Franklin whom Jefferson had met when Williams served as Franklin's assistant in Paris; Williams was the author of a treatise on the use of thermometers in navigation. Jefferson worked with him to design the curriculum for the engineering school at West Point—a diminished version of what Hamilton had envisioned for the academy, among other reasons because the entire military establishment was being scaled back during peacetime.[14]

Jefferson also became friends in this period with Samuel L. Mitchill, the New York physician and editor who had won a seat in the House of Representatives and whom Jefferson dubbed "the Congressional Dictionary" for his encyclopedic knowledge. He showed Mitchill samples of silk made in Virginia, demonstrated the waterproofing qualities of imported British cloth, and showed him models of his own newest design for the moldboard plow and for an ambitious dry docks project. Latrobe, who worked on the dry docks project with him, had made the model, which Jefferson kept on his desk. Mitchill had some technical and some economic concerns about the dry docks, as did others in Congress; as a result, the project often called visionary was referred to a House committee and died there.

HISTORIAN OF SCIENCE GERALD HOLTON suggests that Jefferson's approach to research combined the approaches of two of his trinity of greatest minds, Newton and Bacon; while Newton sought to learn about the world, and Bacon to find practical uses for that learning,

Jefferson located "the center of research in an area of basic scientific ignorance that lies at the heart of a social program." The epitome of this
approach was Jefferson's design of the expedition to explore the territory
west of the Mississippi.[15]

In 1801, Jefferson's longtime desire for an exploratory expedition to
the American West and his belief that the destiny of the United States
of America was to control the land area from the Atlantic to the Pacific,
were heightened by the publication of an account by a Canadian trader
of a journey to the Oregon area and the Columbia River. Faced with the
threat of British control of the upper Northwest, and claims from Spain
on the Southwest and from France to the Midwest, Jefferson keenly felt
the need for an expedition to advance American hegemony over these
areas. Also a naturalist expedition, it would collect and identify flora and
fauna and gather information on Native tribes and languages, his particular hobbyhorse.

To lead that expedition, in 1802 Jefferson chose his private secretary,
Captain Meriwether Lewis, the son of an old Jefferson friend.[16] Lewis
had wanted to be in charge of the 1793 expedition for which the APS had
chosen André Michaux as leader; at that time Jefferson had vetoed the
idea of Lewis's leading it because he was an inexperienced teenager. At age
twenty-eight in 1802, Lewis had proved his mettle in army battles and,
more recently, had proved his loyalty to Jefferson, providing the president
with an insider's knowledge of the army in the congressionally mandated
thinning of the ranks for a peacetime force. Although not a trained naturalist, Lewis was a quick study. For Jefferson, who habitually interwove
several motives into his actions, Lewis was the perfect choice as expedition leader. As he would write in introducing Lewis to the scientific community, it was "impossible to find a character who to a compleat science
in botany, natural history, mineralogy & astronomy, joined the firmness
of constitution and character, prudence, habits adapted to the woods, &
a familiarity with the Indian manners and character, requisite for the
undertaking," and so, since Lewis possessed the "latter qualifications,"
it would be up to the scientific community to tutor him in the others.[17]

To send soldiers as a Corps of Discovery required Congressional approval, and the president conveyed his plan in a confidential letter to
Congress. He sought $2,500 to establish better trading relations with
the Native tribes, "encourage them to abandon hunting," and take up

farming, "thereby to prove to themselves that less land and labor will maintain them;" and to emplace "trading houses" that would put "within their reach those things which will contribute more to their domestic comfort." Under this rubric,

> an intelligent officer, with ten or twelve chosen men, fit for the enterprise . . . might explore the whole line, even to the Western Ocean, have conferences with the natives on the subject of commercial intercourse, get admission among them for our traders . . . and return with the information acquired, in the course of two summers. . . . While other civilized nations have encountered great expense to enlarge the boundaries of knowledge by undertaking voyages of discovery . . . our nation seems to owe to the same object, as well as to its own interests, to explore this, the only line of easy communication across the continent, and so directly traversing our own part of it.[18]

Mitchill headed the House committee and worked closely with Jefferson to shepherd the bill to passage. The money sought was a pittance compared to the $9 million Jefferson had recently asked for as potential payment to France for the acquisition of New Orleans. The Corps of Discovery bill was signed on February 28, 1803, while negotiations were being carried out in France to buy New Orleans and also—what Congress did not yet know—for the purchase of the vastly larger Louisiana Territory that France had acquired from Spain in December 1802. In Washington, Jefferson met with the Spanish and French ambassadors, who agreed to have their countries supply visas for safe passage through the territories they controlled; Jefferson told each ambassador that the ultimate destination of the expedition was the Pacific. The only affected country not so apprised was Great Britain.[19]

Lewis set out for the Harpers Ferry Armory in Virginia and made plans to engage as his co-commander his former army superior, William Clark, younger brother of George Rogers Clark, whom Jefferson had twenty years earlier asked to explore the West on a journey that had not taken place.

In those twenty years, America's scientific and technological establishments had matured enough to be of material assistance to the new expedition. At Harpers Ferry, Lewis ordered variations on the now-reliable Pennsylvania rifle and had the artisans construct an iron boat that he and

Jefferson had designed that was sturdy enough to hazard difficult rivers but not too heavy for portage.[20] Lewis then proceeded to Lancaster for arms training and to be taught surveying and the use of astronomical implements by Ellicott. While Lewis was in Lancaster, Jefferson sent him a cipher for use with sensitive information, a 28-column alphanumeric table keyed to the secret word "artichoke." The president even wrote out a sample sentence for Lewis to code: "I am at the head of the Missouri. All is well, and the Indians so far friendly."

Even though Jefferson's library was the most extensive on the continent regarding its geography and natural history, he made several mistaken assumptions about the country west of the Mississippi and its inhabitants. Principal among them was that a passage of linked rivers could be found that would lead to the Pacific Ocean. Others were a belief in active volcanoes near the upper Missouri and a mile-long salt mountain. In accordance with his biblical beliefs—still preventing him from fully accepting the mounting evidence for extinction, evolution, and descent from multiple original ancestors—Jefferson continued to hope that the expedition would find live mammoths and no fauna that were precisely the same as Europe's, and that the far western Native American tribes would provide linguistic and other evidence of descent from the lost tribes of Israel.

In Philadelphia, Lewis became the sole student of a three-week cram course by the country's leading professors. European scientific field expeditions were usually carried out by members of the Royal Society or the Académie des Sciences; appropriately for America, this one would be done by laymen. But its leaders needed training in making proper observations, collecting specimens, and writing reports. Lewis's principal tutors were the medical doctors Benjamin Rush, Caspar Wistar, and Benjamin Smith Barton—all correspondents of Jefferson's. Rush was an expert in Native and European medicine, Wistar on fossils and anatomy, and Barton on botany and Native languages. Lewis attended the professors' university lectures and private sessions in their homes, and accompanied Barton to Peale's museum, Bartram's gardens, and the nearby Woodlands arboretum. Rush, Wistar, and Barton also reviewed the draft of Jefferson's instructions for Lewis and suggested some changes. These instructions meshed with the questionnaires that Lewis would carry, written mostly by Rush, to extract information from Native tribes along the way. Secretary of the Treasury Albert Gallatin commissioned a map for Lewis that encompassed the findings of all prior expeditions to the Pacific Northwest, and other cabinet members also contributed to the enterprise.

The discoverers would carry Barton's new botany text, dictionaries of Native languages, and a gloss on Linnaeus, but would not have the benefit of Nathaniel Bowditch's *Navigator,* as it was not yet well known to land voyagers. Rush, in addition to teaching Lewis what he would need to know to keep his corps healthy, supplied the expedition with plenty of his patented purges and emetics, the pills known as "Thunderclappers," as well as opium for "nervousness" and medicinal wine. Along with an extensive cache of presents for the Natives, including tomahawks, Lewis and Clark would also carry cowpox matter, kits for smallpox vaccination, and instructions on teaching the Natives to administer them.

Another Lewis tutor was mathematician Robert Patterson, who also guided him in buying equipment for ascertaining his location in the wilderness. Lewis reported to the president that his teachers thought the Jefferson-recommended theodolite too delicate for travel, so he was instead procuring sturdy sextants and chronometers. Perhaps the most important device the expedition would carry was not for measurement but for demonstrations, an "air gun," a rifle that used for power a hand-cranked vacuum pump instead of gunpowder.[21]

During March and April 1803, as Lewis readied himself and the expedition, Robert Livingston and Secretary of State James Monroe concluded negotiations in Paris to have the United States acquire title to the 828,000 square miles of the Louisiana Territory at a cost of about three cents an acre. The transfer by treaty was agreed to on April 30, 1803. News of this huge acquisition, with its immense promise, colored Jefferson's formal instructions to Lewis, dated June 20. The president stressed the need for good scientific note-taking on all sorts of subjects in words that reflected Jefferson's concerns in his *Notes on Virginia,* his near obsession with precise record-keeping and copious detail, and the types of data that he had been collecting at Monticello for decades. To enable commerce with the Natives, Lewis must find out everything about them, their names and numbers,

> the extent & limits of their possessions; their relations with other tribes or
> nations; their language, traditions, monuments; their ordinary occupations

in agriculture, fishing, hunting, war, arts, & the implements for these; their food, clothing, & domestic accommodations; the diseases prevalent among them, & the remedies they use . . . peculiarities in their laws, customs & dispositions; and articles of commerce they may need or furnish, & to what extent.

Similarly, the expedition must take detailed note of the geography, flora, and fauna,

especially those not known in the U.S. the remains & accounts of any which may be deemed rare or extinct; the mineral productions of every kind; but more particularly metals, limestone, pit coal & saltpetre; salines & mineral waters . . . [and] climate as characterized by the thermometer, by the proportion of rainy, cloudy & clear days, by lightening, hail, snow, ice, by the access & recess of frost, by the winds, prevailing at different seasons, the dates at which particular plants put forth or lose their flowers, or leaf, times of appearance of particular birds, reptiles or insects.[22]

At Pittsburgh, Lewis was joined by Clark and the chosen soldiers, and once again had the iron boat constructed. He nearly aborted the expedition by a mishap with the air gun. Just south of Pittsburgh, he was invited ashore a small island by three men to demonstrate the device. While one of them was holding the gun, it accidentally discharged, and the ball passed through the bonnet of a woman forty yards away. "She fell instantly, and the blood gushing from her temple we were all in the greatest consternation supposed she was dead [but] in a minute she revived, to our inexpressible satisfaction," the wound only minor.[23]

IN 1803, PRESIDENT JEFFERSON READ Priestley's recently published *Socrates and Jesus Compared* and was inspired by it to complete an assignment set for him by Benjamin Rush in 1798, to write out in some detail his views on Christianity. He prepared for Rush "A Syllabus of an Estimate of the Merit of the Doctrines of Jesus, Compared with those of Others," a tightly reasoned two pages, and then began to consider expanding his thoughts about organized religion. One product was what has become known as the "Jefferson Bible," *The Life and Morals of Jesus of Nazareth.* Using a razor, Jefferson cut out and then pasted together only those sections of the New Testament that dealt with Jesus's life and teachings, eliminating all references to his divinity and miracles as well as most references to supernatural matters. It concluded with Jesus's death on the cross and made no mention of resurrection. Jefferson would later write that determining which were and were not Jesus's words and thoughts was not hard, for the former were "as easily distinguished as diamonds in a dunghill."

In May 1804, while awaiting the return of Lewis and Clark from the West, Jefferson entertained Alexander von Humboldt; fresh from a five-year expedition in the Caribbean and Central and South America, Humboldt was escorted to Washington by Charles Willson Peale and other APS members. He displayed some of his detailed maps for Jefferson, Gallatin, and other high-ranking officials. One map, not yet published, was of New Spain's territories. Humboldt agreed to lend it with the caveat that no copies be made. Gallatin secretly made a copy. Jefferson asked Humboldt for help in delineating the southern and western boundaries of the Louisiana Purchase and for his estimate of the populations of "white, red, or black people" in its border areas. They also discussed several American expeditions to the Red River under Zebulon Pike, William Dunbar, and Isaac Briggs. Pike's expedition would carry the Gallatin copy of the Humboldt map. All three explorers had some scientific credentials: Pike had published an article in Mitchill's *Medical Repository,* Dunbar had corresponded with Jefferson for years about meteorological matters, and Briggs was a surveyor.[24]

The viewpoint afforded to Jefferson by the presidency of the whole of the American country and enterprise altered some of his prior conceptions. Asked about revising the *Notes on Virginia* twenty years after its publication, Jefferson said that he would have to change a chapter in which he had rejected the sort of manufacturing that was done in European capitals as unworthy of American morals; now, he wrote in 1805, "our manufacturers are as much at their ease, as independent and moral as our agricultural inhabitants, and they will continue so long as there are vacant lands for them to resort to; because whenever it shall be attempted by the other classes to reduce them to the minimum of subsistence, they will quit their trades and go to laboring the earth."[25]

ALTHOUGH JEFFERSON HAD RUN with Aaron Burr as vice president in 1800, he determined in 1804 to have Governor George Clinton of New York on his ticket. Burr, the sitting vice president, had been vying with Clinton for the governorship and was feeling maligned by both Clinton and Alexander Hamilton, who wrote nasty articles about Burr's gubernatorial candidacy. In July 1804, Burr challenged the former secretary of the treasury to a duel. Hamilton, fatally wounded, was borne from the dueling ground to the offices of Dr. David Hosack, who attended him as he had attended the death by duel of Hamilton's son, Philip, three years earlier.

The duel also resulted in the effective ending of Burr's political career.

JEFFERSON'S EASY RE-ELECTION further sharpened John Adams's ire at his former friend, and in 1805 he reacted by renewing correspondence with some old once-radical friends, principal among them Benjamin Rush. Eventually, the two became close enough that Rush would relate his dreams and Adams would respond in kind. Rush was also corresponding separately with Jefferson—and trying to figure out how to re-unite his two correspondents who were just at opposite ends of the spectrum of American political thought.

"IN OBEDIENCE TO YOUR ORDERS we have penetrated the Continent of North America to the Pacific Ocean," read the opening line of Meriwether Lewis's letter to Jefferson on his return to St. Louis on September 23, 1806. Jefferson received it, he replied, with "unspeakable joy," since "the unknown scenes in which you were engaged, & the length of time without hearing of you had begun to be felt awfully." To Congress, Jefferson declared that the expedition "has had all the success which could have been expected," having traced the Missouri to its source, traversed the Rocky Mountains, and "descended the Columbia to the Pacific" in addition to having "learned the character of the country, of its commerce, and inhabitants."[26]

The accomplishments of the Lewis and Clark expedition in science as well as in politics were enormous, although not fully appreciated at the time. The explorers had traced the Missouri to its source, revealed the Columbia River as far larger than had previously been understood, and ended speculation of a northwest passage to the Pacific. They had determined that the continent was wider than previously thought, and that the Rockies and the Cascades—no white man before them had known that there were two mountain ranges, not one—were greater obstacles to "communication" with the Far West than had been imagined. More about Native tribes had been discovered than any white man had ever known; Lewis and Clark brought back the first ethnographical studies of a half-dozen tribes including the Shoshone, Nez Perce, and Yakima, and the first studies of six different Native linguistic groups. Of the approximately one hundred questions drawn up for them by Rush, Wistar, and Jefferson, the explorers had found substantial answers to almost all from the forty-eight tribes with whom they had made contact. They also brought back enough material to eventually identify 179 previously unknown species of plants and 122 similarly unknown species of birds, fish, and animals. Both leaders had kept extensive diaries—nearly a million words. As an academic evaluation of these journals would assert in 1874, "The more closely they are scanned, in light of present knowledge, the more luminous they appear." Lewis used more than 200 technical terms in his descriptions; these helped to identify plants and animals for which no specimens were available. As the scientific reports based on the trove were written, Jefferson had copies put on the desks of each Congressman—reports such as "A Statistical View of the Indian Nations Inhabiting the Territory of Louisiana and the Countries Adjacent to Its Northern and Western Boundaries."[27]

Much of the collected material was sent to Philadelphia, starting with a first batch in 1805. Some material went to Barton and some to Peale, which brought into the open their latent rivalry. Wistar examined the fossils, and the Bartram and Woodlands gardens received some seeds and cuttings for propagation. Benjamin Vaughan and chemist Adam Seybert examined the soils, rocks, and minerals. A visiting Scottish botanist identified and sketched some of the plants from dried specimens; of the 150 specimens, the botanist later wrote, more than 90 percent were previously unknown. Peale's museum was the largest beneficiary of the scientific loot, receiving many skins, skeletons, and other specimens for mounting and display. These ranged from Pacific Coast otters to bighorn sheep, mule deer, grizzly bear, bushy-tailed wood rat, prairie rattler, and many birds. Lewis commissioned bird portraits from Alexander Wilson, portraits of Native chiefs from a visiting French artist, and illustrations of waterfalls from a third artist. A West Point professor corrected the longitude observations.[28]

Three important scientific caches were lost. The first, mostly plant specimens, had been stored below ground and was washed away by a flood; the second, fossils that included a mastodon head, were taken without permission from a temporary depot and found their way to cabinets in Europe; and the third, Lewis's notes on Native languages, was with Jefferson's papers in a trunk taken by robbers and dumped in the James River while on its way to Monticello.

Jefferson's big questions, shared by Rush, Priestley, Peale, Barton, Mitchill, and others, received partial answers from the observations of the Corps of Discovery. An autopsy of a western magpie determined it to be nearly identical to the European bird, undermining Jefferson's belief that God had placed different fauna in the Americas than on the European continent. The notion that some animals had become extinct gained considerable traction, because while fossils were unearthed, no living Megalonyx or mammoth was spotted. The idea of evolution—still decades away from articulation by Charles Darwin—was advanced slightly by observations of regional variations in animals. The concept of the Natives as descendants of the lost tribes of Israel received no verification.

Lewis, rewarded by Jefferson with appointment as governor of the Louisiana Territory, experienced a tremendous emotional letdown, not becoming the hero he had imagined because of competition from Lieutenant Stephen Decatur and others who had defeated the Barbary pirates in military action. He had great difficulty in writing and died in 1809 before completing his text. Clark, appointed brigadier general and Indian agent for the Louisiana Territory, did somewhat better, but even so, his materials would not be published for some years. Eventually, Nicholas Biddle of the APS would edit the journals and interview Clark to supplement them, and the results would become available to the public.

A major achievement of the Lewis and Clark expedition was the transmuting of the act of discovery of new lands into a durable and inspirational American legend. Jefferson's signal scientific achievement as president, it was also the symbol of the country's transition from being a society in which science was a somewhat passive enterprise of reportage and minimal analysis to a society that used a scientific mindset to actively explore previously unknown parts of that world, and did so with a focus on the potential utility of what was being discovered.

AS WITH JEFFERSON'S DREAM of an expedition to the West, the steamboat dream was nearly three decades in coming to fulfillment—and neither John Fitch nor James Rumsey would get the credit for it. The "projector" in the winning endeavor—the man most responsible for its coming to pass—was Chancellor Robert R. Livingston of New York; a partisan of Jefferson's, the senior jurist had been appointed minister to France in 1801. Long interested in using steamboats on the Hudson River, in the 1790s he had obtained a license to do so from New York State, conditional on his delivering a boat that could make four miles an hour going against the current. Prior to embarking for France in late 1801, he had not been able to deliver a satisfactory boat. In March 1802, while in Paris, he met Robert Fulton, whose checkered career had involved attempting to build a submarine and underwater bombs for both the British and the French to use against one another's navies, as well as years as a portrait painter and as the successful designer of a machine for cutting marble and of a cordelier, a machine for twisting strands into rope. None of those inventions or arts had brought in much money, but Fulton had recently been raking in substantial sums from public admittance fees to the panoramas he had designed and emplaced in the Montmartre section of Paris.[29]

Fulton and Livingston each provided what the other lacked, enabling the combination to create a commercially viable steamship enterprise. As Fulton acknowledged, he was not the sort of inventor who started from nothing and made something entirely new. He functioned as an aggregator, evaluating the effectiveness of designs and combining them. This became a creed: "The mechanic should sit down among levers, screws, wedges, wheels, etc., like a poet among the letters of the alphabet, considering them as the exhibition of his thoughts; in which a new arrangement transmits a new idea to the world," he wrote.[30]

While Fulton was working on a steamboat, Livingston was parleying with Napoleon to purchase first New Orleans and then the entire Louisiana Territory. In August 1803, shortly after Livingston and Monroe concluded the Louisiana Purchase, Fulton conducted on the Seine a trial of a 75-foot-long paddlewheel steamboat. It managed three miles per hour, not fast enough to fulfill the terms of Livingston's agreement with New York. But the trial taught Fulton what had eluded Rumsey and Fitch: that in calculating the resistance of the water to paddles and hull, he must factor in that water gave way in reaction to the thrust, meaning that even more power was required to move the boat than was previously understood. Shortly, as a result of a deal made with the British government to terminate his prior contracts with them, he was allowed to have Boulton-Watt make him such an engine. In late 1806, when Fulton returned to New York, he found that engine waiting for him in a warehouse and with it began work on a new steamboat.

In early 1807, Fulton and Livingston attended a dinner in Washington, DC, to honor the returning Lewis. President Jefferson evidenced more interest in having Fulton supervise the building of a canal to connect Lake Pontchartrain and the Mississippi than in the steamboat. Fulton turned down the commission, pleading that he was too busy. However, during this visit to Washington, and through the poet Joel Barlow—the Barlows and Fulton had lived together in France—Fulton met and charmed William Thornton, the first architect of the Capitol, who had once worked with Fitch and whom Jefferson had appointed as chief patent officer. In that capacity, Thornton allowed Fulton to look at all twelve prior patent applications for steamboats in the government's files. "Not one," Fulton wrote to Livingston, "approaches practicality."

In late June 1807, off Norfolk, a British ship that had been refused permission to search the U.S.S. *Chesapeake* for deserters attacked, killing three American seamen, wounding the captain and sixteen others, and taking prisoners. It was the opening salvo in a series of escalating skirmishes that would consume the remainder of Jefferson's presidency and culminate in the onset of the War of 1812. Fulton, in reaction to the news, postponed a steamboat trial to concoct a demonstration of his torpedoes—Jefferson was appealing to Congress for funds to arm the country for a possible war, and Fulton hoped for a big payday. He demonstrated the underwater bombs for an audience that included official representatives of the US Navy, but they did not work well. In the *Salmagundi* magazine, Washington Irving wrote that all that was necessary for the bombs to succeed was that "the [target] ships must come to anchor in a convenient place; watch must be asleep . . . fair wind and tide—*no moonlight*—machines well-directed—mustn't flash in the pan—bang's the word." To counter his bad press, Fulton wrote Jefferson that the eventual blowing up of the target was evidence of the technique's success; by return mail Jefferson urged him to continue, and to do so as well with the submersible as a bomb-delivery device. Later Fulton would write in regard to these under-sea devices that only those individuals among the public who had traced "the progress of the useful arts, know the years of toil, experiment, and difficulties which frequently pass, before the utility and certain operation of new discoveries have been established."[31]

Turning once more to the steamboat, Fulton completed it in short order and, after some difficulty, on August 17, 1807, set out with the boat soon to be known as the *North River* for Albany, 150 miles upstream. Because of the recent torpedo embarrassment, the crowds at the dock when Fulton and the crew set out jeered rather than cheered him, anticipating a failure. They were disappointed. Stopping overnight at Clermont, Livingston's manor, Fulton supposedly met his future wife, Livingston's niece. Next morning the steamboat, with Livingston also aboard, completed the trip to Albany at better than four miles per hour, three times as fast as sailing ships in the river's currents. "The power of propelling boats by steam has now been fully proved," Fulton told Barlow.[32] Within months, the steamboat was in regular use on the Hudson, carrying passengers and freight to and from Albany; and Livingston and Fulton were encouraged to establish a similar route on the Mississippi between New Orleans and St. Louis. The ability of the Hudson steamboats to make quick and relatively inexpensive passage for goods to and from Albany to New York City hastened the building of the Erie Canal and the connecting of the Great Lakes and the Midwest with the Atlantic Ocean. Steamboats on the Hudson, the Mississippi, and the Great Lakes were the most important factors in the spectacular increase in the volume and power of the American economy in the new century.

The true triumph of the Lewis and Clark expedition similarly lay in what it enabled. By dispelling the darkness of myths and providing in their place scientifically observed information on geography, Native tribes, fauna, flora, the location and extent of rivers, ore deposits, soils, and the like, Lewis and Clark enlightened and enriched the United States of America, turning the country decisively in the direction of becoming a continent-wide power, able to sustain many more people than Europe's principalities, and possessed of vast natural resources on which to base a massive economy that would henceforth ensure the country's continued independence and vitality.

EPILOGUE

The INTERWEAVING

A COMET BLAZED ACROSS THE CONNECTICUT sky early one morning in December 1807. That it was not presumed by many observers to be a sign from God reflected the new attitudes toward natural phenomena that were continuing to evolve during President Thomas Jefferson's second term. The comet's physical point of origin, which remained very much subject to dispute, presented to Benjamin Silliman, the young professor of chemistry at Yale, a once-in-a-lifetime opportunity. "I did not dream of being favored by an event of this kind in any vicinity [near me], and occurring on a scale truly magnificent," he would write. Solving the meteor's origin was a task in which the scientific resources of the United States, as well as those of the twenty-eight-year-old professor, would be put to the test.[1]

As had Lewis and Clark and before them John Bartram and the kite-flying Benjamin Franklin, Silliman deliberately set out to delve into the unknown, to dispel the myths around a phenomenon, and to examine it in situ insofar as possible. Previous meteor fragments in Europe had been analyzed in laboratories, but Silliman sought to marshal a resource that Europeans often ignored or mistrusted, ordinary individuals' capacities for accurate observation. When reports began to come in that a half dozen fragments of the meteor, some as large as thirty-five pounds, had landed in fields near Weston, Connecticut, and had crashed through the roof of one building, Silliman assiduously traversed the area to collect samples of the meteor and firsthand reports of its path in the sky and to personally track the scorch and roll patterns. Newly returned from study in London and Edinburgh with chemists who were also field geologists, he had the critical chemical and geological skills and, thanks to Yale's interest in the teaching of science, a laboratory capable of performing sophisticated analyses. His goal, like Franklin's in experimenting with electricity sixty years earlier, was to amass detail to refute theories that he thought were wrong but that had persisted. If most enlightened people no longer thought of comets as divine messengers, they still believed that comets originated in either earthly or lunar volcanoes, or were in some way formed in the clouds. None of those notions had any empirical support. Looking to demolish them as hypotheses, Silliman used eyewitness descriptions and charred-earth trails to reconstruct the meteor's path across the sky, including the duration of flight and the angles of travel and descent. He theorized that the meteor had most likely come from a belt of large fragments orbiting the earth far above the clouds. The fiery tail attested to such an origin, as it likely resulted from friction, generated by the comet's passage through the atmosphere, burning its flammable portions and melting its ores. He found that the chunk of the meteor brought in for analysis was twice the density of most earthly rocks due to its high proportion of iron. In combination with the meteor's speed of transit, which he had already deduced, this high density signaled that the meteor could not have come from an earthly or lunar source. A projectile from an earthly volcano would have produced an arc more perpendicular to the landing sites, and a lunar volcano could not have spewed out a rock of that size and density with enough force to propel it at high velocity through the earth's atmosphere. Finally, no clouds could contain such heavy matter and remain aloft. Eliminating those possible origins, Silliman used the known workings of centripetal force and gravity and mathematical formulae describing the relationship of velocity and mass to the curvature of an object's path to conclude that the meteor must have weighed several thousand pounds when it entered the earth's atmosphere and that it must have traveled through that atmosphere at a rate of tens of thousands of miles per hour before breaking into many pieces.

Working quickly, on December 29, 1807, Silliman published a first article about his findings in the *Connecticut Herald* and was invited to read a more formal paper to the APS in March 1808. The night before that presentation, Silliman dined in Philadelphia with chemists Adam Seybert and Thomas Cooper, and reported on the dinner to his research collaborator: "With an air of ridicule and self-importance, [Cooper] . . . intimated incredulity on several chemical and astronomical points . . . but . . . the Doctor being really as ignorant as he was vain and impertinent, I found no difficulty laying him on his back."

Silliman's nonstandard assertion regarding the meteorite's origin also startled Cooper's friend President Jefferson. The president had already commented on Silliman's early newspaper report, telling a friend, "A thousand phenomena present themselves daily which we cannot explain, but where facts are suggested, bearing no analogy with the laws of nature as yet known to us, their verity needs proofs proportioned to their difficulties." Jefferson requested that Nathaniel Bowditch, the famed mathematician, navigator, and astronomer, check Silliman's conclusions. After retracing how Silliman had reached his conclusions, Bowditch agreed with the Yale professor: the meteor's path and speed indicated that it had to have originated in outer space. Count Rumford also praised the Silliman work on the Weston meteor—it was one more validation of Rumford's theory that heat was produced by friction—and Silliman's APS paper was further praised by French physicist Marc-Auguste Pictet, who had it republished in the *Annales de chimie,* the world's leading chemistry publication. Acceptance of Silliman's work by the Académie des Sciences and the Royal Institution elevated contemporary American work in the sciences in the eyes of Europe; it revolutionized the scientific understanding of the heavens and the study of astral bodies without fixed orbits.[2]

SILLIMAN'S TRIUMPH WAS EVIDENCE that the United States was now reaping the benefits of having fully met Peter Collinson's conditions for scientific progress: a critical mass of adepts, continual conversations among them, and appropriate publications in which to present their findings and theories. Shortly, Silliman would underwrite and edit a new forum for such discussion, the *American Journal of Science,* which specialized in the earth sciences, primarily in the nascent science of geology.

American universities by then employed about two dozen full-time professors of the sciences, none of whom were required, as their predecessors had been, to teach everything from astronomy to zoology—a reflection of the growing acknowledgment that it was no longer possible for any one person to know everything about every science. In the same era, the Academy of Natural Sciences was formed in Philadelphia, as were the Elgin Botanical Garden in New York, the Colombian Institute in Washington, and other scientific institutions with specific rather than general purposes. Boston, New Haven, New York, Philadelphia, Washington, Savannah, and Charleston could boast of functioning scientific societies. Benjamin Smith Barton, Benjamin Rush, Caspar Wistar, David Hosack, and Alexander Wilson, among others, readied seminal works for publication; Rush's on mental diseases was the first extended study of these in the United States. The number of scientific journals published in the country would soon triple. The separation of chemistry from physics, of biology from botany, and of applied mathematics and engineering from mathematical theory ushered in specialization in the sciences and competition among them for research materials and funding.

WHEN WILLIAM CLARK RETURNED from his expedition to the Pacific, Jefferson asked him to mount a separate expedition to excavate and retrieve fossils from the Big Bone Lick. The task was not easy to accomplish, Clark reported to Jefferson, for "this Lick has been pillaged so frequently that but few valuable bones are to be found entire." When he did manage to exhume an intact mammoth head, exposure to the air and removal of the surrounding mud caused it to crumble.[3] Nonetheless, he sent bones and fragments, including some intended for Jefferson's private collection, down the river to New Orleans and thence by ship around the Florida peninsula to Philadelphia. They were accompanied by Clark's detailed listing and analysis, a document whose scope, fine observations, and scientific descriptions were testament that he, as well as Lewis, had mastered the lessons in how to be a field scientist. In "a few desultory remarks and conjectures," Clark opined to Jefferson that the unearthed bones settled one important question: "Can any doubt exist after this of the existence in this Country at some former period of both the Mammoth and the Eliphant, as also of three or four other Animals Now extinct in the U. States! as well as the Horse and other Animals Common in America at this day." He provided details, having compared the length of the lower limb bones, the number and size of the teeth, ribs, shoulder bones, and other parts of various animals.

During the following year, Wistar and Jefferson corresponded regarding the fossils. Some had been intended for Jefferson's personal use, others for the APS. Many were put on public display in the President's House in Washington, and in July 1808 Jefferson dispatched half of the specimens to France, intending them for what had once been the Jardin du Roi. In doing so, he was making good on an old promise to the long-deceased Buffon, but he had not realized that in consequence of the French Revolution, that institution had been reorganized and folded into the Museum of Natural History. The bones were deposited there. Georges Cuvier validated Clark's guesses by positively identifying some larger bones as those of an American mastodon and others as belonging to an American mammoth; Cuvier regarded them all as additional evidence that extinction of species was a facet of the world's history.[4]

TECHNOLOGY TOO WAS IN TRANSITION. Formerly, technology had meant the inventing of new tools. Now it was beginning to mean the replacing of what a worker had previously accomplished through skill, augmented by tools in hand, by machines that did those same tasks with few or no workers to tend them. Automated flour mills of the Oliver Evans design were proliferating as farming spread west through the Louisiana Purchase in the wake of the Lewis and Clark expedition. In the Northeast, going beyond the success of Samuel Slater's semi-automated mills in Rhode Island, Boston-area merchant Francis Cabot Lowell and a group of associates took steps toward establishing the next generation of even more automated textile factories in Waltham, Massachusetts, utilizing carding, drawing, and roving machines as well as looms, which enabled their factory to do weaving, which Slater's had not done. Contemporaneously, the Harpers Ferry Armory in Virginia ushered in a new system for more highly compartmentalized manufacture; under their new system the making of rifles no longer required workers who were highly skilled artisans; less-well-trained men using machine tools were able to make standardized interchangeable parts and assemble them into a weapon in far less time, and with the expenditure of far fewer man-hours, than was possible under the old method. The armories (including one at Springfield, Massachusetts) invited private manufacturers to view their processes and counseled them on how to adapt the techniques to non-military manufacture. Near New Haven, Eli Whitney, using the new technologies, was able to manufacture

30,000 muskets in two years. Mass production employing machines and only moderately skilled workers soon became known as "the American system" and would be widely utilized in many industries.

THROUGHOUT JEFFERSON'S SECOND TERM as president, Benjamin Rush and John Adams carried on their correspondence, confiding to one another thoughts that they seldom conveyed to others. Rush told Adams, for instance, that he had almost inadvertently become wealthy enough to retire—having taught 3,000 young physicians—and thought of doing so in favor of a son who would take over his practice, but he wanted to collect his thoughts on mental diseases and found other reasons to continue as a professor. Adams placed his political hopes in the rise of his son, John Quincy Adams, a Harvard professor, even though Quincy had recently changed parties and joined Jefferson's. As Quincy was doing so, in the spring of 1808, during an election year in which Jefferson's successor would be chosen, Rush wrote to Adams, "Were Mr. Jefferson now asked how he liked his present seat at the helm of our government, he would probably answer as Sancho [Don Quixote's squire] did after having occupied a similar situation, 'Give me (not my shoes and stockings, which were the words of Sancho) but give me my telescope and mathematical instruments.'" Adams responded that he hoped such instruments would secure Jefferson's "felicity," but "how he will be rid of his remorse [for his actions as president] in his retirement, I know not." A year later, as mounting tensions with Great Britain headed the country toward war, Jefferson was not at all reluctant to hand the presidency to his secretary of state and friend James Madison. Preparing to retire, Jefferson responded to a letter from Humboldt, "You have wisely located yourself in the focus of the science of Europe. I am held by the cords of love to my family & country, or I should certainly join you. Within a few days I shall now bury myself in the groves of Monticello, & become a mere spectator of the passing events."[5]

In correspondence with Adams, Rush increasingly referred to his dreams; in one, Rush was president and signed into law an alcohol abstinence edict that unexpectedly created havoc by upsetting the "empire of habit." Adams cheered him on: "That Rosicrucian sylph, that Fairy Queen Mab, or . . . whatever it is that inspired your nightly dreams, I would not exchange . . . for the Daemon of Socrates. You have more wit and humor and sense in your sleep than other people, I was about to say, than you have yourself when awake."[6] Such exchanges established the ground for Adams's acceptance of Rush's ultimate dream, upon Jefferson's retirement in 1809, in which Rush envisioned a reestablishing of cordial relations between Adams and Jefferson after a decade of bitterness between them. At Rush's urging, the two Founders did eventually resume correspondence, beginning with Adams sending along two pieces of what he called "homespun," John Quincy Adams's two-volume *Lectures on Rhetoric and Oratory*—Jefferson had been quite fond of the adolescent Quincy when they had all been in Paris nearly thirty years earlier. The volumes' receipt by Jefferson opened the floodgates, and the two Founders resumed an exchange of ideas that continued to energize and enlighten them to the end of their days. In the letters, Adams was a bit wistful about not having pursued science, which Jefferson characterized as a continual source of excitement and intellectual challenge. They traded recollections, disagreeing about specific content of memories but agreeing that they had been on the same side, fellow patriots. It became clear that these two Founders still considered the governance structure of the United States as an experiment, a test of theory that was under continual challenge and subject to expected and welcomed tinkering and refinement.[7]

Among the subjects they discussed was Jefferson's devotion in retirement to founding what would eventually become the University of Virginia at Charlottesville. He had been ruminating on such an institution since his term as governor (1779–1781) and his attempts to upgrade the College of William & Mary. In 1800, seeking to lure Joseph Priestley to Virginia, he had outlined a scheme to replace William & Mary, in a better climate, with "an university on a plan so broad & liberal & *modern*, as to be worth patronizing with the public support, and be a temptation to the youth of other states to come and drink of the cup of knowledge & fraternize with us." The curriculum would center on what he thought of as the sciences, "Botany, Chemistry, Zoology, Anatomy, Surgery, Natl Philosophy, Agriculture, Mathematics, Astronomy, Geology," in addition to history, ethics, law, and the fine arts. "We should propose that the professors follow no other calling, so that their whole time may be given to their academical functions."[8] He also discussed the project with E. I. Du Pont, whom he had known in Paris. Du Pont enthusiastically seconded the idea, arguing that Europe's universities had become "extinguishers of intelligence" and that America's could surely do better. He suggested four schools within the university, for medicine, mines, law, and mathematically based sciences—the last he labeled the School of Transcendental Geometry and hoped that it would include military engineering—and further envisioned the university as part of a system that would include a national library, a national botanical garden, and a national museum.[9]

By the time Jefferson retired to Monticello, his vision for the university was more practical and localized; he drew up the plans, both architectural and in terms of organization and curriculums, for an ideal university whose instruction would be more oriented toward the sciences than that of any other American university. Classical education, of the sort he had received in his youth from Reverend Maury and William Small, would have to be left behind as inapplicable to youth in the growing United States of America. The establishment of the university would remain Jefferson's major focus for the rest of his life.

IN 1812, HALFWAY THROUGH James Madison's two-term presidency, what Americans then referred to as the second war for independence began; it ended as Madison was preparing to hand over the presidency to his secretary of state, James Monroe. That divisive war left much rebuilding to do, for instance of the President's House and other public buildings in the District of Columbia that had been burned by the British. Accompanying this physical rebirth was the widespread understanding that the era of the Founding Fathers was drawing to a close.

The benefits of having science-minded individuals involved in the framing of the Revolution, in organizing and fighting the war for independence, and in leading the American republic through its nascent phases had been many, and they were markedly formative and pattern-setting. Underlying them was the recognition by the polity that democracy was compatible with and received sustenance from enlightened scientific thinking. The new nation's citizens shared the sense that the country's governance required what science demanded of its adherents, perpetual attention to facts, and consideration of alterations to its laws to encompass new facts and challenges. Also emerging was the sense that the future growth and prosperity of the country was interwoven with and tied to the continuing evolution of its science and technology.

The Founders had been overwhelmingly involved in establishing principles, fashioning a government expressive of those principles, and forming that government's basic institutions. After the War of 1812, it was widely understood that the objectives and tasks of the next generation of presidents had to be quite different from those of the Founders; the new generation's concerns had to be reaping the promise of the future by expanding the United States of America to its continental borders and by enabling the bulk of its citizens, not only its elites, to prosper. The ability of James Monroe, John Quincy Adams, and Andrew Jackson to make progress toward these goals was enhanced by their being able to rely on the tradition of science-influenced experimentation at the heart of the exercise of democratic governance, and on the linked expectation that each new generation's accomplishments could and should surpass those of the previous ones.

ACKNOWLEDGMENTS

MY FIRST FORAY INTO THE REVOLUTIONARY ERA after decades of writing about more recent history, it was made measurably easier and more productive by the assistance given to me by many individuals and institutions. Among the institutions, my foremost debt is to the New York Public Library, my second home, for use of its Wertheim Room for research in its collections. I thank Jay Barksdale of the NYPL for his help. Another such home has been The Writers Room in New York; the staff, headed by Donna Brodie, and my fellow board members, have consistently encouraged me through this extended project.

Once again, as it has on my previous science history project, the book and documentary films *Absolute Zero and the Conquest Of Cold*, the Alfred P. Sloan Foundation's Program for the Public Understanding of Science and Technology enabled me through a generous grant to complete a project dear to my heart and that, I hope, reaches toward our jointly held goal of raising the level of understanding about scientific subjects among non-scientists. My thanks to vice-president Doron Weber for championing this grant.

A grant from the Jack Miller Foundation, in association with the Huntington Library, as part of their seminar "Sacred and Secular Revolutions," allowed me to spend a month researching the Huntington's vast holdings in the history of science and in the American Revolutionary era. My thanks to Pamela Edwards of the Miller Center, Steve Hindle of the Huntington, my fellow panelists, and to the Library's very knowledgeable and helpful staff.

I was also ably assisted at the American Philosophical Library, the Historical Society of Pennsylvania, the Jefferson Library at Monticello, the Swem Library at the College of William and Mary, the Library of the University of Virginia at Charlottesville, the American Antiquarian Library, and the Massachusetts Historical Society. My hometown library, the Scoville Library in Salisbury, CT, obtained difficult-to-find materials through Connecticut's interlibrary loan system.

My thanks to longtime agent, Mel Berger of WME, and to the editing staff at Palgrave Macmillan, especially editor Elisabeth Dyssegaard, for their professionalism, enthusiasm, and attention to detail.

My wife, Harriet Shelare, and my sons, Noah and Daniel Shachtman, have acted as sounding boards, early readers, and prescient critics throughout the composition of the book. Chapters have also been read and helpful critiques provided to me by Larry Bader, Robyn Davis, Lee Dembart, Ken Knoespel, William Kremer, Bruce McEver, Glenn Moots, Edward Nickerson, Steve Usselman, Jon Wilkman, and Walter Woodward. Whatever errors remain in the manuscript are mine alone.

Tom Shachtman—Salisbury, CT, March 2014

A WORD ABOUT SOURCES

THIS IS THE GOLDEN AGE FOR COMPUTER-connected research into the works of the Founding Fathers. The important papers and correspondence of Washington, Jefferson, Adams, Franklin, Hamilton, and Madison are mostly in print and increasingly online. More than 149,000 such documents, mostly the letters, are now available at http://founders.archives.gov/, a collaboration between the National Archives and the University of Virginia Press. Since it is possible to locate in that archive and to view in their entirety most of the Founders' documents referred to in the notes, I have not listed each document's online reference coordinates but refer to it by date, author, and recipient. Also, in the notes, the most frequently-cited letter-writers and recipients are referred to by initials: JA, John Adams; JB, John Bartram; PC; Peter Collinson; BF, Benjamin Franklin; AH, Alexander Hamilton; TJ, Thomas Jefferson; JM, James Madison; TP, Thomas Paine; DR, David Rittenhouse; BR, Benjamin Rush; GW, George Washington. The Founders' papers are referred to in the Notes by the following abbreviations: The Works of John Adams, WJA; The Papers of Benjamin Franklin, PBF; The Papers of Thomas Jefferson, PTJ; The Papers of James Madison, PJM; The Papers of Benjamin Rush, PBR; the Papers of George Washington, PGW.

Also digitized are some of the Founders' papers but they are not in the above-mentioned database, and for those I have listed the alternate source. Also digitized are the *England Courant* and early volumes of the *Philosophical Transactions of the Royal Society*. Virtually all periodic material (newspapers, pamphlets, broadsides, and some books) published in the American colonies and the United States of America prior to 1800 have been digitized and are available through such depots as the New York Public Library.

The provenance of physical documents, when not obvious, is noted as residing in the various archives in which I viewed them, among these the American Philosophical Society (APS), the Huntington Library, the American Antiquarian Society (AAS), the Swem Library of the College of William & Mary, the Historical Society of Pennsylvania, the Massachusetts Historical Society, and the Jefferson Library at Monticello.

To reduce the size of the bibliography, I list in it only books and articles that I found to be highly relevant and readily available. Those secondary materials referred to only once in my text are listed fully in the notes rather than in the bibliography.

COLLECTED PAPERS

The Works of John Adams, abbreviated in the Notes as WJA
The Papers of Benjamin Franklin, PBF
The Papers of Thomas Jefferson, PTJ
The Papers of James Madison, PJM
The Papers of George Washington, PGW, in various series such as Colonial, Revolutionary War.
The Papers of Benjamin Rush, PBR

NOTES

FOREWORD

1. Quoted in Hindle, *The Pursuit of Science in Revolutionary America*, p. 67.
2. Kant, "What is Enlightenment?" 1784. Translated by Mary C. Smith. Online at: http://www.columbia.edu/acis/ets/CCREAD/etscc/kant.html.
3. Church assistant, in Carl and Jessica Bridenbaugh, *Rebels and Gentlemen*, p. 99.
4. Michel Foucault, "What Is Enlightenment?" in *The Foucault Reader.*
5. JA to Waterhouse, April 23, 1785, in W. C. Ford, ed., *Statesman and Friend,*
6. TJ to Caspar Wistar, June 10, 1817.
7. Foucault, *The Order of Things*, p. 73.
8. John William Draper, *History of the Conflict Between Religion and Science* (New York: D. Appleton, 1874).
9. Frazer, *The Religious Beliefs of America's Founders*, p. 14.
10. Becker, *The Declaration of Independence*, p. 37; Morgan, "Puritan Ethic," p. 6.
11. *Diary and Autobiography of John Adams*, vol. 1 of *WJA*, entry of May 1, 1755.
12. Franklin, *The Autobiography of Benjamin Franklin*, p. 43.
13. "Articles of Belief and Acts of Religion," 1728, *PBF*, vol. 1, pp. 101–109.
14. TJ to BR, September 23, 1800.
15. Frazer, pp. 197–203.
16. Wood, *The Radicalism of the American Revolution*, p. 5.
17. See T. H. Breen, *The Marketplace of Revolution;* and Young and Nobles, *Whose American Revolution Was It?*
18. Shapin and Schaffer, *Leviathan and the Air Pump*, p. 337.
19. Francis Bacon, *The New Atlantis*, 1624. Online edition at: http://oregonstate.edu/instruct/phl302/texts/bacon/atlantis.html.
20. d'Alembert, quoted in Thomas L. Hankins, *Science and the Enlightenment* (Cambridge: Cambridge University Press, 1985), p. 1.

CHAPTER 1: CHILDHOODS OF THE FOUNDING FATHERS

1. See Mintz, *Huck's Raft.*
2. Robert L. Griswold, *Fatherhood in America, A History*, p. 11; Mintz and Kellogg, *Domestic Revolutions*, pp. 37–40.
3. Clayne L. Pope, "Adult Mortality in America before 1900: A View from Family Histories," in *Strategic Factors in Nineteenth Century American Economic*

History, ed. Claudia Goldin and Hugh Rockoff (Chicago: University of Chicago Press, 2002).

4. Joseph H. Pleck, "American Fathering in Historical Perspective," in *Changing Men: New Directions in Research on Men and Masculinity,* ed. Michael S. Kimmel (Newbury Park, CA: Sage, 1987).

5. Ibid.

6. TJ to BR, August 17, 1811, http://www.constitution.org/tj/jeff13.txt, pp. 74–75.

7. Dean Keith Simonton, *Scientific Genius: A Psychology of Science* (Cambridge: Cambridge University Press, 1988); TJ to TJ Randolph Washington, November 24, 1808. Online at: http://www.let.rug.nl/usa/presidents/thomas-jefferson /letters-of-thomas-jefferson/jefl187.php.

8. Bacon, *The New Atlantis.*

9. Hughes, *Surveyors and Statesmen,* p. 28.

10. *PGW.* Colonial Series, vol. 1.

11. Hughes, *Surveyors and Statesmen,* p. 128.

12. Ibid., p. 93.

13. *PGW,* vol. 1, pp. 196–197, letter of August 1754.

14. *The Diaries of George Washington, 1748–1799,* ed. John C. Fitzpatrick, vol. 1, 1748–1770 (Boston: Houghton Mifflin, 1925), p. 21.

15. Bruce A. Ragdale, "George Washington, the British Tobacco Trade, and Economic Opportunity in Prerevolutionary Virginia," *Virginia Magazine of History and Biography* 97, no. 2 (April 1989): 158.

16. *Adams Diary,* vol. 3, pp. 256–258; Shute, *The Scientific Work of John Winthrop;* poem, in Cohen, *Some Early Tools of American Science.*

17. JA to Richard Cranch, October–December 1758.

18. See Walter W. Woodward, *Prospero's America.*

19. JA to Waterhouse, April 23, 1785, in W. C. Ford, ed., *Statesman and Friend.*

20. See Cohen, *Science and the Founding Fathers,* pp. 198–204.

21. Quoted in Shute, *The Scientific Work of John Winthrop.*

22. *Adams Diary,* vol. 1, entry of November 18, 1755; Winthrop lecture, reprinted in Shute, *The Scientific Work of John Winthrop;* JA notes on Winthrop lecture, cited in Cohen, *Science and the Founding Fathers,* pp. 213–214.

23. *Earliest Diaries,* draft letter of 1758, pp. 70–71.

24. Buchan, *Crowded with Genius,* p. 336.

25. Jefferson, "Autobiography," http://avalon.law.yale.edu/19th_century/jeffauto .asp; Kimball, *Jefferson: The Road to Glory,* p. 37. See also Dumas Malone, *Jefferson the Virginian* (Boston: Little, Brown, 1948).

26. TJ to John Harvie, January 14, 1760.

27. Francis Bacon, *The Great Instauration,* 1620. Part I, p.12. Online at: http://www .constitution.org/bacon/instauration.htm; Claggett, "William Small, 1734– 1744: Teacher, Mentor, Scientist."

28. TJ to L. H. Girardin, January 15, 1815. Online at: http://thomasjeffersonleader ship.com/blog/were-you-this-clever-at-age-16/.

29. *Autobiography* and Girardin letter.

30. Edgehill Randolph to William Small, June 25, 1767, in William Small Files, Swem Library, College of William & Mary.

31. Franklin, quoted in Uglow, *The Lunar Men,* p. 82; TJ to TJ Randolph, November 24, 1808. See also Schofield, *The Lunar Society of Birmingham.*

32. Walsh, *Education of the Founding Fathers,* p. ix., pp. 14–23.

33. Cohen, *Science and the Founding Fathers,* pp. 265–267.

34. JM to William Bradford, April 1, 1774.

35. AH letter, quoted in Chernow, *Alexander Hamilton.*
36. Chernow, *Alexander Hamilton;* James Thomas Flexner, *The Young Hamilton: A Biography* (Boston: Little, Brown, 1978).
37. Isenberg, *Fallen Founder;* York, *Mechanical Metamorphosis,* p. 28.
38. Rittenhouse, "An Oration, Delivered February 24, 1775, before the American Philosophical Society," Philadelphia, APS, 1775. See chapter 5, *infra,* for an extended review of this oration.
39. Questebrune, *A Short Introduction to Natural Philosophy.*

CHAPTER 2: "VARIOLA" IN BOSTON, 1721–1722

1. Franklin, *Autobiography.* See also Isaacson, *Benjamin Franklin,* pp. 13–20.
2. Isaacson, *Benjamin Franklin,* p. 19; Chaplin, *The First Scientific American,* pp. 9–27.
3. "Silence Dogood" letter to *New England Courant,* May 14, 1722. Online at: http://www.ushistory.org/franklin/courant/silencedogood.htm.
4. Chaplin, *The First Scientific American,* pp. 18–19.
5. Franklin's reading, *Autobiography;* Josiah Franklin experiment, "Report of Peter Kalm," extract, October 12, 1749, in *Pennsylvania Gazette,* online at: http://franklinpapers.org/franklin/framedVolumes.jsp?vol=4&page=061a.
6. Stanley M. Aronson and Lucile Newman, "God Have Mercy on This House: Being a Brief Chronicle of Smallpox in Colonial New England." Online at: http://www.brown.edu/Administration/News_Bureau/2002-03/02-017t.html.
7. Zabdiel Boylston, *Historical Account of the Small-pox Inoculated* (London: S. Chandler, 1726).
8. Silverman, *The Life and Times of Cotton Mather,* pp. 252–254.
9. Mather open letter, quoted in Silverman, p. 338.
10. Douglass, quoted in Hoermann, *Cadwallader Colden.*
11. Douglass, "A Practical Essay Concerning the Smallpox," p. 12.
12. Landsman, *From Colonials to Provincials,* pp. 60–61.
13. Silverman, p. 350.
14. Biographical entry in James Thacher, *American Medical Biography,* vol.1 (Boston: Richardson & Lord, 1828). Online at: www.celebrateboston.com/biography/zabdiel-boylston.htm.
15. *Courant* epidemic coverage, in Richard Hildreth, *The History of the United States of America,* vol. 1 (New York: Harper & Bros., 1851-2), pp. 300–302.
16. Leonard, "Harvard's First Science Professor," pp. 135–168. Online at: http://pds.lib.harvard.edu/pds/viewtext/2573358?op=t&n=14097.
17. *PBF,* vol. 1, various.
18. Aronson and Newman, "God Have Mercy on This House."
19. Leonard, "Harvard's First Science Professor."
20. Silverman, pp. 360–363.

CHAPTER 3: GODFATHERS OF AMERICAN SCIENCE

1. Pickstone, *Ways of Knowing,* p. 60.
2. Baltzell, *Puritan Boston and Quaker Philadelphia,* p. 166.
3. Brinton, *Friends for 300 Years,* p. 140.
4. Logan, quoted in Tolles, *James Logan,* p. 91.
5. Roy N. Lokken, ed., "The Scientific Papers of James Logan," *Transactions of the American Philosophical Society* 62, part 6 (1972).

6. Wollaston, *The Religion of Nature Delineated*, pp. 16–63. Italics in original.

7. Logan, quoted in Tolles, *James Logan*, p. 199; Logan, "Some Experiments concerning the Impregnation of the Seeds of Plants, as Communicated in a Letter to Peter Collinson." *Philosophical Transactions of the Royal Society* 38, no. 440 (January–February–March 1736).

8. Ship captain letter, in George F. Frick, "The Royal Society in America," in *The Pursuit of Knowledge in the Early American Republic*, ed. Oleson and Brown, pp. 80–81.

9. Foucault, "What Is Enlightenment?," p. 54.

10. Logan to Halley, quoted in Nathan Spencer, "Thomas Godfrey and the Invention of the Quadrant," extracted from the *American Magazine*, July 1758, in 1809 (APS Files).

11. See Dava Sobel, *Longitude: The True Story of a Lone Genius Who Solved the Greatest Scientific Problem of His Time* (New York: Walker, 1995).

12. Tolles, *James Logan*, pp. 202–204.

13. Bridenbaugh and Bridenbaugh, *Rebels and Gentlemen*, p. 308.

14. Slaughter, *The Natures of John and William Bartram*, p. 49.

15. Chaplin, *The First Scientific American*, p. 65.

16. "Proposal to Myself," James Logan Collection, Historical Society of Pennsylvania.

17. Tolles, *James Logan*, pp. 208–214.

18. Questions for the Junto come from the notes of the later "Baby Junto," the American Society for the Promotion of Useful Knowledge, APS Archives I, 1758.

19. Bridenbaugh and Bridenbaugh, *Rebels and Gentlemen*, p. 309.

20. Jill Lepore, *Book of Ages: The Life and Opinions of Jane Franklin* (New York: Alfred A. Knopf, 2013).

21. Stearns, *Science in the British Colonies of America*, p. 515; Stearns, Raymond P., "Colonial Fellows of the Royal Society of London, 1661–1788," *William and Mary Quarterly*, series 3 (1946): 208–268.

22. William Bartram, "Some Account of the Late Mr. John Bartram, of Pennsylvania," *Philadelphia Medical and Physical Journal*, part 1, vol. 1, sec. 2 (1804): 116–117.

23. Alan W. Armstrong, "John Bartram and Peter Collinson: A Correspondence of Science and Friendship," in *America's Curious Botanist*, Hoffman and Van Horne, eds., p. 23; James Logan letters to PC and to JB of June 1736, quoted in Wulf, *The Brother Gardeners*, pp. 32, 62; PC to JB, quoted in William Darlington, *Memorials of John Bartram and Humphrey Marshall* (Philadelphia: Lindsay & Blackiston, 1849), p. 152.

24. PC to JB, January 24, 1735. APS file B.C.692a, folder IV, 1721–1735.

25. APS letter file B.C.692a, folder IV, letters 1736–1740.

26. JB to Catesby, March 1740, *Correspondence*, p. 152.

27. Ibid.

28. William H. Goetzmann, "John Bartram's Journey to Onondaga in Context," in *America's Curious Botanist*, Hoffman and Van Horne, eds., pp. 97–106; quotes from Bartram's *Journey from Pennsylvania to Onondaga*. "Wonderful productions" from JB to Mark Catesby, March 1741, *Correspondence*, p. 152.

29. JB to PC, November 17, 1742. *Correspondence*, pp. 208–209.

30. PC to JB, April 12, 1739, in Darlington, *Memorials of John Bartram and Humphrey Marshall*, pp. 128–133.

31. "Proposal for the American Philosophical Society," 1743. Online at: http://nationalhumanitiescenter.org/pds/becomingamer/ideas/text4/amerphilsociety.pdf

32. Ibid.
33. JB to Colden, April 7, 1745, copy at APS.
34. JB to Colden, April 29, 1744. Gratz Collection, Historical Society of Pennsylvania.
35. Jane Colden, Hoermann, *Cadwallader Colden*, pp. 32–33; and Sara Stidstone Gronim, "What Jane Knew: A Woman Botanist in the Eighteenth Century," *Journal of Women's History* 19, no. 3 (Fall 2007).
36. Newton and Colden quotes and explanations, Hoermann, *Cadwallader Colden*, pp. 80–87.
37. Garden and BF, quoted in Hoermann, *Cadwallader Colden*, p. 95.
38. Parrish, *American Curiosity*, p. 133.
39. Garden to British botanist John Ellis, quoted in Daniels, *Science in American Society.*
40. Garden to Colden, November 4, 1754, in Gray, ed., *Selections from the Scientific Correspondence of Cadwallader Colden.*
41. Various Colden letters quoted in Slaughter, *The Natures of John and William Bartram*, p. 96.
42. JB to Colden, January 24, 1745. *Correspondence of Bartram*, pp. 271–272.
43. Stearns, *Science in the British Colonies*, p. 601.
44. Gronim, "What Jane Knew," p. 33; Parrish, *American Curiosity*, pp. 196–197.
45. Garden to Linnaeus, March 15, 1755, quoted in Parrish, *American Curiosity.*

CHAPTER 4: THE BOLT FROM THE BLUE

1. PC to Colden, March 30, 1745, *Colden Papers*, vol. 3, pp. 109–110.
2. BF to Cadwallader Colden, February 1746, *PBF*, vol. 3, p. 67.
3. Priestley, *The History and Present State of Electricity.*
4. Newton, quoted in Zev Bechler, "Newton on Electricity and the Aether," in *Electricity and Experimental Physics in Eighteenth-Century Europe*, ed. R. W. Home (Aldershot, Hampshire: Ashgate, 1992).
5. Charles François de Cisternay Dufay, "A Discourse Concerning Electricity," *Philosophical Transactions* 38 (1734).
6. Desaguliers, *A Dissertation concerning Electricity.*
7. Musschenbroek, quoted in Heilbron, *Elements of Early Modern Physics*, pp. 314–315, 323.
8. Hornberger, *Scientific Thought in the American Colleges, 1638–1800*, pp. 44–45; Isaac Greenwood, *An Experimental Course of Natural Philosophy* (Boston, Bartholomew Green, 1726).
9. Leonard, "Harvard's First Science Professor," pp. 135–168.
10. Neither Chaplin nor Isaacson, the most recent Franklin biographers, attribute any influence on Franklin to Greenwood or Desaguliers.
11. Albrecht von Haller, "Historical Account of the Wonderful Discoveries Made in Germany, &c., concerning Electricity," *Gentleman's Magazine* 15, no. 4 (1745).
12. Lemay, *Ebenezer Kinnersley, Franklin's Friend.*
13. Priestley, *The History and Present State of Electricity.*
14. BF to PC, May 25, 1747, *PBF*, vol. 3, pp. 126 *et seq.*
15. BF to PC, ibid.
16. Cohen, *Benjamin Franklin's Experiments*, p. 64, and citing BF to PC.
17. BF to PC, May 25, 1747, *PBF*, vol. 3, pp 131–133.
18. Ibid., p. 133.
19. Cohen, *Benjamin Franklin's Experiments*, p. 64; BF to PC, August 14, 1747, *PBF*, Vol. 3.

20. Franklin, *Experiments and Observations on Electricity*, p. 29.
21. Ibid., pp. 37–38.
22. Lemay, *Ebenezer Kinnersley, Franklin's Friend*, pp. 62–63.
23. Kinnersley, *A Course of Experiments*.
24. Delbourgo, *A Most Amazing Scene of Wonders*, pp. 93–98.
25. *New York Gazette*, June 1, 1752, quoted in Lemay, *Ebenezer Kinnersley, Franklin's Friend*, p. 77.
26. Delbourgo, *A Most Amazing Scene of Wonders*, p. 97.
27. Quoted in Cohen, *Benjamin Franklin's Experiments*, p. 95.
28. Voltaire, quoted in Maluf, "Jean Antoine Nollet and Experimental Natural Philosophy in Eighteenth Century France."
29. Riskin, *Science in the Age of Sensibility*.
30. Buffon's preface, 1752, quoted in Roger, *Buffon: A Life in Natural History*, p. 26.
31. This discussion draws on Maluf, J. Roger, I. B. Cohen, Chaplin, and Heilbron.
32. BF to PC, October 19, 1752, *Experiments*, p. 111.
33. PC to BF, July 20, 1753, quoted in Cohen, *Benjamin Franklin's Experiments*, p. 116.
34. David Colden to BF, December 4, 1753, and John Canton to the Royal Society, December 6, 1753, printed in Franklin, *New Experiments and Observations on Electricity*, pp. 131–149.
35. Kuhn, *The Structure of Scientific Revolutions*, p. 18.
36. Latour and Woolgar, *Laboratory Life: The Construction of Scientific Facts*.
37. BF to Jan Ingenhousz, October 2, 1781.
38. Robert Boyle, "The Publisher to the Reader," in *New Experiments and Observations Touching Cold*, 2nd ed. (Oxford: Richard Davis, 1683), p. 2.

CHAPTER 5: TRACKING THE HEAVENS FROM THE COLONIES

1. Anderson, *The Day the World Discovered the Sun;* Wulf, *Chasing Venus*.
2. Buffon, quoted in Jacques Roger, *Buffon: A Life in Natural History*, pp. 83–84, 110.
3. BF, Stiles, and Alison letters quoted in Schlenther, *Charles Thomson*.
4. "Junto and American Society," in "Papers Concerning the American Society for Useful Knowledge." Archives I, no. 1 and 2, American Philosophical Society.
5. Manuel and Manuel, *James Bowdoin and the Patriot Philosophers*, p. 64.
6. PC to BF, July 7, 1750. Franklin, *Letters*, vol. 4, pp. 3–6; and excerpt of letter from Penn to Governor Hamilton, February 12, 1750.
7. Hindle, *The Pursuit of Science in Revolutionary America*, pp. 105–126.
8. Anderson, *The Day the World Discovered the Sun;* and Wulf, *Chasing Venus*.
9. Edwin Danson, *Drawing the Line: How Mason and Dixon Surveyed the Most Famous Border in America* (New York: John Wiley, 2001).
10. Buffon passages from J. Roger, *Buffon: A Life in Natural History*, pp. 82-84; Dugatkin, *Mr. Jefferson and the Giant Moose*, pp. 10-30.
11. BR to Ebenezer Hazard, November 9, 1765. *Letters of Rush*, vol. 1., p. 18.
12. Voltaire note, in Morgan diary 1764, cited in Bell, *Patriot-Improvers: Biographical Sketches of the Members of the American Philosophical Society*, vol. 2.
13. John Morgan, "Discourse upon the Institution of Medical Schools in America, with a Preface Containing . . . the author's Apology for attempting to introduce the regular mode of practicing physics in Philadelphia." Philadelphia, 1765.
14. Schlenther, *Charles Thomson: A Patriot's Pursuit*, p. 75.
15. "Papers Concerning the American Society."

16. Ibid.
17. Quoted in Schlenther, *Charles Thomson: A Patriot's Pursuit*, p. 76
18. Bridenbaugh and Bridenbaugh, *Rebels and Gentlemen*, pp. 335–336.
19. Colden to PC, January 14, 1766. Huntington Library HM 8256.
20. See, e.g., JB to BF, Nov. 5, 1768, and BF to JB, Jan. 9, 1769.
21. Stiles, 1765, quoted in Daniels, *Science in American Society*, p. 136.
22. Rittenhouse description and British comment, in Howard C. Rice Jr., *The Rittenhouse Orrery, Princeton's Eighteenth-Century Planetarium, 1767–1954* (Princeton: Princeton University Press, 1954).
23. West, 1769, in Donald Fleming, "Science and Technology in Providence."
24. Morgan, *The Gentle Puritan*, p. 155.
25. Maskelyne letter, "Early Proceedings of the American Philosophical Society . . . compiled . . . from the Manuscript Minutes of its Meetings from 1744 to 1838," *Proceedings of the APS*, 1884.
26. Ibid.
27. Cited in S. Brown, *Benjamin Thompson*, p. 22
28. Hindle, *The Pursuit of Science in Revolutionary America*, p. 189.
29. APS Minutes, 1769–1774.
30. Bartram to BR, December 5, 1767. *Correspondence*, pp. 690–691.
31. *Proceedings of the APS*, 1884, *op. cit.*

CHAPTER 6: "EXPRESSIONS OF THE AMERICAN MIND"

1. Jürgen Habermas, *The Structural Transformation of the Public Sphere: An Inquiry into a Category of Bourgeois Society* (Cambridge, MA: MIT Press, 1989), pp. 27–43.
2. David Zaret, "Religion, Science and Printing in the Public Spheres in Seventeenth-Century England," in *Habermas and the Public Sphere*, ed. Craig Calhoun (Cambridge, MA: MIT Press, 1992).
3. Wood, *Radicalism*, pp. 218–219; Boorstin, *The Lost World of Thomas Jefferson*, pp. 243–244.
4. Adams, *WJA*, vol. 2, p. 513.
5. William Bradford to JM, August 1, 1774, *PJM*, Vol. 1, pp. 117–120
6. Hindle, *David Rittenhouse*, pp.112–122.
7. David Rittenhouse, 1775 address, APS archives, Mss.520.4.R51ms.
8. T. H. Breen, *The Marketplace of Revolution: How Consumer Politics Shaped American Independence* (New York: Oxford University Press, 2004), p. 205.
9. *Virginia Gazette*, March 1770, cited in Lyons, *The Society for Useful Knowledge*, p. 134; Ragdale, "George Washington, the British Tobacco Trade, and Economic Opportunity in Prerevolutionary Virginia." p. 188.
10. York, *Mechanical Metamorphosis*, pp. 18, 43; and Morgan, "The Puritan Ethic and the American Revolution," p. 9–10.
11. Virginia Society meeting, recorded in *Washington Diary*, entry of June 1774, and in *Virginia Gazette*, June 16, 1774.
12. Ragdale, "George Washington, the British Tobacco Trade, and Economic Opportunity in Prerevolutionary Virginia."
13. Rush speech, Brodsky, *Benjamin Rush*, pp. 118–119.
14. Smith, *An Inquiry into the Nature and Causes of the Wealth of Nations*, 1776. Online at: http://www2.hn.psu.edu/faculty/jmanis/adam-smith/wealth-nations .pdf.
15. York, *Mechanical Metamorphosis*, pp. 18, 26.

16. Chaplin, *The First Scientific American,* pp. 231–232.

17. Worthington C. Ford, ed., *Journals of the Continental Congress, 1774–1789,* vol. 1, pp. 75–80 (Washington, DC: Government Printing Office, 1904).

18. Keane, *Tom Paine,* pp. 83–100.

19. Ibid. and Brodsky, *Benjamin Rush,* pp. 115–117.

20. Thomas Paine, *Common Sense,* 1776, p. 24. Online at: http://www.early america.com/earlyamerica/milestones/commonsense/text.html.

21. JA to Moses Gill, June 10, 1775. *WJA,* vol. 3, pp. 20–22.

22. Keane, *Tom Paine.*

23. Some authors assert that Samuel Adams also reviewed Paine's text before it was published, but Adams's most recent biographer, Mark Puls, only credits Adams with actively supporting the pamphlet once it was published. Mark Puls, *Samuel Adams: Father of the American Revolution* (New York: Palgrave Macmillan, 2006), p. 181.

24. Wood, *Revolutionary Characters,* p. 250.

25. Sennett, *The Fall of Public Man,* p. 79.

26. Various quotations from *Common Sense,* p. 22.

27. Washington quotation, Keane, *Benjamin Rush,* p. 111.

28. Bailyn, *The Ideological Origins of the American Revolution,* pp. x, 18–19.

29. Locke, *An Essay Concerning Human Understanding,* 4, IV, 3.

30. Eric Nelson, "Hebraism and the Republican Turn of 1776: A Contemporary Account of the Debate over *Common Sense," William and Mary Quarterly* (October 2013): 807; Congressional action, March 1776, quoted in Kasson, *Civilizing the Machine,* p. 11.

31. May 15 declaration, Maier, *Ratification: The People Debate the Constitution, 1787–1788,* pp. 37–38; Adams to Jefferson, cited in Meacham, *Thomas Jefferson: The Art of Power,* p. 103.

32. TJ to Henry Lee, May 8, 1825. At: http://www.let.rug.nl/usa/presidents/thomas -jefferson/letters-of-thomas-jefferson/jefl282.php.

33. These and other quotes are from Jefferson's "rough draft," online at: http:// www.ushistory.org/declaration/document/rough.htm.

34. Wills, *Inventing America,* pp. 93–94.

35. JA to T. Pickering, August 6, 1822, *WJA,* vol. 2, p. 512.

36. TJ, letter to Lee.

37. Becker, *The Declaration of Independence,* p. 44.

38. Frazer, *The Religious Beliefs of America's Founders,* pp. 214–218; Maier, *American Scripture,* p. 148; Becker, *The Declaration of Independence,* p. 37.

39. Locke, *Second Treatise on Civil Government,* 1689. At: www.constitution.org /jl/2ndtreat.htm.

40. Jefferson "rough draft," Boorstin, *The Lost World of Thomas Jefferson,* p. 61.

41. Himmelfarb, *The Roads to Modernity,* p. 204.

42. Wollaston, *The Religion of Nature Delineated,* pp. 18–31.

43. For a discussion of the philosophic antecedents of this view of happiness as a pursuit, see Darrin M. McMahon, *Happiness: A History* (New York: Grove Atlantic, 2006).

CHAPTER 7: "THIS MOST DANGEROUS ENEMY"

1. The most extensive description of 1740s variolation technique is in Fenn, *Pox Americana.*

2. Chaplin, *The First Scientific American*, p. 66; Howard Markel, "Life, Liberty, and the Pursuit of Vaccines," *New York Times*, February 28, 2011.

3. Franklin, introduction to William Heberden, "Some Account of the Success of Inoculation for the Small-Pox in England and America Together with Plain Instructions, By Which Any Person May Be Enabled to Perform the Operation, and Conduct the Patient through the Distemper." London, 1754. Online at: http://www.historyofvaccines.org/content/blog/library-treasures-benjamin-franklin-smallpox-pamphleteer.

4. Rush, *Medical Inquiries and Observations*, vol. 3, p. 125.

5. Fenn, *Pox Americana*, pp. 33–35, 79, 84.

6. Bedini, *Thomas Jefferson: Statesman of Science*, pp. 46–47.

7. Dewey, "Thomas Jefferson's Law Practice."

8. Griffenhagen, "Drug Supplies in the American Revolution."

9. A. Becker, "Smallpox in Washington's Army"; Fenn, *Pox Americana*, pp. 44–48.

10. Jasper Copping, "George Washington Named Britain's Greatest Ever Foe," *Morning Telegraph*, April 4, 2012. Online at: http://www.telegraph.co.uk/history/9204961/George-Washington-named-Britains-greatest-ever-foe.html.

11. GW to Congress, July 21, 1775, online at: http://founders.archives.gov/documents/Washington/03-01-02-0085.

12. Mark Puls, *Samuel Adams: Father of the American Revolution* (New York: Palgrave Macmillan, 2006), pp. 172–173.

13. Gillett, "The Army Medical Department, 1775–1818."

14. GW to John Hancock, September 25, 1776.

15. Oscar Reiss, *Medicine and the American Revolution: How Diseases and Their Treatments Affected the American Army* (Jefferson, NC: McFarland & Co., 1998), pp. 25–26.

16. Gillett, "The Army Medical Department," p. 53.

17. Griffenhagen, "Drug Supplies in the American Revolution," pp. 114–115.

18. Chernow, *Washington: A Life*, pp. 199–200.

19. *March to Quebec: Journals of the Members of Arnold's Expedition* (New York: Doubleday Doran, 1954), pp. 238–240, 372–375; Fenn, *Pox Americana*, pp. 62–70.

20. Gillett, "The Army Medical Department," pp. 60–61.

21. Fenn, *Pox Americana*, pp. 55–60.

22. Washington, order of March 13, 1776. Quoted in A. Becker, "Smallpox in Washington's Army," p. 402.

23. Ellis, *His Excellency, George Washington*, pp. 86–87; Fenn, *Pox Americana*, pp. 52–53.

24. Fenn, *Pox Americana*, p. 54.

25. John Morgan to JA, February 19, 1776, *WJA*, vol. 4, pp. 30–36.

26. Griffenhagen, "Drug Supplies in the American Revolution," p. 115–116.

27. A. Becker, "Smallpox in Washington's Army," p. 422.

28. Ellis, *His Excellency, George Washington*, p. 87.

29. Fenn, *Pox Americana*; A. Becker, "Smallpox in Washington's Army"; GW to Shippen, March 1, 1777, and January 7, 1777. *PGW, Revolutionary Series*, vol. 8, pp. 476–477.

30. Gillett, "The Army Medical Department, 1775–1818," pp. 74–76.

31. Brodsky, *Benjamin Rush*, pp. 209–216.

32. Rush, "To the Officers in the Army of the United States: Directions for Preserving the Health of Soldiers."

33. Brodsky, *Benjamin Rush*, p. 246.

34. Reiss, *Medicine and the American Revolution*, pp. 26–27.

CHAPTER 8: SEEKING A TECHNOLOGICAL EDGE

1. JA to Moses Gill, June 10, 1775; Orlando W. Stephens, "The Supply of Gunpowder in 1776," *American Historical Review* 30, no. 2 (January 1925): 271; Jimmy Dick, "The Gunpowder Shortage," *Journal of the American Revolution*, September 9, 2013. Online at: http://allthingsliberty.com/2013/09/the-gunpowder-shortage.
2. GW to Congress, *PGW*, Rev. Series, vol. 1, pp. 85–97; December 25 letter, vol. 3, p. 299; Stephens, "The Supply of Gunpowder in 1776," p. 272; Chernow, *Washington*, p. 200.
3. Gary A. O'Dell, "Saltpeter Manufacturing and Marketing and Its Relation to the Gunpowder Industry in Kentucky during the Nineteenth Century," Lexington, University of Kentucky, 1996. Online: http://www.rkci.org/library/odell_ky_saltpeter_1996.pdf.
4. JA, from Joseph Palmer, June 19, 1775, *WJA*, vol. 3, pp. 27–30.
5. Abigail to JA, March 31, 1776. L. H. Butterfield, ed., *Adams Family Correspondence*, vol.1. (Cambridge, MA: Belknap Press, 1963–1993), pp. 369–371. Online at: http://www.pbs.org/wgbh/amex/adams/filmmore/ps_ladies.html.
6. "Several Methods of Making Salt-Petre, Recommended to the Inhabitants of the United Colonies by their Representatives in Congress." Philadelphia, 1775.
7. Brodsky, *Benjamin Rush*, pp. 130–132.
8. Gerald M. Carbone, *Nathanael Greene* (New York: Palgrave Macmillan, 2008); Noah Brooks, *Henry Knox* (1900; repr. New York: Cosimo, Inc., 2007).
9. Diamant, *Dive!*, p. 12.
10. York, *Mechanical Metamorphosis*, pp. 86–111.
11. Ibid., pp. 92–97; Diamant, *Dive!*, pp. 28–32; Hindle, *Pursuit of Science*, pp. 244–245.
12. GW to TJ, September 26, 1785.
13. GW July 10–11, 1775; GW to Hancock, December 31, 1775, *Rev. War Series*, vol. 2, pp. 622–626.
14. Charles H. Bradford, "Dorchester Heights, Prelude to Independence," online at: http://www.dorchesteratheneum.org/pdf/Dorchester%20Heights.pdf.
15. Stacy Schiff, "Franklin in Paris," *American Scholar*, Spring 2009.
16. Francis Casimir Kajencki, *Thaddeus Kosciuszko: Military Engineer of the American Revolution* (El Paso, TX: Southwest Polonia Press, 1998), pp. 56–59.
17. List of provisions in the *Amphitrite*, in notes to Major General William Heath to GW, April 23, 1777. *PGW*, Rev. Series, vol. 9, pp. 244–246.
18. Coudray to GW, August 6, 1777, in Walker, *Engineers of Independence*, p. 151.
19. Daniel Jouve, "Louis Le Bègue Duportail (1743–1801: Washington's Right-Hand-Man and Founder of the United States Army Corps of Engineers," *Les Amis de la Grive*, translated by Alice Jouve. Online at: http://xenophongroup.com/mcjoynt/duport.htm; Duportail memos November 25 and December 3, 1777, in Walker, *Engineers of Independence*, pp. 178–179 and 182–183.
20. Walker, *Engineers of Independence*, p. 178. See also, Duportail to GW, January 18, 1778.
21. York, *Mechanical Metamorphosis*, pp. 112–131.
22. GW to John Armstrong Sr., September 14, 1777.
23. York, *Mechanical Metamorphosis*, p. 45; Matthew S. Henry, "Life of William Henry," typescript, 1860, APS files, B H391; Philip, *Robert Fulton: A Biography*.

24. John G. W. Dillin, *The Kentucky Rifle* (New York: Ludlum & Beebe, 1846), pp. 12–15. HL U897 U5 D5.
25. GW to Hancock of July 10, 1775.
26. John Penn to JA, April 17, 1776.
27. York, *Mechanical Metamorphosis*, pp. 132–137.
28. Kajencki, *Thaddeus Kosciuszko*, pp. 61–120.

CHAPTER 9: SCIENCE RESURFACES

1. TJ to Giovanni Fabbroni, June 8, 1778.
2. DR and TJ letters, quoted in Hindle, *David Rittenhouse.*
3. BF to Colden, October 11, 1759. *Colden Letters,* vol. 4, p. 227.
4. Page and DR letters, in Hindle, ed., *The Scientific Writings of David Rittenhouse.*
5. Ibid., and Hindle, *David Rittenhouse,* pp. 226–229.
6. DR to Reverend Madison, August 27, 1779, in "JM" File, Swem Library.
7. Reverend Madison to DR, November 1779. Misc. collection, APS.
8. JA to Waterhouse, February 24, 1791, in Ford, ed. *Statesman and Friend,* pp. 9–10.
9. Massachusetts Constitution, https://malegislature.gov/laws/constitution.
10. McCullough, *John Adams,* p. 58.
11. JA to Waterhouse, July 1805, in Ford, *Statesman and Friend,* p. 25.
12. Manuel and Manuel, *James Bowdoin,* pp. 19–35.
13. Ibid., pp. 169–172.
14. Owen Biddle, "An Oration, Delivered the Second of March, 1781." Philadelphia, Francis Bailey for the APS, 1781.
15. Jefferson, *Notes on the State of Virginia.* Query 6 includes Raynal's remark.
16. Wilson, "The Evolution of Jefferson's 'Notes on the State of Virginia,'" quoting TJ to d'Anmours, November 30, 1780.
17. O'Shaughnessy, *The Men Who Lost America,* p. 14.
18. Walker, *Engineers of Independence,* pp. 300–312.
19. Wilson, "The Evolution of Jefferson's 'Notes on the State of Virginia.'"
20. Ibid.; summarizes evidence for later composition.
21. Chastellux, *Travels in North America in the Years 1780, 1781, and 1782,* vol. 2, pp. 393–395.
22. TJ to Thomas Walker, Sept. 25, 1783.
23. Benjamin R. Cohen, *Notes from the Ground: Science, Soil, and Society in the American Countryside* (New Haven, CT: Yale University Press, 2009), p. 2.
24. T. Jefferson, *Notes on the State of Virginia.* Online at: http://etext.virginia.edu/toc/modeng/public/JefVirg.html. Buffon and de Pauw said that travelers' reports of Patagonian "giants" could not be true since, in their view, South Americans were all smaller in stature than Europeans or Africans.
25. GW to DR, February 16, 1783.
26. JA to Waterhouse, April 23, 1785, in Ford, *Statesman and Friend.* See also, Marlana Portolano, *The Passionate Empiricist: The Eloquence of John Quincy Adams in the Service of Science* (Albany: State University of New York Press, 2009).
27. David Knight, *The Making of Modern Science: Science, Technology, Medicine and Modernity: 1789–1914* (Cambridge, MA: Polity Press, 2009).
28. "Loose thoughts," *PBF,* vol. 9, pp. 599–600. See also Riskin, *Science in the Age of Sensibility,* pp. 191–225.
29. "Animal Magnetism, Report of Dr. Franklin and Other Commissioners." HL 300570. Pg. 12. Also Riskin, *Science in the Age of Sensibility.*

30. "Animal Magnetism," p. 17.
31. TJ to Hugh Williamson, February 6, 1785.
32. Nicholson, *An Introduction to Natural Philosophy*, p. 150.

CHAPTER 10: MIDCOURSE CORRECTIONS

1. Benjamin Rush, *Address to the People of the United States*, 1777. Online at: http://teachingamericanhistory.org/library/document/address-to-the-people-of-the-united-states/. George Washington, "Circular to the States," June 8, 1783. Online at: http://press-pubs.uchicago.edu/founders/documents/v1ch7s5.html.
2. Gordon S. Wood, *The Radicalism of the American Revolution* (New York: Alfred A. Knopf, 1991), p. 229; J. Hector St. John de Crèvecoeur, *Letters From an American Farmer* (1782), Letter 3. Online at: http://avalon.law.yale.edu/subject_menus/letters.asp.
3. Washington, "Circular to the States," *op. cit.; Federalist Paper* #1, 1788. Online at: http://avalon.law.yale.edu/18th_century/fed01.asp.
4. Webster, quoted in Hindle, *The Pursuit of Science in Revolutionary America*, pp. 257–258.
5. St. George Tucker, quoted in Kasson, *Civilizing the Machine*, p. 15.
6. Morris, *The Forging of the Union*, p. 131; Tench Coxe, "Address to the Board of Managers of the Pennsylvania Society for the Promotion of Manufactures and the Useful Arts," printed in the *American Museum* 2, no. 4 (1787).
7. Kant, quoted in Dugatkin, *Mr. Jefferson and the Giant Moose*, p. 106.
8. TJ to Chastellux, June 7, 1785. Dugatkin, *Mr. Jefferson and the Giant Moose*, pp. 81–100; K. Thomson, *Jefferson's Shadow*, pp. 9–13.
9. For Charles Thomson, see Schlenther, *A Patriot's Pursuit*, pp. 200–201.
10. K. Thomson, *Jefferson's Shadow*, pp. 151–160; Bedini, *Thomas Jefferson*, pp. 183–184.
11. Suzanne Olson, "Thomas Jefferson's Collection of Scientific Instruments." In three volumes, unpublished, at Jefferson Library, Monticello, 1997.
12. Benjamin R. Cohen, *Notes from the Ground: Science, Soil, and Society in the American Countryside* (New Haven, CT: Yale University Press, 2009), pp. 18, 27.
13. GW to Levi Hollingsworth, September 20, 1785.
14. Wulf, *Founding Gardeners*, quoting Young and GW letter to George William Fairfax, June 30, 1785.
15. Arthur Young to GW, January 7, 1786.
16. GW Diary entry, May 2, 1787. *Diaries*, vol. 5, pp. 147–149.
17. David Rittenhouse, "Structure of the Surface of the Earth in Pennsylvania," *Columbian Magazine*, October 1786.
18. David Ramsay to BR, July 11, 1783, quoted in John M. Kloos Jr., *A Sense of Deity: The Republican Spirituality of Dr. Benjamin Rush* (Brooklyn, NY: Carlson Publishing, 1991), p. 37.
19. BR to John Armstrong, March 19, 1783, *Letters*, vol. 1, pp. 294–295; "A Plan of Education for Dickinson College." 1785. (Anniversary Edition, Carlisle, Pennsylvania, 1973). HL 433189.
20. Peres Fobes to Corporation of Rhode Island College, August 25, 1802, quoted in Fleming, "Science and Technology in Providence."
21. Sellers, *Mr. Peale's Museum;* Ward, *Charles Willson Peale*.
22. Paine to BF, December 31, 1785, and June 6, 1786 (APS); Keane, *Tom Paine*, pp. 267–282.

23. TJ to Paine, December 23, 1788. See also "Thomas Paine, Bridge Builder," *Virginia Quarterly Review*, Autumn 1927, pp. 571–584. Online at: http://www.vqronline.org/essay/thomas-paine-bridge-builder.

24. Greville Bathe and Dorothy Bathe, *Oliver Evans: A Chronicle of Early American Engineering* (Philadelphia: Historical Society of Pennsylvania, 1935), quoting Evans, "A Young Mill-wright's Guide."

25. Quotations from GW letters to Lafayette and others, in Achenbach, *The Grand Idea.*

26. GW Diary entry of September 6, 1784.

27. Sutcliffe, *Steam*, pp. 5–6.

28. Wood, *The Radicalism of the American Revolution*, pp. 207–208.

29. TJ to Hugh Williamson, February 6, 1785.

30. Sutcliffe, *Steam*, pg. xii, *et seq.*

31. JA to Cotton Tufts, June 1, 1786.

32. I. B. Cohen, *Science and the Founding Fathers*, p. 210.

33. Adams, *A Defence of the Constitutions of Government of the United States of America*, 1787 *et seq.*, online at: http://www.constitution.org/jadams/john_adams.htm.

34. McCullough, *Adams*, p. 375.

35. Hindle, *The Pursuit of Science in Revolutionary America*, p. 378.

36. Coxe, "Address to the Board of Managers," *op. cit.*; Kasson, *Civilizing the Machine*, pp. 28–32.

37. Leo Marx, *The Machine in the Garden: Technology and the Pastoral Idea in America* (New York: Oxford University Press, 1964), pp. 153–156.

38. Gutzman, *James Madison and the Making of America*, p. 136.

39. Khan, *The Democratization of Invention*, p. 8.

40. GW to Rev. John Lathrop, June 22, 1788.

41. Maier, *Ratification: The People Debate the Constitution, 1787–1788.*

42. Rush, "Observations on the Federal Procession in Philadelphia," in *Letters*, pp. 470–477, reprinted from the *American Museum*, July 1788; Rigal, *The American Manufactory*, pp. 21–54.

CHAPTER 11: PATENTS, INNOVATIONS, AND FIRST STEPS

1. R. Thomson, *Structures of Change in the Mechanical Age*, p. 17.

2. Crèvecoeur; Hindle, *Emulation and Invention*, p. 3; Norman R. Wilkinson, "Brandywine Borrowings from European Technology," in *Technology and American History*, ed. Stephen H. Cutliffe and Terry S. Reynolds (Chicago: University of Chicago Press, 1997); Leonard Moseley, *Blood Relations: The Rise and Fall of the du Ponts of Delaware* (New York: Athenaeum, 1980), pp. 23–26.

3. GW to TJ, February 13, 1789.

4. TJ to John Trumbull, February 15, 1789; TJ to Joseph Willard, March 24, 1789.

5. Washington's First Inaugural Address, online at: http://www.archives.gov/exhibits/american_originals/inaugtxt.html; GW to Senate and House, January 8, 1790.

6. TJ to Isaac McPherson, August 13, 1813.

7. Khan, *The Democratization of Invention*, p. 8.

8. *New American State Papers: Science and Technology*, vol. 4, listing patents of the 1790s. (Wilmington, DE: Scholarly Resources, 1973).

9. Dupree, *Science in the Federal Government*, p. 12.

10. Sutcliffe, *Steam*, pp. xiii, *et seq.*

11. *Federalist Papers,* #49; TJ to JM, September 6, 1789. See Himmelfarb, *The Roads to Modernity,* pp. 194–198.

12. Hessian Fly discussion, and quotes from *American Museum* and TJ letter, online at: http://www.monticello.org/site/house-and-gardens/hessian-fly.

13. Bedini, *Thomas Jefferson,* pp. 220–222.

14. Benjamin Banneker to TJ, August 19, 1791.

15. Ferguson, "Oliver Evans, Inventive Genius;" Ruth Schwartz Cowan, *A Social History of American Technology* (New York: Oxford University Press, 1997), pp. 69–73.

16. TP to TJ, June 17, 1789.

17. William Bartram, unpublished essay, in *William Bartram: The Search for Nature's Design; Selected Art, Letters, and Unpublished Writings,* ed. Thomas Hallock and Nancy E. Hoffmann (Athens: University of Georgia Press, 2010), pp. 352–353.

18. Hamilton, "Report on Manufactures," 1791. Online at: http://www.archive .org/stream/alexanderhamilt00caregoog/alexanderhamilt00caregoog_djvu .txt.

19. Hamilton, *Report on Manufactures;* Chernow, *Alexander Hamilton,* pp. 370–378.

20. Weber, "The Patent Office, Its History, Activities and Organization," pp. 4–6.

21. Subscription list and charter for Michaux Expedition (1793), APS Files.

22. Chaplin, *Anxious Pursuit,* pp. 312-319.

23. Apel, "Feverish Bodies, Enlightened Minds," p. 3.

24. Brodsky, *Benjamin Rush,* pp. 326–337; Letters of Julia Rush to BR, APS File B R894; Excerpt from *Autobiography,* vol. 5, p. 188. American Philosophical Society, 1813; Princeton University Press, 1948.

25. TJ to Bishop Madison, March 4, 1798; Jefferson, "A Memoir of the Discovery of Certain Bones of an Unknown Quadruped, of the Clawed Kind, in the Western Part of Virginia," *Transactions of the APS* 4 (1799): 246–260.

26. Schlenther, *Charles Thomson,* pp. 186–208.

27. Nicholson, *An Introduction to Natural Philosophy,* 1795 edition; Anonymous, "A Compendious View of Natural Philosophy: For the Use of Both Sexes" (Boston: Spottiswood, 1796). American Antiquarian Society.

28. Graham, *Revolutionary in Exile,* pp. 21–69.

29. Woodward, "Joseph Priestley and Scientific Research on the American Frontier"; Schofield, *The Enlightened Joseph Priestley,* quotes Priestley to BR, p. 281.

30. Cooper, quoted in Dumas Malone, *The Public Life of Thomas Cooper 1783–1839* (New Haven, CT: Yale University Press, 1926), pp. 101–102.

31. S. Brown, *Benjamin Thompson,* pp. 112, *et seq.*

32. Brodsky, *Benjamin Rush,* p. 342.

CHAPTER 12: THE SCIENCE-MINDED PRESIDENCY

1. TJ to JM, May 26, 1800.

2. K. Thomson, *Jefferson's Shadow,* p. 37.

3. Rigal, *The American Manufactory,* pp. 91–113; Semonin, *American Monster,* pp. 315–340.

4. Rigal, *The American Manufactory;* Semonin, *American Monster;* Sellers, *Mr. Peale's Museum.*

5. Quotations from Waterhouse letter, Hawes, *Benjamin Waterhouse,* p. 36.

6. TJ to Waterhouse, October 1, 1801, in Robert Halsey, "How the President, Thomas Jefferson, and Doctor Benjamin Waterhouse Established Vaccination as a Public Health Procedure." Halsey, privately printed, New York, 1936. NY.

7. Bedini, *Thomas Jefferson*, pp. 310–315.

8. Priestley to Barton, November 27, 1800, quoted in Ewan and Ewan, *Benjamin Smith Barton*, p. 317.

9. Berry, *Yankee Stargazer.*

10. Christina Chapman Robbins, *David Hosack: Citizen of New York* (Philadelphia: American Philosophical Society, 1964).

11. Silliman, "Letters of Shahcoolen"; C. M. Brown, *Benjamin Silliman.*

12. Samuel L. Mitchill, "A Discourse on the Character and Services of Thomas Jefferson," pp. 39–40.

13. TJ to Robert Patterson, April 17, 1802, cited in Bedini, *Thomas Jefferson*, p. 238.

14. John W. Francis, *Reminiscences of Samuel Latham Mitchill* (New York: J. F. Trow, 1859). Online at: http://collections.nlm.nih.gov/catalog/nlm:nlmuid-10 1179317-bk

15. Gerald Holton, "On the Jeffersonian Research Program," in Holton, *Science and Anti-Science*, pp. 109–125.

16. The section on the training of the Lewis and Clark expedition draws on discussions in Ambrose, *Undaunted Courage;* Bedini, *Thomas Jefferson;* K. Thomson, *Jefferson's Shadow;* Wood, *Empire of Liberty;* Greene, *American Science in the Age of Jefferson;* Ewan and Ewan, *Benjamin Smith Barton;* and Sellers, *Mr. Peale's Museum.*

17. TJ to Barton, February 27, 1803, cited in Ewan and Ewan, Benjamin *Smith Barton*, p. 541; Jenkinson, *The Character of Meriwether Lewis.*

18. Jefferson, Confidential Message to Congress, January 18, 1803. Online at: www .monticello.org/site/jefferson/jeffersons-confidential-letter-to-congress.

19. Bedini, *Thomas Jefferson*, pp. 339–340, citing notes of Spanish and French ambassadors.

20. Quoted in M. R. Smith, *Harpers Ferry Armory and the New Technology*, p. 53.

21. Woodward, "Joseph Priestley's Laboratory," *op. cit.*, Woodward, Walter W. "The Dickinson College Thomas Cooper Collection: Joseph Priestley and Scientific Research on the American Frontier." In *Joseph Priestley, a Celebration of His Life and Legacy,* edited by James S. Birch and Joe Lee. Lancaster, UK: Scotforth Books/The Priestley Society, 2007. Woodward states that the air gun was provided to the expedition by Priestley, who was in close correspondence with Jefferson; other sources state that it was produced at the Harpers Ferry Armory and returned by Lewis to that depot after the expedition.

22. TJ Instructions to Lewis, June 20, 1803, online at: www.monticello.org/site /jefferson/jeffersons-instructions-to-meriwether-lewis.

23. Lewis Journals, August 30, 1803. Online at: http://lewisandclarkjournals.unl .edu/read/?_xmlsrc=1803-08-30.xml.

24. John Logan Allen, "Pike and American Science," in *Zebulon Pike, Thomas Jefferson, and the Opening of the American West,* ed. Matthew L. Harris and Jay H. Buckley (Norman: University of Oklahoma Press, 2012).

25. TJ to Mr. Lithson, January 4, 1805. *Writings*, vol. 11, p. 55.

26. TJ and Lewis letters, and Jefferson message to Congress, at www.monticello .org/site/return-lewis-and-clark.

27. Paul Russell Cutright, *Lewis & Clark, Pioneering Naturalists* (1969; repr. Lincoln: University of Nebraska Press, 1989), pp. 393–398.

28. Greene, *American Science in the Age of Jefferson*, pp. 198–207.

29. Sutcliffe, *Steam*, pp. 161–185; Sale, Kirkpatrick. *The Fire of his Genius: Robert Fulton and the American Dream*. New York, Free Press, 2001, pp. 10–28; Philip, *Robert Fulton*.

30. Quoted in Sale, p. 23.

31. Irving quotation, Sutcliffe, *Steam*, p. 185; Fulton, "Torpedo War and Submarine Explosions" (New York: William Elliott, 1810).

32. Fulton to Barlow, quoted in Sutcliffe, *Steam*, pg. 185.

EPILOGUE: THE INTERWEAVING

1. For the section on Silliman and the meteor, see Cathryn J. Prince, *A Professor, a President, and a Meteor: The Birth of American Science* (Amherst, NY: Prometheus Books, 2011); C. M. Brown, *Benjamin Silliman;* and Greene, *American Science in the Age of Jefferson.*

2. TJ to Daniel Salmon, February 15, 1808. Other Silliman quotes in Prince, *A Professor, a President, and a Meteor.*

3. William Clark to TJ, September 20, 1807, in Rice, "Jefferson's Gift of Fossils to the Museum of Natural History in Paris."

4. Rice Jr., *op. cit.*

5. BR to JA, April 5, 1808; JA to BR, April 18, 1808; TJ to Alexander von Humboldt, March 6, 1809.

6. BR to JA, September 16, 1808; JA to BR, September 18, 1808.

7. Lester J. Cappon, ed., The *Adams-Jefferson Letters: The Complete Correspondence between Thomas Jefferson and Abigail and John Adams*. Vol. 2. (Chapel Hill: University of North Carolina Press, 1959).

8. TJ to Priestley, January 18, 1800.

9. Jennings L. Wagoner Jr., *Jefferson and Education* (Chapel Hill: University of North Carolina Press, 2004), pp. 55–56.

BIBLIOGRAPHY

BOOKS

Achenbach, Joel. *The Grand Idea: George Washington's Potomac and the Race to the West.* New York: Simon & Schuster, 2004.

Ambrose, Stephen. *Undaunted Courage: Meriwether Lewis, Thomas Jefferson, and the Opening of the American West.* New York: Simon & Schuster, 1996.

Anderson, Mark. *The Day the World Discovered the Sun.* New York: DaCapo Press, 2012.

Armstrong, Alan A., ed. *"Forget not mee and my garden—" Selected Letters of Peter Collinson, F. R. S.* Philadelphia: American Philosophical Society, 2002.

Bailyn, Bernard. *The Ideological Origins of the American Revolution.* Cambridge, MA: Harvard University Press, 1992.

———. *The Peopling of North America.* New York: Alfred A. Knopf, 1986.

Baltzell, E. Digby. *Puritan Boston and Quaker Philadelphia: Two Protestant Ethics and the Spirit of Class Authority and Leadership.* New York: The Free Press, 1979.

Becker, Carl L. *The Declaration of Independence: A Study in the History of Political Ideas.* New York: Alfred A. Knopf, 1942. First published 1922.

Bedini, Silvio A., *Thomas Jefferson: Statesman of Science.* New York: Macmillan, 1990.

Bell, Whitfield J., *Patriot-Improvers: Biographical Sketches of the Members of the American Philosophical Society.* Vols. 1–3. Philadelphia: American Philosophical Society, 1997.

———. *The College of Physicians of Philadelphia: A Bicentennial History.* Canton, MA: Science History Publications, 1987.

Berkeley, Edmund, and Dorothy Smith Berkeley, eds. *The Correspondence of John Bartram, 1734–1777.* Gainesville: University Press of Florida, 1992.

Berry, Robert Elton. *Yankee Stargazer: The Life of Nathaniel Bowditch.* New York: Whittlesey House/McGraw-Hill, 1941.

Bolton, Henry Carrington, ed. *Scientific Correspondence of Joseph Priestley.* New York, privately printed, 1892. New York: Klaus Reprint, 1969.

Boorstin, Daniel. J. *The Lost World of Thomas Jefferson.* Chicago: University of Chicago Press, 1993.

Bowers, Claude G. *The Young Jefferson, 1743–1789.* Boston: Little Brown, 1945.

Boyle, Robert. *New Experiments and Observations Touching Cold.* 2nd ed. Oxford: Richard Davis, 1683.

Breen, T. H. *The Marketplace of Revolution: How Consumer Politics Shaped American Independence* (New York: Oxford University Press, 2004),

Bridenbaugh, Carl, and Jessica Bridenbaugh. *Rebels and Gentlemen: Philadelphia in the Age of Franklin.* 1942. Reprint. Westport, CT: Greenwood Press, 1978.

Brinton, Howard. *Friends for 300 Years: The History and Beliefs of the Society of Friends Since George Fox Started the Quaker Movement.* New York: Harper, 1952.

Brodsky, Alyn. *Benjamin Rush: Patriot and Physician.* New York: St. Martin's Press, 2001.

Brown, Chardos Michael. *Benjamin Silliman: A Life in the Young Republic.* Princeton: Princeton University Press, 1989.

Brown, Sanborn C. *Benjamin Thompson, Count Rumford.* Cambridge, MA: MIT Press, 1979.

Butterfield, L. H., ed. *Letters of Benjamin Rush.* Philadelphia: American Philosophical Society, 1951.

Carter, Edward C., II. *"One Grand Pursuit": A Brief History of the American Philosophical Society's First 50 Years, 1743–1993.* Philadelphia: American Philosophical Society, 1993.

Chaplin, Joyce E. *The First Scientific American: Benjamin Franklin and the Pursuit of Genius.* New York: Basic Books, 2006.

———. *An Anxious Pursuit: Agricultural Innovation and Modernity in the Lower South, 1730-1815.* Chapel Hill, University of North Carolina Press for the Omohundro Institute, 1993.

Chernow, Ron. *Washington: A Life.* New York: Penguin Press, 2010.

———. *Alexander Hamilton.* New York, Penguin Press, 2004.

Chastellux, François Jean, Marquis de. *Travels in North America in the Years 1780, 1781, and 1782.* Vol. 2. Chapel Hill: University of North Carolina Press, 1963.

Clagett, Martin. *Scientific Jefferson Revealed.* Charlottesville: University of Virginia Press, 2009.

Cohen, Benjamin R. *Notes from the Ground: Science, Soil, and Society in the American Countryside.* New Haven, CT: Yale University Press, 2009.

Cohen, I. Bernard. *Science and the Founding Fathers: Science in the Political Thought of Thomas Jefferson, Benjamin Franklin, John Adams, and James Madison.* New York: Norton, 1995.

———. *Some Early Tools of American Science: An Account of the Early Scientific Instruments and Mineralogical and Biological Collections in Harvard University.* Cambridge, MA: Harvard University Press, 1950.

———, ed. *Benjamin Franklin's Experiments.* Cambridge, MA: Harvard University Press, 1941.

Daniels, George H. *Science in American Society, A Social History.* New York: Alfred A. Knopf, 1971.

Danson, Edwin. *Drawing the Line: How Mason and Dixon Surveyed the Most Famous Border in America.* New York: John Wiley, 2001.

Delbourgo, James. *A Most Amazing Scene of Wonders: Electricity and Enlightenment in Early America.* Cambridge, MA: Harvard University Press, 2006.

Desaguliers, J. T., *A Dissertation Concerning Electricity.* London: Innys and Longman, 1742.

———, *A Course of Experimental Philosophy.* London: Senex et al., 1734.

Diamant, Lincoln. *Dive! The Story of David Bushnell and his Remarkable 1776 Submarine.* Fleishmanns, NY: Purple Mountain Press, 2003.

Dibner, Bern. *Benjamin Franklin, Electrician.* Norwalk, CT: Burndy Library, 1976.

Dugatkin, Lee Alan. *Mr. Jefferson and the Giant Moose: Natural History in Early America.* Chicago: University of Chicago Press, 2009.

Dupree, A. Hunter. *Science in the Federal Government.* Cambridge, MA: Harvard University Press, 1957.

Ellis, Joseph J. *His Excellency, George Washington.* New York: Alfred A. Knopf, 2004.

Ewan, Joseph, and Nesta Dunn Ewan. *Benjamin Smith Barton: Naturalist and Physician in Jeffersonian America.* St. Louis: Missouri Botanical Gardens Press, 2007.

Fenn, Elizabeth A. *Pox Americana: The Great Smallpox Epidemic of 1775–82.* New York: Hill & Wang, 2001.

Ferguson, Robert A. *The American Enlightenment, 1750–1820.* Cambridge, MA: Harvard University Press, 1994.

Foucault, Michel. *The Order of Things: An Archaeology of the Human Sciences.* Rev. ed. New York: Random House, 1994.

Flexner, James Thomas. *The Young Hamilton.* Boston: Little, Brown, 1978.

Ford, Worthington Chauncey, ed. *Statesman and Friend: Correspondence of John Adams with Benjamin Waterhouse.* Boston: Little, Brown, 1927.

Franklin, Benjamin. *New Experiments and Observations on Electricity.* London, R. Cave, 1752.

———. *Benjamin Franklin's Autobiography.* Edited by Joyce E. Chaplin. New York: Norton, 2012.

Frazer, Gregg L. *The Religious Beliefs of America's Founders: Reason, Revelation, and Revolution.* Lawrence: University Press of Kansas, 2012.

Gay, Peter. *The Enlightenment: An Interpretation.* Vol. 2, *The Science of Freedom.* New York: Alfred A. Knopf, 1969.

Graham, Jenny. *Revolutionary in Exile: The Emigration of Joseph Priestley to America, 1794–1804.* Philadelphia: The American Philosophical Society, 1995.

Gray, Asa, ed. *Selections from the Scientific Correspondence of Cadwallader Colden.* New Haven, CT. 1843. Reprint from the *American Journal of Science and Arts.*

Greene, John C. *American Science in the Age of Jefferson.* Ames: Iowa State University Press, 1984.

Greenwood, Isaac. *A Course of Mathematical Lectures and Experiments.* Boston, 1735.

Griswold, Robert L. *Fatherhood in America: A History.* New York: Basic Books, 1983.

Gutzman, Kevin R. C. *James Madison and the Making of America.* New York, St. Martin's Press, 2012.

Habermas, Jürgen. *The Structural Transformation of the Public Sphere: An Inquiry into a Category of Bourgeois Society.* Cambridge, MA: MIT Press, 1989.

———. *The Philosophical Discourse of Modernity: Twelve Lectures.* Translated by Frederick G. Lawrence. Cambridge, MA: MIT Press, 1987.

Hawes, Lloyd E. *Benjamin Waterhouse, M.D.* Boston: The Francis A. Courtenay Library of Medicine, 1974.

Hedeen, Stanley. *Big Bone Lick: The Cradle of American Paleontology.* Lexington: University Press of Kentucky, 2008.

Heilbron, J. H. *Elements of Early Modern Physics.* Berkeley: University of California Press, 1982.

———. *Electricity in the Seventeenth and Eighteenth Centuries.* Berkeley: University of California Press, 1979

Himmelfarb, Gertrude. *The Roads to Modernity: The British, French, and American Enlightenments.* New York: Alfred A. Knopf, 2003.

Hindle, Brooke. *Emulation and Invention.* New York: New York University Press, 1981.

———. *David Rittenhouse.* Princeton: Princeton University Press, 1964.

————. *The Pursuit of Science in Revolutionary America*. Chapel Hill: University of North Carolina Press, 1956.

————. ed. *The Scientific Writings of David Rittenhouse*. New York: Arno Press, 1980.

Hoermann, Alfred E. *Cadwallader Colden: A Figure of the American Enlightenment*. Westwood, CT: Greenwood Press, 2005.

Hoffman, Nancy E., and John C. Van Horne, eds. *America's Curious Botanist: A Tercentennial Reappraisal of John Bartram, 1699–1777*. Philadelphia: American Philosophical Society, 2004.

Holton, Gerald. *Science and Anti-Science*. Cambridge, MA: Harvard University Press, 1993.

Hornberger, Theodore. *Scientific Thought in the American Colleges, 1638–1800*. Austin: University of Texas Press, 1945.

Hughes, Sarah S. *Surveyors and Statesmen: Land Measurement in Colonial Virginia*. Richmond, VA: Virginia Surveyors Foundation, 1979.

Isaacson, Walter. *Benjamin Franklin: An American Life*. New York: Simon & Schuster, 2003.

Isenberg, Nancy. *Fallen Founder: The Life of Aaron Burr*. New York: Viking Penguin, 2007.

Jefferson, Thomas. *Writings*, including "Autobiography." New York, Library of America, 1984 edition.

Jenkinson, Clay S. *The Character of Meriwether Lewis*. Washburn, ND: Dakota Institute Press, 2011.

Jones, Landon Y., ed. *The Essential Lewis and Clark*. New York: HarperCollins, 2002.

Judd, Richard. *The Untilled Garden: Natural History and the Spirit of Conservation in America, 1740–1840*. Cambridge: Cambridge University Press, 2009.

Kajencki, Francis Casimir. *Thaddeus Kosciuszko: Military Engineer of the American Revolution*. El Paso, TX: Southwest Polonia Press, 1998

Kasson, John F. *Civilizing the Machine: Technology and Republican Values in America, 1776–1900*. New York: Hill and Wang, 1999.

Keane, John. *Tom Paine: A Political Life*. London: Bloomsbury, 1995.

Khan, B. Zorina. *The Democratization of Invention: Patents and Copyrights in American Economic Development, 1790–1920*. Cambridge: Cambridge University Press, 2005.

Kimball, Marie. *Jefferson: The Road to Glory, 1743 to 1776*. New York: Coward-McCann, 1943.

Kinnersley, Ebenezer. *A Course of Experiments, in That Curious and Entertaining Branch of Natural Philosophy, Called Electricity; Accompanied with Explanatory Lectures; In Which Electricity and Lightning, Will Be Proved to Be the Same Thing*. Philadelphia: Armbruster, 1764.

Kuhn, Thomas S. *The Structure of Scientific Revolutions*. Chicago: University of Chicago Press, 1962.

Landsman, Ned C. *From Colonials to Provincials: American Thought and Culture, 1680–1760*. New York: Twayne, 1997.

Latour, Bruno. *We Have Never Been Modern*. Translated by Catherine Porter. Cambridge, MA: MIT Press, 1993.

————, and Steve Woolgar, *Laboratory Life: the Construction of Scientific Facts*. 2nd ed. Princeton: Princeton University Press, 1985.

Lemay, J. A. Leo. *Ebenezer Kinnersley, Franklin's Friend*. Philadelphia: University of Pennsylvania Press, 1964.

Lewis, Andrew J. *A Democracy of Facts: Natural History in the Early Republic*. Philadelphia: University of Pennsylvania Press, 2011.

Locke, John. *An Essay Concerning Human Understanding.* Oxford: Clarendon Press, 1975. First published 1689.

Lyons, Jonathan. *The Society for Useful Knowledge: How Benjamin Franklin and Friends Brought the Enlightenment to America.* New York: Bloomsbury, 2013.

Maier, Pauline. *Ratification: The People Debate the Constitution, 1787–1788.* New York: Simon & Schuster, 2010.

———. *American Scripture: Making the Declaration of Independence.* New York: Alfred A. Knopf, 1997.

———, Merritt Roe Smith, Alexander Keyssar, and Daniel J. Kevles. *Inventing America: A History of the United States.* Vol. 1, *To 1877.* 2nd ed. New York: Norton, 2006.

Malone, Dumas. *Jefferson the Virginian.* Boston: Little, Brown, 1948.

———. *The Public Life of Thomas Cooper, 1783–1839.* New Haven, CT: Yale University Press, 1926.

Manuel, Frank E., and Fritzie P. Manuel. *James Bowdoin and the Patriot Philosophers.* Philadelphia: American Philosophical Society, 2004.

McCullough, David. *John Adams.* New York: Simon & Schuster, 2001.

Miller, Perry. *The Life of the Mind in America, from the Revolution to the Civil War.* New York: Harcourt, Brace, 1965.

———. *The New England Mind: From Colony to Province.* Cambridge, MA: Harvard University Press, 1953.

Mintz, Steven. *Huck's Raft: A History of American Childhood.* Cambridge, MA: Harvard University Press, 2006.

———. and Susan Kellogg. *Domestic Revolutions: A Social History of American Family Life.* New York: The Free Press, 1988.

Mokyr, Joel. *The Gifts of Athena: Historical Origins of the Knowledge Economy.* Princeton: Princeton University Press, 2002.

Morgan, Edmund S. *The Gentle Puritan: A Life of Ezra Stiles, 1727–1795.* New Haven, CT: Yale University Press, 1962.

Morris, Richard B. *The Forging of the Union, 1781–1789.* New York: Harper & Row, 1987.

Myers, Amy R. W. *Knowing Nature: Art and Science in Philadelphia, 1740–1840.* New Haven, CT: Yale University Press, 2011.

Myrsiades, Linda. *Medical Culture of Revolutionary America.* Madison, NJ: Fairleigh Dickinson University Press, 2009.

Nicholson, William. *An Introduction to Natural Philosophy.* 2 vols. 3rd ed. Philadelphia: T. Dobson 1795. First published in 1781.

Oleson, Alexandra, and Sanborn C. Brown, eds. *The Pursuit of Knowledge in the Early American Republic: American Scientific and Learned Societies from Colonial Times to the Civil War.* Baltimore: Johns Hopkins University Press, 1976.

O'Neill, Jean, and Elizabeth P. McLean. *Peter Collinson and the Eighteenth Century Natural History Exchange.* Philadelphia: American Philosophical Society, 2008.

O'Shaughnessy, Andrew Jackson. *The Men Who Lost America: British Leadership, the American Revolution, and the Fate of the Empire.* New Haven, CT: Yale University Press, 2013.

Parrish, Susan Scott. *American Curiosity: Cultures and Natural History in the Colonial British Atlantic World.* Chapel Hill: University of North Carolina Press, 2006.

Philip, Cynthia Owen. *Robert Fulton: A Biography.* New York: Franklin Watts, 1985.

Pickstone, John V. *Ways of Knowing: A New History of Science, Technology, and Medicine.* Chicago: University of Chicago Press, 2001.

Priestley, Joseph B. *The History and Present State of Electricity.* London, J. Dodsley, 1767.

Prince, Cathryn J. *A Professor, a President, and a Meteor: The Birth of American Science.* Amherst, NY: Prometheus Books, 2011.

Prince, Sue Ann, ed. *Stuffing Birds, Pressing Plants, Shaping Knowledge: Natural History in North America, 1730–1860.* Philadelphia: American Philosophical Society, 2003.

Puls, Mark. *Samuel Adams: Father of the American Revolution.* New York: Palgrave Macmillan, 2006.

Regis, Pamela. *Describing Early America: Bartram, Jefferson, Crèvecoeur, and the Rhetoric of Natural History.* DeKalb: Northern Illinois University Press, 1992.

Rigal, Laura. *The American Manufactory: Art, Labor, and the World of Things in the Early Republic.* Princeton: Princeton University Press, 1998.

Riskin, Jessica. *Science in the Age of Sensibility.* Chicago: University of Chicago Press, 2002.

Robbins, Christine Chapman. *David Hosack, Citizen of New York.* Philadelphia: American Philosophical Society, vol. 6, 1974.

Roger, Jacques. *Buffon: A Life in Natural History.* Translated by Sarah Lucille Bonnefoi. Ithaca, NY: Cornell University Press, 1997.

Roger, Philippe. *The American Enemy: A Story of French Anti-Americanism.* Chicago: University of Chicago Press, 2005.

Rothenberg, Marc, ed. *The History of Science in the United States.* New York: Garland, 2001.

Rush, Benjamin. *Medical Inquiries and Observations.* Philadelphia: Hopkins & Earle, et al., 1805.

Sale, Kirkpatrick. The Fire of his Genius: Robert Fulton and the American Dream. New York, Free Press, 2001.

Schlenther, Boyd Stanley. *Charles Thomson: A Patriot's Pursuit.* Newark: University of Delaware Press, 1990.

Schofield, Robert E. *The Enlightened Joseph Priestley: A Study of His Life and Work from 1773 to 1804.* University Park: Pennsylvania State University Press, 2004.

———. *The Lunar Society of Birmingham, A Social History of Provincial Science and Industry in Eighteenth-Century England.* Oxford: Clarendon Press, 1963.

Schultz, John A., and Douglass Adair, eds. *The Spur of Fame: Dialogues of John Adams and Benjamin Rush, 1805–1813.* San Marino, CA: Huntington Library, 1966.

Sellers, Charles Coleman. *Mr. Peale's Museum: Charles Willson Peale and the First Popular Museum of Natural Science and Art.* New York: Norton, 1980.

Semonin, Paul. *American Monster: How the Nation's First Pre-Historic Creature Became a Symbol of National Identity.* New York: New York University Press, 2000.

Shapin, Steven. *The Scientific Revolution.* Chicago: University of Chicago Press, 1998.

———, and Simon Schaffer, *Leviathan and the Air-Pump: Hobbes, Boyle, and the Experimental Life.* Princeton: Princeton University Press, 1985.

Shute, Michael N. *The Scientific Work of John Winthrop.* New York: Arno Press, 1980.

Silliman, Benjamin. *Letters of Shahcoolen, A Hindu Philosopher, Residing in Philadelphia: to His Friend El Hassan, an Inhabitant of Delhi.* Boston: Russell and Cutler, 1802.

Silverman, Kenneth. *The Life and Times of Cotton Mather.* New York: Harper & Row, 1984.

Slaughter, Thomas P. *The Natures of John and William Bartram*. New York: Alfred A. Knopf, 1996.

Smith, Adam. *An Inquiry into the Nature and Causes of the Wealth of Nations*. London: Strahan & Cadell, 1776.

Smith, Merrit Roe. *Harpers Ferry Armory and the New Technology*. Ithaca, NY: Cornell University Press, 1977.

Stearns, Raymond P. *Science in the British Colonies of North America*. Urbana: University of Illinois Press, 1970.

Sutcliffe, Andrea. *Steam: The Untold Story of America's First Great Invention*. New York: Palgrave Macmillan, 2005.

Thomson, Keith. *Jefferson's Shadow: The Story of His Science*. New Haven, CT: Yale University Press, 2012.

———. *A Passion for Nature: Thomas Jefferson and Natural History*. Monticello Monograph Series. Charlottesville, VA: Thomas Jefferson Foundation, 2008.

Thomson, Ross. *Structures of Change in the Mechanical Age: Technological Innovation in the United States, 1790–1865*. Baltimore, Johns Hopkins University Press, 2009.

Tolles, Frederick B. *James Logan and the Culture of Provincial America*. Boston: Little, Brown, 1957.

Torlais, Jean. *Un physicien au siècles des lumières: l'Abbé Nollet, 1700–1770*. Elbeuf-sur-Andelle: Jonas Editeur, 1987

Uglow, Jenny. *The Lunar Men: Five Friends Whose Curiosity Changed the World*. New York: Farrar, Straus, and Giroux, 2003.

Walker, Paul A. *Engineers of Independence: A Documentary History of the Army Engineers in the American Revolution, 1775–1783*. Honolulu, HI: University Press of the Pacific, 2005.

Walsh, James J. *Education of the Founding Fathers of the Republic: Scholasticism in the Colonial Colleges*. New York: Fordham University Press, 1935.

Ward, David C. *Charles Willson Peale: Art and Selfhood in the Early Republic*. Berkeley: University of California Press, 2004.

Watts, Ruth. *Women in Science: A Social and Cultural History*. Abingdon, Oxon: Routledge, 2007.

Wheatland, David. *The Apparatus of Science at Harvard, 1765–1800*. Cambridge, MA: Harvard University Press, 1968.

White, Edward A. *Science and Religion in American Thought: The Impact of Naturalism*. Stanford, CA: Stanford University Press, 1952.

Wills, Garry. *Inventing America: Jefferson's Declaration of Independence*. Garden City, NY: Doubleday, 1978.

Wollaston, William. *The Religion of Nature Delineated*. London, privately printed, 1724. Reprint. Delmar, NY: Scholars' Facsimiles and Reprints, 1974.

Wood, Gordon S. *Empire of Liberty: A History of the Early Republic, 1789–1815*. New York: Oxford University Press, 2009.

———. *Revolutionary Characters: What Made the Founders Different*. New York: Penguin, 2007.

———. *The Radicalism of the American Revolution*. New York: Alfred A. Knopf, 1992.

Wulf, Andrea. *Chasing Venus: The Race to Measure the Heavens*. New York: Alfred A. Knopf, 2012.

———. *Founding Gardeners: The Revolutionary Generation, Nature, and the Shaping of the American Nation*. New York: Alfred A. Knopf, 2011.

———. *The Brother Gardeners: Botany, Empire, and the Birth of an Obsession.* New York: Alfred A. Knopf, 2009.

York, Neil Longley. *Mechanical Metamorphosis: Technological Change in Revolutionary America.* Westport, CT: Greenwood Press, 1985.

Young, Alfred F., and Gregory Nobles. *Whose American Revolution Was It?* New York: New York University Press, 2011.

CHAPTERS, ARTICLES, PAMPHLETS, DISSERTATIONS

Anonymous. "Analysis of Certain Parts of a Compendious View of Natural Philosophy: For the Use of Students of Both Sexes." Boston: Spottiswood, 1796. (AAS)

Anonymous. "Animal Magnetism, Report of Dr. Franklin and Other Commissioners, Charged by the King of France with the Examination of the Animal Magnetism as Practiced at Paris." Philadelphia: Perkins Co., 1837.

Apel, Thomas. "Feverish Bodies, Enlightened Minds: Yellow-Fever and Commonsense Natural Philosophy in the Early American Republic." PhD diss., Georgetown University, 2012.

Becker, Ann M. "Smallpox in Washington's Army: Strategic Implications of the Disease during the American Revolutionary War." *Journal of Military History* 68, no. 2 (April 2004): 381–430.

Biddle, Owen. "Annual Address to the American Philosophical Society, 1781." Philadelphia, privately printed, 1781. (APS)

Boylston, Zabdiel. "Historical Account of the Small-Pox Inoculated in New England." London, privately printed, 1726. Evans 3259.

Chinard, Gilbert. "Jefferson and the American Philosophical Society." *Proceedings of the American Philosophical Society* 87, no. 3, Bicentennial of Thomas Jefferson (July 14, 1943): 263–276.

———. "The American Philosophical Society and the World of Science, 1768–1800." *Proceedings of the American Philosophical Society* 87, no. 1, The Early History of Science and Learning in America (July 14, 1943): 1–11.

Claggett, Martin. "William Small, 1734–1755: Teacher, Mentor, Scientist." PhD diss., Virginia Commonwealth University, 2002.

Clark, Charles E., "Science, Reason, and an Angry God: The Literature of an Earthquake," *New England Quarterly* 28, no. 3 (1965): 340–362.

———, and Charles Wetherell. "The Measure of Maturity: The Pennsylvania Gazette, 1728–1765." *William and Mary Quarterly,* 3rd series, vol. 46, no. 2 (April 1989): 279–303.

Cooke, Jacob E. "Tench Coxe, Alexander Hamilton, and the Encouragement of American Manufactures." *William and Mary Quarterly,* July 1975, pg. 369-392.

D'Elia, Donald J. "Jefferson, Rush, and the Limits of Philosophical Friendship." *Proceedings of the American Philosophical Society* 117, no. 5 (October 1973): 333–343.

Dewey, Frank L. "Thomas Jefferson's Law Practice: The Norfolk Anti-Inoculation Riots." *Virginia Magazine of History and Biography* 91 (1983).

Douglass, William. "A Practical Essay Concerning the Smallpox." London, privately printed, 1730.

Ewing, Galen W. "Early Teaching of Science at the College of William and Mary," *Bulletin of the College of William and Mary* 32, no. 4 (April 1938): 3–29.

Ferguson, Eugene S. "Oliver Evans: Inventive Genius of the American Revolution." Greenville, DE: Hagley Museum, 1980.

Fleming, Donald. "Science and Technology in Providence, 1760–1914." Brown University, 1952.

Foucault, Michel. "What Is Enlightenment?" In *The Foucault Reader,* edited by Paul Rabinow, pp. 32–50. New York: Pantheon Books, 1984.

Genuth, Sara Schechner. "From Heaven's Alarm to Public Appeal: Comets and the Rise of Astronomy at Harvard." In *Science and Harvard University,* edited by Clark A. Elliot and Margaret W. Rossiter. Bethlehem, PA: Lehigh University Press, 1992.

Gillett, Mary C. "The Army Medical Department, 1775–1818." Washington, DC: U.S. Army Medical Department, 1981. Online at: http://history.amedd.army.mil /booksdocs/rev/gillett1/ch3.html

Gray, Asa. "Selections from the Scientific Correspondence of Cadwallader Colden." Reprint from the *American Journal of Science and the Arts,* 1843.

Griffenhagen, George B. "Drug Supplies in the American Revolution." Contributions from the Museum of History and Technology, paper 16, pp. 110–133. *United States National Museum Bulletin 225.* Washington, DC: Smithsonian Institution, 1961.

Gronim, Sara Sidstone. "What Jane Knew: A Woman Botanist in the Eighteenth Century." *Journal of Women's History* 19, no. 3 (Fall 2007).

Hackmann, W. D. "Scientific Instruments: Models of Brass and Aids to Discovery" In *The Uses of Experiment,* edited by David Gooding, Trevor Finch, and Simon Schaffer. Cambridge: Cambridge University Press, 1989.

Hindle, Brooke. "Cadwallader Colden's Extension of the Newtonian Principles." *William and Mary Quarterly,* 3rd series, vol. 13, no. 4 (October 1956): 459–475.

Hull, Gillian. "William Small 1734-1775: No Publications, Much Influence." *Journal of the Royal Society of Medicine* 90 (February 1997): 102–105.

Kant, Immanuel. "What Is Enlightenment?" *Berlinische Monatschrifft,* November 1784. Translated by Mary C. Smith. Online at: http://www.columbia.edu/acis /ets/CCREAD/etscc/kant.html.

Leonard, David C. "Harvard's First Science Professor: A Sketch of Isaac Greenwood's Life and Work." *Harvard Library Bulletin* 29, no. 2 (April 1981): 135–168.

Lesley, Peter, ed. "Early Proceedings of the American Philosophical Society for the Promotion of Useful Knowledge, Compiled by One of the Secretaries from the Manuscript Minutes of Its Meetings from 1744 to 1838." *Proceedings of the American Philosophical Society* 22, part 3 (July 1885).

Logan, James. "Some Experiments concerning the Impregnation of the Seeds of Plants, as communicated in a letter to P. Collinson." *Transactions of the Royal Society* 38, no. 440 (Janurary–February–March 1736).

Lokken, Roy S., ed. "The Scientific Papers of James Logan." *Transactions of the American Philosophical Society.* New Series, vol. 62, part 6, 1972.

Maluf, Ramez Bahige. "Jean Antoine Nollet and Experimental Natural Philosophy in Eighteenth Century France." PhD diss., University of Oklahoma, 1985.

Mitchill, Samuel L. "A Discourse on the Character and Services of Thomas Jefferson, More Especially as a Promoter of Natural and Physical Science." Address at the New York Lyceum of Natural History of New York, October 11, 1826.

Morgan, Edmund S., "The Puritan Ethic and the American Revolution," *William and Mary Quarterly,* 3rd. ser., no. 24 (January 1967).

Olson, Susanne. "Thomas Jefferson's Collection of Scientific Instruments." Unpublished research paper, 3 vols., Monticello Library, 1997.

Pleck, Joseph H. "American Fathering in Historical Perspective." In *Changing Men: New Directions in Research on Men and Masculinity,* edited by Michael S. Kimmel. Newbury Park, CA: Sage Publications, 1987.

Pope, Clayne L. "Adult Mortality in America before 1900: A View from Family Histories." In *Strategic Factors in Nineteenth Century American Economic History,* edited by Claudia Goldin and Hugh Rockoff, pp. 278–292. Chicago: University of Chicago Press, 2002.

Questebrune, John. "A Short Introduction to Natural Philosophy." Scotland. Handwritten. 1718–1720. (APS)

Ragdale, Bruce A. "George Washington, the British Tobacco Trade, and Economic Opportunity in Prerevolutionary Virginia," *Virginia Magazine of History and Biography* 97, no. 2 (April 1989).

Rice, Howard C., Jr. "Jefferson's Gift of Fossils to the Museum of Natural History in Paris," *Proceedings of the APS* 95, no. 6 (December 1951).

Rittenhouse, David. "An Oration, Delivered February 24, 1775, Before the American Philosophical Society, Held at Philadelphia, for Promoting Useful Knowledge." Philadelphia, privately printed, 1775.

Rush, Benjamin. "Observations on the Duties of a Physician, and the Methods of Improving Medicine. Accommodated to the Present State of Society and Manners in the United States." Philadelphia, privately printed, 1789.

———. "Directions for Preserving the Health of Soldiers." Lancaster, PA, 1778.

Schaffer, Simon. "Glass Works: Newton's Prisms and the Uses of Experiment." In *The Uses of Experiment,* edited by David Gooding, Trevor Finch, and Simon Schaffer. Cambridge: Cambridge University Press, 1989.

Schultz, Constance B. "Of Bigotry in Politics and Religion: Jefferson's Religion, the Federalist Press, and the Syllabus." *Virginia Magazine of History and Biography* 91 (1983).

Smith, Beatrice Sheer. "Jane Colden (1724–1766) and Her Botanic Manuscript." *American Journal of Botany,* Vol. 75, No. 7 (Jul., 1988), pp. 1090–1096.

Stearns, Raymond P. "Colonial Fellows of the Royal Society of London, 1661–1788." *William and Mary Quarterly,* 3rd series, 1946.

Tilton, Eleanor M. "Lightning Rods and the Earthquake of 1755." *New England Quarterly* 13, no. 1 (March 1940): 85–97.

Van der Wetering, Maxine. "A Reconsideration of the Inoculation Controversy." *New England Quarterly* 58, no. 1 (March 1985): 46–67.

Van Doren, Carl. "The Beginnings of the American Philosophical Society." *Proceedings of the American Philosophical Society* 87, no. 3 (1943): 277–289.

Weber, Gustavus A. "The Patent Office, Its History, Activities and Organization." Institute for Government Research, Service Monograph no. 31, 1924.

Wilson, Douglas L. "The Evolution of Jefferson's 'Notes on the State of Virginia.'" *Virginia Magazine of History and Biography* 112, no. 2 (2004).

Woodward, Walter W. "The Dickinson College Thomas Cooper Collection: Joseph Priestley and Scientific Research on the American Frontier." In *Joseph Priestley, a Celebration of His Life and Legacy,* edited by James S. Birch and Joe Lee. Lancaster, UK: Scotforth Books/The Priestley Society, 2007.

INDEX